Education and Analog Role-Playing Games

Education and Analog Role-Playing Games: Theory and Pedagogy brings together scholars and educators who explore the educational potential of analog role-playing games (tabletop role-playing games and live action role-play) through the lens of pedagogical theory. These games trace their roots to educational war games and teaching aids. This volume goes further and takes a deeper dive into why they are such effective tools for learning, imagination, and identity development. This volume offers a multidisciplinary analysis that draws on philosophy, history, psychology, and critical pedagogy. Contributors examine how analog role-playing games intersect with educational theories such as constructivism, pragmatism, and experiential learning and explore classroom and nontraditional learning contexts. The rich insights position analog role-playing games as rich sites for identity exploration, deliberation, and transformative practice. Rather than simply advocating for gamification or offering how-to guides, this book critically interrogates how these games work, what they offer learners, and what pedagogical challenges they help us address. It is a valuable resource for educators, game scholars, and instructional designers interested in leveraging narrative, collaboration, and play for powerful learning experiences.

Susan Haarman, Ph.D., is Associate Director at Loyola University Chicago's Center for Engaged Learning, Teaching, and Scholarship. She facilitates the university's service-learning program and publishes on community-based learning. Her real love is her research on the capacity of tabletop role-playing games as formative tools for civic identity and imagination. She serves on the editorial board of the *International Journal of Role-Playing* and is also a professional improviser and a licensed therapist.

Education and Analog Role-Playing Games

Theory and Pedagogy, Volume 1

Edited by Susan Haarman
Additional editing by Kari Gustafson

CRC Press
Taylor & Francis Group
Boca Raton London New York

CRC Press is an imprint of the
Taylor & Francis Group, an **informa** business

Designed cover image: Beth Sparks

First edition published 2026
by CRC Press
2385 NW Executive Center Drive, Suite 320, Boca Raton FL 33431

and by CRC Press
4 Park Square, Milton Park, Abingdon, Oxon, OX14 4RN

CRC Press is an imprint of Taylor & Francis Group, LLC

ISBN: 9781041076124 (hbk)
ISBN: 9781041076070 (pbk)
ISBN: 9781003641353 (ebk)

DOI: 10.1201/9781003641353

Typeset in Minion
by codeMantra

Contents

About the Contributors

Sarah Lynne Bowman is a scholar, game designer, and event organizer. Currently, she is an Associate Professor and Docent in Game Design at Uppsala University Campus Gotland. She formerly served as Coordinator for the Peace & Conflict Studies program at Austin Community College, where she teaches Humanities. Bowman is a founding member of the Transformative Play Initiative, who research analog role-playing games as vehicles for personal and social change. She co-edited *The Wyrd Con Companion Book* (2012-2015) and currently edits for the *International Journal of Role-Playing* and Nordiclarp.org. Bowman has co-organized several conferences, including Living Games (2014, 2016, 2018), Role-playing and Simulation and Education (2016, 2018), the Edu-Larp Conference (2025) and the Transformative Play Initiative Seminar (2022, 2025).

David Brockway received his M.A. in English from Missouri State University in May 2025. At MSU, he had diverse academic interests and taught a variety of composition classes. His contribution to this book began with a presentation he gave at the Popular Culture Association National Conference in 2024. David is a tabletop gamer, designer, and game master. He lives in Springfield, Missouri, with his wife and pets.

Kari Gustafson, Ph.D. (they/she) is an instructor, researcher, role-playing gamer, and parent, working in the crossroads of neurodiversity and disability studies, education, and role-playing games. Kari has a Ph.D. in Philosophy of Education from Simon Fraser University, and an M.A. in Educational Psychology from Aarhus University. Their dissertation explores role-playing games, relationality, and inclusion, and asks what we can learn from role-playing games about welcoming students for their strengths, and creating collaborative learning spaces together. Kari is Assistant Professor in the School of Education at University of the Fraser Valley.

Susan Haarman Ph.D., is Associate Director at Loyola University Chicago's Center for Engaged Learning, Teaching, and Scholarship. She facilitates the university's service-learning program and publishes on community-based learning. Her real love is her research on the capacity of tabletop role-playing games as formative tools for civic identity and imagination. She serves on the editorial board of the International Journal of Role-Playing and is also a professional improviser and a licensed therapist.

Mátyás Hartyándi is a mental health specialist, psychodramatist, and currently a Ph.D. candidate in leadership development methodologies at Corvinus University of Budapest, Hungary. His research focuses on the history, theory, and application of various pretensive methodologies, including various forms of role-playing, applied drama, and gaming simulations, with the aim of bridging and integrating their differences. He is a member of ISAGA and serves as an associate editor of the *Simulation & Gaming* journal. As a leadership development trainer and change management consultant at Grow Group, Hungary, his professional references include local NGOs and multinational companies such as Audi and Bosch.

Jessica Hautsch is a teaching assistant professor of Humanities, where she teaches writing, film, and science fiction. She earned her Ph.D. from Stony Brook University. Her work offers a phenomenological interrogation of fan communities, exploring how the cognitive humanities, performance studies, and fandom intersect.

Karin Johansson is a researcher, professional larp designer, and educator. With a teacher's degree, she taught political science and sociology for several years, incorporating role-playing into her teaching. From there, she moved to work professionally developing edu-games with role-playing components for stakeholders such as the Swedish Museum of World Cultures, WWF, IKEA, The House of Peace, and the Swedish International Development Cooperation Agency. Karin has also worked for two years as a professional larp designer and educator at LajvVerkstaden. Having been a creative industry partner in several research projects, Karin is now pursuing a Ph.D. in Human-Computer Interaction at the Department of Informatics and Media, Uppsala University. Her thesis work focuses on designing for engagement together with value-driven stakeholders, exploring how playful interventions like larp can be used for these purposes as both a process and as design outcome. Karin is part of the Larpocracy EU horizon project.

Johanna Koljonen is a doctoral candidate in game studies at Tampere University, and co-founder of Participation Design Agency, a boutique experience design consultancy based in Sweden. She lectures internationally on participatory culture and on the future of the audiovisual industries, and advises cultural institutions, policymakers and film industry stakeholders on media transformation and immersive experience design. An occasional writer of non-fiction, drama, comics, and digital games, her first career was in broadcasting. In 2011, she received the Swedish Grand Journalism Award in the Innovator category. She holds a B.A. (First Class Honours) in English Literature from Oxford University, and an M.A. in Media Studies from Malmö University. Her latest book is *Larp Design: Creating Role-Play Experiences* (2019), for which she was lead editor.

Stephen Russell Mallory is an Assistant Professor of Game Design and Co-Director of the Game Design Program at Lawrence Technological University in Southfield, Michigan. A professional game designer for over a decade prior to academia, Stephen's research occurs at the intersection of game studies, game design and development, and games as informal learning technologies. He has published works on engagement and play through games as effective teaching and learning technologies, streaming as sites of informal education and apprenticeship learning, and the deployment of games in the service of critical pedagogy. His current research explores how history games normalize reactionary extremist political agendas and activities.

Leland Masek is a Doctoral Candidate at Tampere University's program in Media, Communications and Performing Arts. His dissertation is on definitions of playfulness and wellbeing across disciplines and cultures. He also directs the Games As Art Center in Tampere, Finland, which hosts hundreds of public events a year on aesthetic and important play in games.

The Games As Art Center also is an active researching institution developing a scientific arts research method with games termed Ludic Inquiry. Leland Masek also runs the Oasis Research Group at Tampere University which studies the empirical well being effects of playful behavior in games. He is a professional game designer with 14 years experience and over 40 professional projects, predominantly in games for education, pervasive games, interactive theater, and experimental game design.

PerOla Öberg has published research on public administration, interest groups, corporatism, lobbying, trust, and deliberation. His current research concerns expertise and public policy, civil society, deliberative governance, cotizen participation, civic values, and the use of learning, experience and knowledge in public policy. He has published in journals such as *The Journal of European Public Policy, Public Administration, Policy Sciences, Public Administration Review, Political Studies, Policy Studies Journal, West European Politics, Governance,* and *European Political Science Review.* Öberg has contributed handbook chapters with research on science and policy design, deliberation, local policy analysis, lobbying and public policy, and interest group politics.

Albert R. Spencer holds a Ph.D. in Philosophy from Baylor University and specializes in Inter-American Philosophy. In his first book, *American Pragmatism: An Introduction* (Polity Press, 2020), he provides an accessible, diverse, and inclusive survey of the origins and development of American philosophy as a reaction to the historical and ongoing consequences of settler-colonialism. He is also the author of several e-Textbooks with Kendall Hunt: *Philosophy of Sports (2021), Philosophy or Sex & Love (2022), Philosophy of War (2023) and Philosophy of Games (2025). His forthcoming book, The Philosophy of Role-Playing Games: Art, Inquiry, & Ritual (Bloomsbury 2025),* is the culmination of his personal passion for RPGs and his professional study of pragmatism (Peirce) and psychoanalytic (Lacan) thought.

Jaakko Stenros (Ph.D.) is a University Lecturer in Game Studies working at Game Research Lab, Tampere University. He has published

11 books and a hundred articles and reports, and has taught game studies for over 15 years. Stenros studies play and games; his research interests include norm-defying play, game rules, queer play, role-playing games, pervasive games, game jams, and playfulness. Stenros has also collaborated with artists and designers to create ludic experiences and has curated many exhibitions at the Finnish Museum of Games.

Josefin Westborg is one of the world's leading designers in edu-larps. She has studied game design and has a master's degree in education. She used to run her own company, working professionally with edu-larp for 10 years before going into academia. She has been a teacher in game design at both Chalmers University of Technology and the University of Gothenburg. Now she is part of the Transformative Play Initiative at Uppsala University in the Department of Game Design, where she has been part of creating the world's first master's program in analog role-playing games. Throughout her career, she has met thousands of students of all ages and run and designed larps for them. When she is not involved with games, you will probably find her at the dance studio ballroom dancing.

Annika Waern is a professor of Human-Computer Interaction at Uppsala University. Annika has a background in computer science and human-computer interaction. Annika has studied pervasive games as well as hybrid play design for children, adults and families. Annika is the scientific coordinator of Larpocracy, a project researching live role-playing to develop democratic values and skills. She is a DiGRA (Digital Games Research Association) distinguished scholar and a HEVGA (Higher Education Video Game Alliance) fellow.

Introduction to Education and Analog Role-Playing Games

Theory and Pedagogy

Susan Haarman

In recent years, analog role-playing games (RPGs) like tabletop RPGs and live action role-play (larp) have leapt from the margins of hobby culture into mainstream consciousness. But what may seem like a renaissance of fantasy, imagination, and communal storytelling is, in fact, a return to something deeply pedagogical. Long before polyhedral dice and character sheets, educators have used role-playing, whether in the form of war games, therapeutic simulations, or civic exercises, to cultivate empathy, build communities of inquiry, and prepare students for the complexities of the world. These games are sites of deep meaning-making, and a growing body of research now confirms the potential of RPGs to teach empathy, collaboration, and critical thinking (Cullinan and Genova, 2023 ; Zagal & Deterding, 2018). From classrooms and museums to therapy groups and corporate leadership programs, analog RPGs are being used to explore a range of topics, including historical consciousness, social justice, and negotiating trauma, to name a few.

DOI: 10.1201/9781003641353-1

Additionally, these learning experiences are occurring even in games played purely for leisure. Players engaged in recreational campaigns are still negotiating identities, building communities, experimenting with ethical choices, and collaboratively shaping narratives – often without framing these activities as educational. Research has shown that even when RPGs are not designed with explicit learning outcomes in mind, they foster meaningful personal and interpersonal development (Hammer et al., 2018). Analog RPGs promote collaborative storytelling, which cultivates empathy, identity exploration, and social cohesion (Baird, 2022; Berge, 2025; Bowman et al., 2024 Garcia, 2017). Players make complex decisions within game worlds that mirror ethical dilemmas, prompting reflection and critical thinking. These practices reflect forms of embodied, affective, and cognitive learning that is occurring outside formal learning environments. This suggests that analog RPGs can cultivate embodied, affective, and cognitive growth even with the absence of intentional instructional design, offering rich ground for further pedagogical reflection.

This volume, *Education and Analog Role-Playing Games: Theory and Pedagogy*, emerges from the conviction that we must move beyond merely demonstrating the educational efficacy potential of these games. We must now ask *why* they do it so well. They are as powerful tools of education, therapy, social analysis, and cultural critique. The chapters in this collection interrogate co-creation through a wide range of disciplinary and theoretical lenses, asking how analog RPGs function as educational tools, what kinds of learning they support, and how they complicate and expand our understanding of pedagogy itself.

Rather than replicating the instrumental logic of gamification, this volume leans into the vibrant and critical potential of role-playing to create ludic pedagogical experiences. Analog RPGs offer a singularly rich site for pedagogical inquiry. These games are built not on experience that is negotiated, embodied, relational, and recursive. In these spaces, learning is not merely absorbed content, but a co-created experience. Contributors explore how tabletop RPGs and larps support *learning* – not just as knowledge acquisition, but also as identity formation, ethical development, and social imagination. This volume brings together scholars and practitioners who not only believe in the educational potential of these games but also rigorously investigate how and why they educate so effectively. Rather than offering a "how-to" manual or a defense of games in classrooms, this book explores what analog RPGs reveal about pedagogy itself and how they can help us reimagine teaching and learning in a myriad of spaces for a more collaborative, inclusive, and imaginative future.

RECASTING PEDAGOGY THROUGH PLAY

Drawing on a myriad of traditions, including constructivism, experiential education, critical pedagogy, care ethics, material cognition, historiography, and positive psychology, contributors interrogate the unique affordances of analog RPGs: co-created narratives, improvisational learning, embodied cognition, and collective worldbuilding. These games are not merely educational tools; they are pedagogical spaces in which participants live through dilemmas, negotiate meaning, and co-produce knowledge. As John Dewey argued, "education is not an affair of 'telling' and being told, but an active and constructive process" (1938, 38). Analog RPGs embody this ethos, cultivating what Dewey called "communities of inquiry" grounded in shared experience. The chapters in this volume explore that potential through diverse theoretical lenses and practical contexts.

PART I: WISDOM CHECK: PEDAGOGY AND THEORY

Before exploring the many places analog RPGs have taken root, we begin with the foundational question: what kind of pedagogy do these games enact? The chapters in this section investigate the theoretical underpinnings of analog RPGs as educational spaces. Drawing from traditions such as Deweyan pragmatism, material cognition, organizational learning, and instructional design, the contributors interrogate how learning occurs within RPGs, and what that reveals about the nature of education itself. Whether through classroom-based simulations, edu-larps, home games, or corporate retreats, these essays show that analog RPGs are not just tools to be deployed – they are theories in action, shaping how we understand power, community, and transformation. The section's title, "Wisdom Check," nods to the games' own vocabulary of discernment, asking what it means to think wisely about learning through play.

Susan Haarman opens this volume with "Teaching Rolls: The Practice of Teaching and Game Mastering through the Lens of John Dewey," arguing that the game master (GM) role is strikingly similar to Dewey's conception of a teacher – both serve as co-creators of experience, balancing authority with responsiveness and shared meaning-making. Both GMs and teachers (as Dewey envisioned them) must balance the authority they have over their players or students in a way that neither abdicates power nor diminishes agency in others. By placing the roles in conversation with one another, this chapter presents a vision of generative authority in both spaces through three core practices: co-creation, community norming, and scaffolded challenge.

In "We Are Playing in a Material World: Thinking and Learning through the Physical Objects of Tabletop Role-Playing Games," **Jessica Hautsch** challenges the assumption that tabletop RPGs are purely mental or imaginative. Drawing on cognitive science and philosophy, she argues that players don't just think *about* rulebooks, character sheets, and dice, they think *with* them. Through distributed cognition, material culture becomes central to how players learn and act in-game. This chapter reframes learning in analog RPGs as materially mediated, emphasizing the cognitive work of embodied interaction with tools and space.

Mátyás Hartyándi, in "From Diverse Roots to Dual Classing: Crystallizing the Role of Tabletop Role-Playing Games in Education, with Examples from Corporate Learning & Development," bridges the world of leisure RPGs and corporate learning and development. Tracing role-playing's history from psychodramatic training tools in the 1950s to today's HR practices, he argues that tabletop RPGs uniquely support probabilistic thinking and complex decision-making, and cognitive engagement. Using a three-layered analytical model (social, ludic, diegetic), he argues that RPGs enable probabilistic thinking, scenario modeling, and identity experimentation. By examining business simulations and psychodrama traditions, this chapter reveals that corporate learning is often already ludic in nature, even when disguised as "serious" work. His concept of "dual classing" captures the blending of game mechanics and real-world skills, demonstrating that RPGs can be both playful and pedagogically robust.

In "Edu-larp: The Promise and Pitfalls of the Method," **Josefin Westborg** offers a thoughtful analysis of what makes edu-larps such effective educational tools, and what missteps lead to poor execution. Drawing on interviews with practitioners across Europe and North America, she outlines common challenges such as institutional resistance, emotional risk, and insufficient scaffolding. Westborg surfaces pitfalls such as over-association with frivolity, implementation challenges, and difficulties in curricular alignment and offers concrete mitigation strategies. The precarity experienced by educators who use larps in formal settings is also honestly grappled with, as the piece's thoughtful analysis of edu-larps' shortcomings and practitioners' blind spots helps strengthen the method's practice.

PART II: A PLACE AT THE TABLE: INCLUSIVE AND TRANSFORMATIVE LEARNING THROUGH TABLETOP ROLE-PLAYING GAME

Who gets to learn? Who gets to play? The chapters in this final section explore the radical inclusivity of analog RPGs and the transformative possibilities they offer for players and educators alike. From neurodivergent joy to queer storyworlding, these essays foreground the affective, embodied, and identity-shaping dimensions of play. They examine how tabletop RPGs can challenge dominant narratives, create safer spaces for emotional risk-taking, and reimagine literacy and participation for marginalized learners. "A Place at the Table" signals the commitment to hospitality and shared authorship that defines this work: RPGs not only make space for new voices, they depend on them. In this section, role-playing becomes not just a pedagogy, but a practice of justice and belonging.

In "Storyworlding Together: Tabletop Role-Playing Games as Inclusive Becoming," **Kari Gustafson** examines how RPGs can disrupt normative educational models. Drawing on post-qualitative research and affect theory, she argues that collaborative storytelling enables what Donna Haraway calls "becoming-with." These are spaces where players construct emergent, co-authored identities. Using feminist philosophy and participatory design, she frames storyworlding as an affective, inclusive process of narrative emergence. This chapter foregrounds how analog RPGs can serve as tools for identity exploration, particularly for queer and marginalized players seeking narrative agency.

Albert R. Spencer, in "Transforming Crisis into Growth: Neurodivergence, Bleed, and Care Ethics in RPGs," presents a moving case study of emotional bleed during a D&D campaign. Spencer's chapter blends critical disability studies and care ethics to examine how neurodivergent players experience bleed – when emotional experiences cross between character and player. Through personal narrative and philosophical analysis, he demonstrates how analog play can foster care practices and ethical relationality. Through a care ethics framework, he argues that RPG safety practices must go beyond consent and toward relational support and highlights how this support can allow for deep learning within the players. His chapter is a call for trauma-informed, inclusive facilitation and reframes neurodivergence not as a barrier but as a transformative lens for gameplay and pedagogy.

The section concludes with **David Brockway**'s "Collaboration and Empowerment for an Inclusive Environment: Social Constructivism in the Composition Classroom and Tabletop Roleplaying Games." Brockway situates tabletop RPGs within constructivist composition pedagogy, arguing that collaborative narrative-building mirrors the recursive, negotiated nature of writing. He demonstrates how collaborative RPG play aligns with the goals of composition pedagogy, especially in classrooms with diverse learners. Brockway argues that TTRPGs promote empowerment by allowing students to take ownership of language and narrative, offering an inclusive alternative to hierarchical classroom norms. RPGs teach audience awareness, rhetorical flexibility, and co-authorship. His classroom case studies show how analog play cultivates the dispositions of reflective writing and metacognitive awareness through experiential learning.

PART III: PROFICIENCY BONUS: DISCIPLINARY CHALLENGES AND OPPORTUNITIES

RPGs do not take place in a vacuum. When they enter classrooms, museums, therapy rooms, or political spaces, they collide with disciplinary norms and institutional expectations. This section explores what happens at those intersections. The authors examine how RPGs function as historiographic tools, psychological interventions, and democratic simulations, showing both their promise and their pressure points. In each case, analog RPGs open new avenues for knowledge creation – but also challenge educators and designers to navigate questions of fidelity, ethics, and engagement. The title "Proficiency Bonus" reflects how expertise in traditional disciplines – history, psychology, political science – can be leveled up and reimagined through the lens of play.

Stephen Mallory's "Historiography and History Tabletop Role-Playing Games: History Is What We Play It" examines how RPGs can serve as vehicles for historical consciousness. He argues that history RPGs create liminal space and tension around documented history, allowing players to reenact, reinterpret, and sometimes distort historical narratives. These games blur the line between history and historical fiction, allowing players to rehearse, interrogate, and rewrite dominant historical narratives. His analysis stresses how counterfactual and speculative play can democratize history-making in the classroom. Mallory says that playing with history in this way creates a dynamic tension between learning and the process of education and asks readers to consider both the affordances and the ethical risks of counterfactual play.

In "Edu-larp and Positive Psychology: Theory, Practice, and Case Study," **Leland Masek** situates a Finnish edu-larp program within three psychological paradigms: behaviorism, cognitivism, and constructivism. Masek weaves positive psychology with edu-larp, suggesting that RPGs support well-being by fostering flow, meaning-making, and social connection. Drawing on a case study of a role-play workshop, this chapter demonstrates how players experience self-actualization, identity rehearsal, and narrative cohesion. RPGs are thus shown not only as educational but also as a form of psychological flourishing.

"Playing a Role in Democracy: Political Live Action Role-Playing Games, Activism, and Deliberation" by **Karin Johansson, Johanna Koljonen, Jaakko Stenros, PerOla Öberg**, and **Sarah Lynne Bowman** offers a sweeping analysis of political larp as a method for civic engagement and democratic education. This chapter explores political edu-larps as incubators of democratic deliberation and civic engagement. Drawing on multiple larp case studies, the authors show how these games simulate activist dilemmas, foster empathy, and create low-risk environments for moral experimentation. This chapter argues that such larps can help cultivate the habits and dispositions of democratic citizens. From simulations of deliberative assemblies to larps on environmental policy, these games create experiential civic laboratories.

In "Mapping the Design Terrain between Live Action Role-Playing Games and Deliberative Events for Democratic Skill Development," **Sarah Lynne Bowman, PerOla Öberg, Karin Johansson**, and **Annika Waern** examine the generative overlap between two seemingly disparate domains: political larps and deliberative democratic events. Drawing on extensive interdisciplinary research, this chapter outlines how both practices cultivate key democratic competencies such as empathy, perspective-taking, reason-giving, and civic agency. The authors argue that the immersive, embodied nature of larp provides a powerful context for rehearsing and refining deliberative skills, while deliberative theory offers normative and structural insights that can enrich larp design. By mapping shared outcomes and distinct challenges (such as the tension between escalation in larp and de-escalation in deliberation), this chapter proposes a new design frontier: deliberative larps. In doing so, it opens a path toward crafting transformative pedagogical experiences that blend narrative immersion with civic formation, offering practical and theoretical implications for educators, designers, and democratic innovators alike.

Together, these two chapters illuminate the evolving potential of political larp as both a reflective and generative space for democratic learning. While "Playing a Role in Democracy" presents compelling case studies of larps functioning as civic laboratories, modeling deliberative processes and fostering moral imagination, the subsequent chapter expands this terrain by systematically theorizing the intersection of larp and deliberative democratic practice. Building on the foundational examples of political edu-larp, "Mapping the Design Terrain…" pushes the conversation further by articulating a shared design language and identifying practical and ethical considerations for integrating deliberative skill development directly into larp experiences. This movement from rich descriptive analysis to conceptual and design synthesis marks a critical step in developing analog RPGs as tools not only for simulating democracy but also for practicing and refining it.

LUDIC PEDAGOGY FOR THIS WORLD AND BEYOND

Across all three sections, a set of shared themes emerges: play as a site of epistemic power, immersion as pedagogy, and vulnerability as educational strength. The chapters in this volume treat games not as simulations of learning, but as learning itself, dynamic, embodied, affective, and deeply human. In doing so, they invite educators, scholars, and designers to embrace analog RPGs not just as tools, but as sites of educational theory in action. This is neither a how-to manual nor a defense of games in education. It is something more ambitious: a theoretical intervention into how we understand learning and a call to embrace the radical potential of imagination, collaboration, and shared storytelling in the pedagogical project. This vision of a *ludic pedagogy* acknowledges the ways in which these games expand the player, enabling deep learning that encompasses and extends beyond content acquisition, and into ethical and identity formation (Haarman, 2023). Ludic pedagogy makes our learning gameful, but more importantly, has the capacity and space to name, claim, and leverage learning in formal and informal educational spaces. Whether the setting is a university classroom, a corporate training retreat, a therapy group, a campground, or a kitchen table, analog RPGs open spaces for collaborative meaning-making, inclusive participation, and imaginative rehearsal for the world as it is and as it could be. We invite you, the reader, to join – not as a spectator but as a participant in an unfolding pedagogical adventure.

Let the games begin.

REFERENCES

Baird, Josephine. 2022. "Learning about Ourselves: Communicating, Connecting and Contemplating Trans Experience through Play." *Gamevironments* 17: 355–402.

Berge, PS. 2025. "The Table and the Tomb: Positioning Trans Power and Play amid Fantasy Realism in *Dungeons & Dragons.*" *Games and Culture* 20 (3): 335–354.

Bowman, Sarah Lynne, Elektra Diakolambrianou, Kjell Hedgard Hugaas, Josefin Westborg, and Josephine Baird. 2024. "Transformative Role-Playing Games: Types, Purposes, and Features." In *Transformative Role-Playing Game Design*, edited by Sarah Lynne Bowman, Elektra Diakolambrianou, and Simon Brind, 80–139. Uppsala: Acta Universitatis Upsaliensis.

Cullinan, Maryanne, and Jennifer Genova. 2023. "Gaming the Systems: A Component Analysis Framework for the Classroom Use of RPGs." *International Journal of Role-Playing* 13: 7–17.

Dewey, John. 1938. *Experience and Education*. New York: Macmillan.

Garcia, Antero. 2017. *Good Reception: Teens, Teachers, and Mobile Media in a Los Angeles High School*. Cambridge: MIT Press.

Greene, Maxine. 1995. *Releasing the Imagination: Essays on Education, the Arts, and Social Change*. San Francisco, CA: Jossey-Bass.

Haarman, Susan. 2023. *Dungeons & Dragons & Dewey: Toward a Ludic Pedagogy of Democratic Civic Life through the Philosophy of John Dewey and Tabletop Role-Playing Games*. PhD diss., Loyola University Chicago.

Hammer, Jessica, Alexandra To, Karen Schrier, Sarah Lynne Bowman, and Geoff Kaufman. 2018. "Learning and Role-Playing Games." In *Role-Playing Game Studies: Transmedia Foundations*, edited by José P. Zagal and Sebastian Deterding, 283–299. New York: Routledge.

Zagal, José P., and Sebastian Deterding, eds. 2018. *Role-Playing Game Studies: Transmedia Foundations*. New York: Routledge.

I

Wisdom Check

Pedagogy and Theory

CHAPTER 1

Teaching Rolls

The Practice of Teaching and Game Mastering Through the Lens of John Dewey

Susan Haarman

One of the most distinguishing elements of most tabletop role-playing games (RPGs) is the existence of some form of game master (or GM). This individual serves as both facilitator and participant. They oversee creating the initial structure, details, and challenges of a given adventure, while maintaining a realistic continuity of events. Nearly every element of gameplay falls under their auspices except the most important one – the players' choices. Some GMs use source material provided by game designers called playbooks or guides containing information like game rules, settings, and even potential plotlines. Other GMs create whole worlds and all the denizens therein whole cloth from their imagination.

While style of play and level of influence can vary from game to game, GMs must juggle a variety of information and skill sets. They must respond to players in real time, determine how their actions impact the game world, and think ahead about where players may go or be led. Daniel Carlson (2020) states that a GM must be able to serve the roles of world builder, adjudicator, and supportive narrator – all of which require skills in creative authority, collaboration, and discerning when to use each.

The GM, players, and chance (manifested by the die) form a web of interactions that serve to drive the gameplay and narrative, while also

DOI: 10.1201/9781003641353-3

serving as checks and balances for each other. The action of one element instigates a reaction from another that typically amplifies or limits the aforementioned catalyzing action. This interplay also frames the structure and limits of power within the game. In most games, the GM has control over every aspect of the world and plot *except* character choices, feelings, and reactions. At the same time, players have no direct control over anything beyond their characters, but they have high levels of influence on the narrative and world (and, by proxy, the behavior of the GM), as the game milieu is forced to define and redefine itself based on player choices (Montola 2009). Consequently, this interplay creates a narrative that stays in flux and cannot become fully determined or rigid unless there is a significant use/abuse of power by one of these elements. While a tremendous amount of that power resides in the hands of the GM, they remain constrained by *the pure necessity of having players*. Because the game does not exist without the players, their choice to "leave the table" (to stop playing) ends the game. Thus, the nearly limitless power that a GM holds over their players ultimately originates in the players themselves.

When viewed through this lens, a GM's role in a tabletop RPG campaign strongly mirrors educational philosopher John Dewey's view of a teacher's role as articulated in *Experience and Education* (Haarman 2023). A GM does not serve as an autocratic ruler or a dispassionate adjudicator; rather, they co-create the world alongside players and actively foster opportunities for their individual and collective growth. This co-creation occurs when GMs take the actions of their players seriously. While the style of play and level of influence can vary from game to game, GMs are as impacted by their players' decisions as players are by theirs. This delicate balance between participation, mutual impact, and power also mimics much of how Dewey described the role of a teacher in a progressive classroom.

Dewey called for teachers to understand themselves as part of the learning community, learning alongside pupils and (within limits) allowing the classroom to be influenced by student interests. He actually said that it was "absurd" to not consider a teacher as part of the community of learners in a classroom (Dewey 1938, 58). This is remarkably similar to *D&D's* definition of the Dungeon Master as "the game organizer and participant in charge of creating the details and challenges of a given adventure, while maintaining a realistic continuity of events" (Wizards of the Coast, 2014, 8). GMs in tabletop RPGs reflect the principles of a Deweyan teacher through the co-creation of the game with players, establishing and fostering the norms of the creative community, and providing scaled and growth-oriented challenges.

This chapter aims to identify the common DNA of collaborative and generative authority that effective GMs possess, and which Dewey hoped teachers would also possess. It is meant to serve as a theory-building piece that invites deeper conversation across both educational theory and game studies. All too often, scholarship on games as learning tools focuses on their simple utility as educational tools and does not explicate the ways in which they mirror, echo, or challenge fundamental precepts of educational philosophy. When used in the classroom, tabletop RPGs must be implemented with care and consideration for their purpose and impact. This chapter does not mean to oversimplify the commonality between the positions of teacher and GM. Rather, it hopes to provide more lines of contemplation for both arenas around where to deepen best practices and to amplify Dewey's seminal insights around how people think and learn.

After providing the necessary background on John Dewey and his vision for education and teachers, I will place the Deweyan Teacher and the GM in conversation with one another, focusing on three themes of best practice that overlap across both roles. I will expand on these themes, including the co-creation of the game with players, establishing and fostering the norms of the creative community, and providing scaled and growth-oriented challenges. Finally, I will highlight how they might challenge each other, and then close with a brief reflection on what it means to learn through experience.

JOHN DEWEY – PALADIN OF PRAGMATIST PHILOSOPHY

Considered a founder of the American pragmatist tradition, John Dewey lived from 1859 to 1952. He was a philosopher, psychologist, and educational and social reformer. He arrived in Chicago in 1894 when the city was dealing with major labor strikes, a huge immigrant influx, and massive industrialization. For the first half of the 20th century, Dewey was an extremely influential public intellectual and served as a co-founder of ACLU, NAACP, and The New School (Lake 2017). He rooted his philosophical work and approach to education in democratic ideals, advocating for communication and ways of association that could create what he called "The Great Community" (Dewey & Rogers 2016).

In his seminal work *Experience and Education*, Dewey said that the transformation of the learner was essentially a social process and that "the quality [of the education] is realized in the degree in which individuals form a community group" (1938, 58). Knowledge is a function of association and communication – of being in relationship with others and interacting with them. It depends upon tradition, tools, and methods socially transmitted, developed, and sanctioned (Dewey & Rogers, 138). However, Dewey was realistic about the ways in which schools hindered students' experiences in the name of teaching supposedly stable absolutes. He believed that traditional schools employed a model of rote instruction from above and outside, focusing on the imposition of knowledge onto passive students. The knowledge conveyed was verified but ossified (Dewey 1938, 18). Schools provided students with further miseducational learning experiences, primarily through memorization and drilling, which made them dislike the subject matter and limited their critical thinking. Dewey referred to rote instruction as fatal to reflection capacity and famously said, "How many students were rendered callous to ideas, and how many lost the impetus to learn because of the way in which learning was experienced by them?" (1938, 26).

WHO'S IN CHARGE? – DEWEYAN TEACHER AND GM AUTHORITY

Teachers in Dewey's ideal classroom were understood to be a part of the educational community, not as a dictator, but still serving as a leader (Dewey 1991). While collaboration and co-learning were essential, he still centered the authority they held in the classroom. Far from being laissez-faire, Dewey believed the teacher served an essential role in helping the community to form through thought and planning. Because education is a social process, the teacher must be considered a member of the same community. However, as the most mature members, teachers needed to guide interactions and help the community form around shared goals. By shifting the frame away from "external boss" to "leader of group activities," an instructor was able to remain fully in the community without exerting their will onto students or abdicating their shared responsibility and expertise (Dewey 1938, 58).

Dewey said instructors were meant to fully engage in the learning process alongside students and to "let [their] mind come to close quarters with the pupil's mind and the subject matter" (1916, 109). Care theorist and fellow educational philosopher Nel Noddings (2010) says that while Dewey's emphasis on the teacher as co-learner and an inquiry approach is important, a care theorist's approach would claim that the relationship between the teacher and student is at the center of any educational experience. For Noddings, as long as the teacher was caring, they would be able to produce excellent educational results with old-fashioned and less experiential methods.

Similar debates around the balance of power and authority also exist around the role of GM. Even the question of their necessity is up for debate, with Jerzy Kociatkiewicz (2000) claiming a GM is, at best, an unnecessary outside authority, and at worst, a privileged individual who exerts coercive power over others. Timothy Christopher claims that GMs tend to fall into one of four categories: guide, host, arbiter, or puppet master, each with its own benefits in running games and providing experience. Like Dewey's admonition to attend to the interests and skills of students in the classroom, Christopher (2012) believes the value of a GM lies in how they respond to the desired experience of players, rather than in an inherent set of abstract gaming values or principles. For instance, a GM who dictates a large amount of action and choices could remove the stress of having to create them from more inexperienced players who might be intimidated by a game's complex rule system. Absolute freedom without direction can often result in players feeling confused or unsure of what to do, leaving them with less agency than they would have if they were operating within a more structured environment with clear guidelines.

Deweyan classroom, like a tabletop RPG, are built on social cooperation. Dewey believed that children were well aware of the dynamics of social cooperation and control needed in the classroom even at a young age. He used the example of gameplay, indicating that most children did not have a problem playing with an agreed-upon rule set. Dewey (1938) insisted that children typically emulate the rules that they saw adults abiding by in games, with their adherence serving as a form of respect for the continuity of traditions. The enforcement of these rules by one individual was not seen as an imposition so long as the game continued to progress fairly, and players could continue to participate. Children understood that without rules, no games would exist. Social control in the classroom was a result not of domination but of students joining in a shared social enterprise, with each person participating.

This shared enterprise also demands responsiveness. As a result of his view of traditional schooling, Dewey believed the ideal model of instruction was not static and rigid, allowing for complex interplays in the classroom community around the subject matter (Nelsen 2016). At the same time, teachers achieved this by being well prepared with an eye to encouraging individual pupils' capacity. They needed to walk the line between good activity management and inspiration that could excite students into deeper learning (Skilbeck 2017). Dewey did not view intellectual capacity as all-encompassing and advised instructors not to make assumptions about students' academic abilities based on their reactions to a single subject matter. Dewey said, "The teacher is not entitled to assume stupidity or even dullness merely because of unresponsiveness to school subjects or the lesson presented by textbook or teacher" (1991, 35). A student may be unresponsive to one lesson but animated by the next because of their own curiosity and desire to deepen experience with the content.

As a result, the teacher needed to be prepared to make adjustments in order to better follow the spirit of excitement and engagement in students as they learned. Attention had to be paid to the environment in which learners existed, as well as their internal capacities and motivations. Dewey (1938) advocated for "mutual adaptation" between the student and the educational experience. It advocated for developmentally appropriate choices. Citing the fact that trigonometry is not taught to elementary children, he maintained that there was no such thing as something having educational value in the abstract. It is the interaction of the position and interest of the learner, the material, and how it is taught that led to educational experiences. Dewey said that there was "no defect in traditional education greater than its failure to secure the active cooperation of the pupil in the construction of the purposes involved in his studying" (1938, 67).

Like Dewey's vision for teachers, GMing is rooted in relationship to those they both serve and hold authority over. Both roles are encouraged to have a high level of attention to and familiarity with their players/ students. Dewey's exhortation to never assume a student lacks the capacity to learn and instead help find subjects that engage them echoes the 2024s *Dungeon Masters Guide* claim that the game should revolve around *the players' decisions*. It reads,

> Your players need to know from the start that you'll run a game that is fun, fair, and tailored for them; that you'll allow each of them to contribute to the story; and that you'll pay attention to them when they take their turns.

There is a common phrase in the larger tabletop RPG community that GMs should "be fans of their players" and see the relationship as collaborative and with an emphasis on curiosity and responsiveness, rather than adversarial and autocratic (White et al. 2022). Responding to player interests and ensuring that their choices matter develops a sense of agency that encourages them to co-create the world alongside the GM (Katifori 2022). Dewey sought to create the same efficacy in learners.

CO-CREATION

That interplay and cooperation are at the heart of the first major theme that overlaps both Deweyan teachers and GMs – that of co-creation. Because of the mechanics of chance and emergent outcomes of choice, GMs must be responsive to game action and practice some level of improvisation to run a game. Although many use sourcebooks with guidelines and extensive material around suggested encounters, ultimately the result of gameplay is uncertain, and both GM and players are negotiating and being impacted by that uncertainty. This necessitates a wide range of skills as GMs respond to the ways that game shifts and moves. Tresca says that GMs must serve in the roles of world builder, adjudicator, and supportive narrator, requiring skills in both creative authority and collaboration.

In addition to being an academic, I am also a professional GM. My tables range from good friends to people who want to learn to play tabletop RPGs for the first time. At all my tables, I have employed a principle of co-creation with my players I call "nothing is wasted." Anything my players say becomes fodder for later moments or sessions. That off-handed comment a player made about being a water ski champion? That is now canon, and I may push the narrative so that they will likely have the opportunity to test that skill later. This approach ensures that players understand their actions and choices have meaning and influence. My players are creating aspects of the world alongside me, and although I may have structured a general narrative in a specific way, refusing to follow emergent outcomes threatens the coherence and believability of the narrative. This respect for emergent material and the input of players echoes Dewey's understanding of education as a social process rooted in experience. Players are not playing "my game" – we are engaging and creating the world together. For Dewey, an instructor who understood the social dynamics of education would see themselves not as "external boss or dictator," but rather one who was leading others through an activity they were experiencing together.

Rene Schallegger (2018) explicitly compares GMing to pragmatist philosophy, saying that negotiation and interpretation, instead of conflict and rigid truth, are the principles and habits that drive the role.

At the same time, much of the enjoyment of games can come from having a GM who is prepared and has a narrative or world into which a player can step. While co-creation certainly leads to a level of wonder, having a rich environment created by the GM to begin with often helps players feel comfortable and build skills in creative thinking and problem-solving. Dewey also emphasized the importance of preparation in creating a classroom community that would support learning. He was careful to indicate that sustained and functioning life together does not organize itself spontaneously and without direction. Dewey said in *Experience and Education*,

> It requires thought and planning ahead. The educator is responsible for a knowledge of individuals and for a knowledge of subject-matter that will enable activities to be selected which lend themselves to social organization, an organization in which all individuals have an opportunity to contribute something, and in which the activities in which all participate are the chief carrier of control.
>
> *(1938, 56)*

Similarly, GMs are tasked with both setting the tone of a gaming environment through balancing player choice with the rule system that structures the game. Steven Dashiell, a sociologist and game scholar, claims that the power that GMs hold begins and ends with both player agency *and* games rules – it is not actually a fully blank slate upon which they may (individually or in collaboration with players) create something from nothing. GMs create the environment not through unequivocal acts of power, but through striking the balance between "the social construct of the rules system and the collective will of the ludic space" (Dashiell 2022, 10).

ESTABLISHING THE NORMS OF THE CREATIVE COMMUNITY

The educational environment in the classroom that John Dewey detailed in his writings was composed not only of the structure and activities chosen by the instructors but also of the students' interactions with one another. Dewey also said that the teacher would need to be particularly attentive not just to content, but to the "interactions and inter-communications which are the very life of the group as a community" (1938, 58). A good teacher helps lay the baseline and monitors the ways in which students interact with one another to foster an environment conducive to learning. This aspect of responsibility for tone setting is echoed in the work of GMs through increasingly common processes, such as safety tools or "session zero." Session zero or prep sessions occur before gameplay technically begins and typically include character introductions, a discussion of the desired tone or focus for the game, and a discussion of boundaries regarding content. Character creation or introduction features players either collectively creating their characters or introducing and discussing how their already created characters may be intertwined. This helps establish the beginnings of a common narrative or bond between characters and, *ipso facto*, the players themselves.

The practice of using safety tools in games is also becoming more and more commonplace with practices such as the X Card and "Lines and Veils" allowing players to indicate what content they do and do not want in the game.

Sean K. Reynolds and Shanna Germain wrote *Consent in Gaming* (2019), a resource around how to both play and run a tabletop RPG in a way that prioritizes the consent of all parties involved. Rather than simply censoring content, these practices actually allow for better development of trust and player agency. It also encourages values clarification amongst players both and individuals and as a group as they make active decisions around what they will and will not participate in.

SCALED AND GROWTH-ORIENTED CHALLENGE

This educational community that Dewey says a teacher should create in the classroom will succeed in part because of the ways in which it is responsive to the interests and developmental needs of students. Dewey says that these needs and capacities should inform both what is taught to both engage students and help scaffold learning and development. As a result, according to Dewey, planning for the classroom must be "flexible enough to permit free play for individuality of experience and yet firm enough to give direction towards continuous development of power" (1938, 58). While Dewey prized imagination and encouraged agency in learners, he also despised the vein of progressive education, which he perceived as lacking focus and intention, and as leaving too much to the whims of children. Educational structure had been too rigid in the past but could not be entirely given up.

A GM is called upon to have foster a similar balance of co-creation and guidance, personalization, and challenge. Most of the time, they are working within a set of rules, using them to both propel the game forward and adjudicate its boundaries. To give players both a sense of agency and an understanding that their actions and choices have meaning, a GM must allow for levels of player influence and co-creation. However, a complete departure from rules or structure in favor of player preference could lead to a collapse of the game itself. Gary Gygax and Dave Arneson, two co-creators of *D&D*, cautioned the importance of scaling player agency and maintaining a sense of structure to ultimately serve larger goals of the game, saying,

> The danger of a mutable system is that you or your players will go too far in some undesirable direction and end up with a short-lived campaign. Participants will always be pushing for a game which allows them to become strong and powerful far too quickly. Each will attempt to take the game out of your hands and mold it to his or her own ends. To satisfy this natural desire is to issue a death warrant to the campaign, for it will either be a one-player affair or the players will desert en masse for something more challenging and equitable.
>
> *(1974, 4)*

Dashiell (2022) says that GMs are able to relax the rules, but never completely dismiss them, as doing so would fully violate the magic circle that they are entrusted to maintain and protect for players.

For both the Deweyan teacher and the GM, structure and rules used alongside freedom allow for the facilitation of experiences that are educative – leading to further growth. GMs are responsible for finding a razor-thin balance between an appropriately leveled challenge that engages players and simultaneously gives them a sense of the game having stakes. Antero Garcia, an education scholar, claims that teachers should explicitly incorporate the best principles of game-based learning (GMing) into their classrooms, arguing that it will enhance the adventurous nature of learning. Antero (2016) says these practices could allow schooling to shift from tedious rote learning and instead become, "a foundation on which students explore ideas, take on new identities, and generally get to try out new experiences in the safe confines of a teacher mediated space."

WHAT CAN GMS AND DEWEYAN TEACHERS
LEARN FROM EACH OTHER?

Just as John Dewey envisioned the teacher as an active participant in the learning community, tabletop GMs can adopt similar principles to enhance player engagement and co-creation. Dewey believed that an effective instructor was not merely a transmitter of knowledge but a facilitator of experience, guiding students through a dynamic learning process that balanced structure with adaptability. GMs can learn from the Deweyan principles of experiential learning to enhance player immersion, foster meaningful collaboration, and create more engaging and transformative gaming experiences.

Incorporating practices of reflection from modern experiential learning (which is deeply rooted in Dewey's educational theories) can help improve communication between GMs and their players, build trust, and even increase the value that players take from their gaming experience. Intentional reflection can be seen in the increasingly more common practice of debriefing at the end of gaming sessions. When GMs, after the conclusion of a gaming session, ask players how they felt about their experiences, what they enjoyed, what they did not like, and what they are taking away from it, metacognition is being sparked.[1] At the most basic implementation, this encourages players to reflect upon their experience of the game and the feelings and responses it elicited as a player as well as a character. Joe Lasley (2020) believes that debrief sessions can extend what he claims is the "holding environment" of the game that allows for personal experimentation and reflection. The extension of this environment into a space where players are invited to engage in an intentional frame shift, reflecting on themselves and their experience, allows for more learning to be leveraged. Building off the need to make this debrief space intentional, Stéphane Daniau (2016) recommends that the debrief session be no longer than half an hour and include specific questions around what skills players feel they utilized or where they were challenged.

By incorporating structured reflection into their sessions, GMs can foster a deeper sense of player investment and agency, reinforcing the collaborative nature of the game. When players are encouraged to articulate their thoughts on the session, they not only process their own experiences more fully but also provide the GM with valuable insights into what aspects of the game are most engaging or challenging. This feedback loop enables the GM to fine-tune future sessions, ensuring that the player needs, interests, and boundaries are acknowledged and integrated into the evolving narrative. Additionally, intentional debriefing can help create a safer and more inclusive space, where players feel empowered to voice concerns and shape the game in a way that best suits the group's collective enjoyment. Much like Dewey's vision of an ideal classroom where learning is shaped by student participation and responsive teaching, campaigns that prioritize reflection and player agency can cultivate richer, more immersive storytelling and stronger group cohesion.

Given their similar struggles and goals, Deweyan teachers can look to GMs for inspiration on how to balance the authority and power at their disposal with a desire to build efficacy in students. Gallons of ink have been spilled in commentary over the years on the appropriate role and style of a GM. Are they meant to adjudicate the rules with an iron fist, or do they create a sandbox and just let players roam? In both binaries, what is not acknowledged is that a GM would not exist without players. Without the consent and participation of the players, a GM serves no function, or worse, is a tyrant. If a GM is forcing players to behave a certain way, can it truly be said that "players" are even playing the game anymore?

Dewey saw instructors as *part* of the classroom learning community, who worked alongside students and owed their role to the presence of the students. A good GM's approach should be reflective of and responsive to the desires of players, as the existence of the game is predicated upon the existence of players, not the will of the GM. Players have the power to leave the table, and it is through their consent that the magic circle of the gaming space is maintained. When they leave the table, the game ends, no matter how "correctly" the GM may have been running it.

The power of the consent that players give GMs is an essential reminder to teachers to cultivate the same trust in their students. When students disengage (whether bodily or mentally), a good teacher knows that learning has stopped. While most students in primary and secondary educational settings do not have the physical ability to leave these spaces without consequence, they can still withdraw and limit their engagement. The existential power of that consent to create the learning/gaming environment is much easier to see in a tabletop RPG. It can remind Deweyan teachers of the importance of establishing ongoing buy-in, trust, and enthusiastic participation from students, even when their ability to "leave the table" is less evident.

PLAY AND EXPERIENCE

The resemblance the role of teacher and GM bear to one another helps us begin to examine how we consider the role of power, authority, and mutual participation in the classroom. It is situated in a larger question around why play is something important to education to begin with. Do learning environments simply need to be more fun for students to engage more deeply in them, or is there an essential aspect of how we learn found in the experience of play itself? Yet again, Dewey's perspective on the essential nature of experience to learning can help frame these questions and encourages us to consider how the experiences of play within an RPG may provide some of the same raw material of experience from which we extract educative moments.

According to Dewey, the experience of play was essential in intellectual formation. Dewey claimed that through play, children experiment with abstract concepts and create a "world of meanings, a store of concepts so fundamental to all intellectual achievement" (1991, 162). Rather than being unconnected with reality, Dewey pointed out that most "free play" connected back to recognizable concepts. A child might imagine a firefighter on the moon in their play, but they were still conceptualizing things like space, fire, job roles, etc. The experimentation with meaning and plasticity was a key element in playfulness – a trait that Dewey believed was an essential attitude of mind. The imaging that players do in a tabletop RPG session may be a bit more on the fantastical side, but they are still toying with frames and understandings gained through experiences in their own lives. Rolling the dice and taking risks, guided along by a GM, can help them continue to stretch their way of understanding the world. Those experiences, even if they only occurred in their imagination and in the shared story created by the group, still have the ability to transform and educate.

Dewey's primary goal for a student's education was growth through experience. It needed to be understood not as a "movement toward a fixed goal" or specific set of benchmarks to achieve, but rather as an end in itself. The growth experienced through education was meant to spark deeper curiosity and desire for more education. In *Education and Experience*, Dewey (1938) said, "Every experience is a moving force. Its value can only be judged by what it moves toward and into" (55). Sarah Stitzlein (2014), educational philosopher and Dewey scholar, highlights that Dewey's conception of growth also entails a deeper and ongoing curiosity about the world, as well as an openness to changing oneself in response to a shifting environment. Experience should yield growth and development in personal habits, which in turn help an individual pursue and reflect upon further experience, leading to a sort of compounding effect. Learning is lifelong not because of the sheer willpower of the learner to continue to pursue new knowledge, but because the act of learning from experience ignites a reaction that fosters more growth within the self and, thereby, more opportunities to learn as you orient this richer self to the world. For Dewey, education can be seen in the growth it ignites and continues to spark, not in the repository of what it has mastered.

The greatest compliment I was ever given as a GM occurred at the end of the last session of a three-year campaign of Monster of the Week, a narrative-focused game that sets players in a *Buffy the Vampire Slayer* or X-Files-like setting to track down the monsters in the modern day. This was a personal campaign started during the pandemic, and after three years, my players had saved Chicago from an evil fae overlord and put narratively satisfying bows on all of their characters' journeys. We all knew it was time for the game to end. As I finished narrating the epilogue and began to pack my notes, I joked that I would no longer know what to do with my time. The game was over. Without skipping a beat, one of my players said, "Just because this story's finished, it doesn't mean we want to stop telling them with you." Tabletop RPGs, like John Dewey's vision of education, are autotelic at their core. The point of both is the doing of both. We learn and we play because we wish to learn and to play, and our lives are made measurably better in the wake of both. GMs and Deweyan teachers are happily entrusted with the sacred duty to both foster and participate in these glorious autotelic pursuits.

NOTE

1 Black Armada Games, "Tools to Use After Play," Blog Entry, https://blackarmada.com/tools-to-use-after-play/.

REFERENCES

Carlson, Daniel. 2020. "D&D Beyond Bikini-Mail: Having Women at the Table," Dialogue: The Interdisciplinary Journal of Popular Culture and Pedagogy: Vol. 7: Iss. 3, Article 4.

Christopher, Timothy. 2012. "Justice Is Not Blind, Deaf, or Willing to Share Its Nachos." In *Dungeons & Dragons and Philosophy: Raiding the Temple of Wisdom*, edited by Jon Cogburn and Mark Silcox, 260. Chicago, IL: Carus Publishing Company.

Daniau, Stéphane. 2016. "The Transformative Potential of Role-Playing Games: From Play Skills to Human Skills." *Simulation & Gaming* 47 (4): 430.

Dashiell, Steven. 2022. "DM Habitus: The Social Dispositions of Game Mastering in Dungeons & Dragons." *Japanese Journal of Analog Role-Playing Game Studies* 3: 3–13.

Dewey, John. 1916. *Democracy and Education*. New York: Free Press.

Dewey, John. 1938. *Experience and Education*. New York: MacMillan.

Dewey, John. 1991. *How We Think*. Amherst, NY: Prometheus Books.

Dewey, John, and Melvin L. Rogers. 2016. *The Public and Its Problems: An Essay in Political Inquiry*. University Park: Penn State Press.

Garcia, Antero. 2016. "Teacher as Dungeon Master." In *The Role-Playing Society: Essays on the Cultural Influence of RPGs*, edited by Andrew Byers and Francesco Crocco, 175. Jefferson, NC: McFarland.

Gygax, Gary, and Dave Arneson. 1974. *Dungeons & Dragons Volume 1: Men & Magic*, 4, Tactical Studies Rules.

Haarman, Susan. 2023. *Dungeons & Dragons & Dewey: Toward a Ludic Pedagogy of Democratic Civic Life Through the Philosophy of John Dewey and Tabletop Role-Playing Games*. PhD diss., Loyola University Chicago.

Katifori, A., Petousi, D., Sakellariadis, P., Roussou, M. & Ioannidis, Y. 2022 September. Tabletop role playing games and creativity: The Game Master perspective. *17th International Conference on the Foundations of Digital Games*, 1–7.Kociatkiewicz, Jerzy. 2000. "Dreams of Time, Times of Dreams: Stories of Creation from Roleplaying Game Sessions." *Studies in Cultures, Organizations and Societies* 6 (1): 71.

Lake, Robert W. 2017. "For Creative Democracy." *Urban Geography* 38 (4): 507–511.

Lasley, Joe. 2020. "An Examination of Gaming Environments in Dungeons and Dragons Groups." PhD diss., University of San Diego.

Montola, Markus. 2009. "The Invisible Rules of Role-Playing: The Social Framework of Role-Playing Process." *International Journal of Role-Playing* 1 (1): 22–36.

Nelsen, Peter. 2016. "Growth and Resistance: How Deweyan Pragmatism Reconstructs Social Justice Education." *Educational Theory* 66 (1–2): 234.

Noddings, Nel. 2010. "Dewey's Philosophy of Education: A Critique from the Perspective of Care Theory." In *The Cambridge Companion to Dewey*, edited by Molly Cochran, 269. Cambridge: Cambridge University Press.

Reynolds, Sean K., and Shanna Germain. 2019. *Consent in Gaming*. Monte Cook Games. https://www.montecookgames.com/store/product/consent-in-gaming/.

Schallegger, Rene Reinhold. 2018. *The Postmodern Joy of Role-Playing Games: Agency, Ritual and Meaning in the Medium*. Jefferson, NC: McFarland.

Skilbeck, Adrian. 2017. "Dewey on Seriousness, Playfulness and the Role of the Teacher." *Education Sciences* 7 (1): 12.

Stitzlein, Sarah. 2014. "Habits of Democracy: A Deweyan Approach to Citizenship Education in America Today." *Education and Culture* 30 (2): 67.

White, William J., Nicolas LaLone, and Nicholas J. Mizer. 2022. "At the Head of the Table: The TRPG GM as Dramatistic Agent." *Japanese Journal of Analog Role-Playing Game Studies* 3: 47.

Wizards of the Coast. 2014. *Dungeon Master's Guide*. Wizards of the Coast.

CHAPTER 2

We Are Playing in a Material World

Thinking and Learning through the Physical Objects of Tabletop Role-Playing Games

Jessica Hautsch

It's Friday night, *Dungeons & Dragons*, and my character Sildar Oussearnith, a half-elf draconic sorcerer, is battling a pair of frost worms. As my turn approaches, I glance at my character sheet to see what spell slots I have available and then flip open my copy of the *Player's Handbook* (*PHB*) – one of the three core *D&D* rule books – to look up spells. When it's Sildar's turn, I double-check placement on the battle map to ensure that I won't incinerate any of my allies currently in melee, before casting "Fireball" at eighth level and rolling my dice.

Very often, when we discuss tabletop role-playing games (tabletop RPGs), like *D&D*, we talk about mental escapism and imagination. These discursive frameworks often depict *D&D* as intangible and immaterial, happening in what is sometimes referred to as the "theater of the mind." However, as this opening anecdote of a single turn in combat suggests, the physical objects we play with are integral to analog tabletop RPGs. In this chapter, I build on the work of scholars who have looked at material culture in tabletop RPGs, drawing on my autoethnographic observations and

DOI: 10.1201/9781003641353-4

comments from *D&D* players posted to various Reddit forums (referred to as subreddits),[1] to argue that physical objects are not only a part of how we play but also how we think. As we reference rule books, consult our character sheets, and add up our dice, they become a part of our cognitive system, integrated into, shaping, and extending our minds. These objects are not just aspects of the game that we think *about*, but that we think *with*. Learning to play entails extending our minds through these material components, distributing cognition across them as we integrate them into our cognitive system.

Since the first studies of analog tabletop RPGs, Scholars have commented on the material components of play. Gary Fine's (1983) seminal ethnographic study, for example, discusses player superstitions around dice (95). Other scholars have focused on how these objects shape our understanding of characters and gameplay. For example, Jeff Rients (2014), Lars Konzack (2013), and Jason Morningstar (2014) discuss how the design of the character sheet influences our understanding of characters and our approaches to tabletop RPGs. In addition, Jamie Banks, Nicholas David Bowman, and Joe A. Wasserman (2017) looked at the material elements of character construction, analyzing how characters are represented through minis, commissioned artwork, and other physical items. Christo Leon, James Lipuma, and Mauricio Rangel Jimenez (2024) describe these elements as "sacred objects," an essential part of the ritual of in-person games. In response to the increase in online play during the COVID-19 pandemic, researchers found that, despite digital counterparts streamlining play, many tabletop RPGers said that they missed physical objects (Scriven 2021). As Antero Garcia (2019) theorizes, "gaming literacies are enacted differently within different spaces and mediated by different tools," asserting "that this focus on materiality and spatiality in analog settings is an important focus for understanding literacies in digital, analog, and hybrid contexts today" (11). Playing and learning in *D&D*, he argues, occur across a network of material and interpersonal interactions. While Garcia uses the term "literacies" to discuss our interaction with the material components of play, I frame it in terms "cognition," to emphasize the integration of these objects into a cognitive system and their role in extending and shaping our thinking as we play.

In a comprehensive examination of physical components in role-playing, Rafael Bienia's (2016) dissertation, "Role Playing Materials," takes a Latourian approach to RPGs, looking at materials as not simply passive objects but actors that shape players through collaborative "inter-relational processes" (15). He asserts that such an approach "expands preconceived notions that define role-playing as a mental process caused by players," arguing instead that play "emerges in and by a group of heterogeneous elements" (14–15). While I agree with Bienia that "materials collaborate with narrative and ludic actors in role-playing games" (15), it is not just that materials and players exist as a social network of actors, but that they form a cognitive system. Physical objects shape our actions (Bienia 2016, 23), because they are integrated into our cognition, enabling it as we think and learn with and through them.

In this chapter, I draw on work being done in the cognitive sciences and philosophy theorizing that our cognition extends into and is distributed across the physical world to explore how players interact with and think through some of the different material elements of analogue *D&D*[2] as they learn and play the game. By examining rule books, character sheets, and dice, I argue that the material objects of the game are not just objects that we use to play with but that we think with, offloading our cognition onto them to facilitate our understanding of the game. I begin by looking at rule books, and how their presence at the table eases the cognitive load of players and helps them to navigate the complex mechanics of the game. Next, I turn to character sheets, discussing how they are designed to help us offload and extend our memory. Finally, I look at dice, the shiny math rocks that determine the outcomes of character actions. I argue that these "math rocks" not only provide the numbers that we need to add up but also can be physically manipulated by players to facilitate the arithmetic necessary for the game. In each case, players and objects form a cognitive system as they think with and through these materials.

LEARNING AND EXTENDED COGNITION

Learning to play *D&D* can feel formidable. As one Reddit user, u/stirfriedpenguin (2024), notes,

> For most people, *D&D* is the most complicated game they have ever, and will ever, play. By far. It might seem approachable and intuitive to veteran players and hardcore gamers, but to most newcomers the Player's Handbook is as arcane and intimidating as a wizard's spellbook.

Just attempting to build their first player character (PC) presents a considerable hurdle for new players, who must make decisions about their PC's background, class, species, and abilities, while also figuring out things like proficiency bonuses, passive perception, and spell DCs (difficulty class). Reddit posts from prospective players demonstrate just how daunting learning the game can be. For example, in "(HELP) I'm scared of getting into *D&D*," u/E-C-3 (2023) expresses his fears about being a Dungeon Master (DM), the player at the table who describes the scene, controls non-player characters (NPCs), calls for dice rolls, and arbitrates the rules. His first time ever playing *D&D*, he watched videos and bought the Wizards of the Coast issued starter pack, but admits

> It's SO complicated. I just feel like the explanations people give are too slim. I see a video that tells me "I'm ready for an adventure" and then realize there's 19390 million more things to learn about the game[…] For example, combat was the most complicated thing ever to understand for me, along with spells and stuff like that. Speed? action? Bonus action? Reaction? Spell slot? Short rest? Long rest? WHAT IS THAT?!

By DMing, u/E-C-3 is taking on an admittedly more complicated role than players who are responsible only for controlling their PC. But even those players might feel overwhelmed their first time playing the game because, as he observes, "There's so many rules and things to learn" (u/E-C-3 2023). This comment brings up important questions about what it means to "learn" to play a tabletop RPG, like *D&D*, and what that suggests about how we learn.

While the material components of the game might be an effective and intuitive cognitive support system for experienced players, for those new to *D&D*, they add additional complexity to an already incredibly complex game. Cognitive scientist David N. Perkins (1993) notes the fallacy of "the 'fingertip effect'" (95), the common assumption that all you need to do is "Simply make a support system available and people will more or less automatically take advantage of the opportunities it affords" (95). But, as anyone who has ever seen a new player struggling to find information in their *PHB* can attest, belief in such an effect is unfounded. It isn't enough for people just to have access to a support system; they need to *learn* how to use it. I argue that learning the game is less about memorizing rules and more about knowing how to structure and interact with the environment in ways that facilitate play through the extension and distribution of cognition across the material components of the game.

Animate Objects

In his introduction to *Distributed Cognitions: Psychological and Educational Considerations*, Gavriel Salomon (1993) notes that "Traditionally, the study of cognitive processes, cognitive development, and the cultivation of educationally desirable skills and competencies has treated cognitive as being *possessed* and residing *in the heads* of individuals" (xii). Such an approach, though, overlooks the role of the environment – both social and material – in how we think and learn. Contrary to the Cartesian disembodied abstraction of the mind, theories of what is referred to as "4-E[3] cognition" maintain that our thinking is deeply embodied, extended into the world, and distributed across social and material environments. While this approach to cognition acknowledges that the brain plays an important role in how we think, it does not reduce cognition to neurons, arguing instead that, as Alva Noë (2010) puts it, "You are not your brain" (7). Human consciousness and cognition are activities that are not contained by "the boundaries of skin and skull" but rather extend into the environment and are distributed across material, social, and cultural networks (Clark and Chalmers 1998, 7). Cognitive philosopher Andy Clark (1997) explains that your "Mind is a leaky organ, forever escaping its 'natural' confines and mingling shamelessly with body and with world" (53). Cognition is not individual, but ecological, a "continuous with processes in the environment" (Clark and Chalmers 1998, 10). Or, as cognitive archeologist Lambros Malafouris (2016) puts it, "Human thinking is, first and above all, thinking *through*, *with*, and *about* things, bodies, and others" (77). Tabletop RPGs, like *D&D*, exist in – to use cognitive scientist Edwin Hutchins's (1995) term – a "cognitive ecology" that is enacted through the interaction of social, cultural, and physical contexts (112–114).

This approach to cognition, then, suggests that learning is embodied, extended into the environment, and distributed across intersubjective interactions. Educators have long noted the social elements of learning. Probably the most well-known theory of the power of socially extended cognition is Lev Vygotsky's (1978) "zone of proximal," which refers to "the distance between the actual development level as determined by independent problem solving and the level of potential development as determined through problem solving under adult guidance or in collaboration with more capable peers" (86). In this formulation, the zone of proximal development demonstrates the way in which cognition is distributed across and extended through interpersonal interactions. While *D&D* and other tabletop RPGs take advantage of this socially distributed cognition, I am focusing on how our cognition might also be extended through the physical world. Like social interaction, material objects can also extend our abilities, helping us to expand them through what Clark (1997) calls "soft scaffolding," noting that "we may often solve problems by 'piggy-backing' on reliable environmental structures" (45). By thinking and learning with and through our environment, we demonstrate conceptual understanding and complete processes that would not be able to without those structures.

In tabletop RPGs, like *D&D*, the objects that we play with provide us with various forms of "soft scaffolding" that help us to learn the game, a task that might be impossible otherwise. For example, despite u/E-C-3's concerns about having to frequently check the *PHB* or *Dungeon Master's Guide* (*DMG*) for rules, veteran players promise him that it's perfectly fine to look things up. Learning to play the game doesn't necessarily mean you have to internalize all the rules; no one does. In fact, attempting to do so could interfere with your ability to learn. As Joshua R. Eyler (2018), notes "intrinsic cognitive load" – which relates to the complexity of new information or processes – "can often be an issue with learners who have less expertise in a particular area" (192–193) because when "an individual's cognitive load crosses the threshold from challenging to overtaxing, learning is affected" (192). Although he is primarily concerned with student learners, his observations also hold true for new *D&D* players; trying to memorize all the rules could actually impede your ability to play.

Learning to play the game has a high intrinsic cognitive load, which environmental supports – like rule books – can help players manage. For this reason veteran players, like u/DrTenochtitlan[4] (Jennings 2023), reassure new players that

> there are LOTS of rules that are very situational. Quite frequently, you won't learn many of these lesser-used rules until you have to use them for the first time. That's ok… just look them up quickly, and go from there.

Jennings (2023)

u/Zohwithpie (2023) offers similar reassurance, "At the end of the day, every player that is on the table (including the DM) will have things that they don't know or don't remember. That's why it is always good to keep the manuals in hand." Between all three *D&D* handbooks, there are over a thousand pages of rules – way too many to memorize. But the handbooks are there so that players don't *have* to; they have environmental support that will do the remembering for them as they learn the game. Playing the game is an open-book – not a closed-book – exam.

For that reason, players' time is more effectively spent not studying the PHB but figuring out how to physically alter their books to integrate them more efficiently into their cognitive system. My *PHB*, for example, has color-coded tabs to help me find key information and sections more quickly. This is not uncommon for players. As Garcia (2019) notes, many players' books are "pocked with myriad sticky notes and paper bookmarks to key pages in the book. Materiality and physical use meant these books were weathered, annotated, and personalized over time" (19). Part of the personalization of these books is about making the information in them more easily accessible, rendering them more effective tools for lessening the cognitive load of play.

Similarly, players and companies create "cheat sheets" to help new players. An Instagram ad by Armor Class (2024) emphasizes the overwhelming amount of information that new players need to get started, offering them a sheet that "goes through *everything* you will need in your campaign and helps remind you of rules that you may have forgotten or need in a quick moment." The cheat sheet by Armor Class – and others like it – has a breakdown of the most common rules of the game: the difference between advantage and disadvantage, what actions you can take in combat, what initiative is, etc. A reference, like this one, lightens the cognitive load of new players, helping them to mentally manage the complexity of the game and preventing it from becoming overtaxing.

Reference pages are valuable cognitive tools, and so I want to push back against the idea that these are "cheat sheets." Despite what this nomenclature suggests, using one isn't "cheating" at all. The reason why other Redditors advised u/E-C-3 to keep the books nearby and why Armor Class and other companies create "cheat sheets" is that we don't need to have all the rules "in our heads" if we have them in our hands. Learning is not just about finding the information in the environment, but about designing material components to help us more efficiently and effectively complete tasks. As Hutchins (1995) notes, "Humans create their cognitive powers by creating the environments in which they exercise those powers" (169). These kinds of sheets aren't "cheating," they are structuring environments to offload cognition, scaffold learning, and extend a new player's cognitive powers. Looking at the role of material components, like these reference books, in how *D&D* is learned can help us to see and rethink the role of physical objects in more formal learning settings – and how we are structuring those environments to facilitate learning. For example, we might reconsider how we frame the "cheat sheets" that we allow students to bring to quizzes or open-book exams. Rather than imply that it is "cheating," we might have students engage in a metacognitive reflection about how their notes function as extensions of their minds, teaching them the most effective ways to format them. Understanding the mind as extending into and distributed across our social and material environments can help us expand what we mean by and how we measure learning.

THE CHARACTER SHEET

Sildar's character sheet is three printed-out pages that include information about his ability scores (20 for Charisma, 8 for Intelligence), language and skill proficiencies, armor class (AC), hit points (HP), melee and ranged attacks, and treasure and equipment. And that's just the first page. Other pages include a summary of his backstory, commissioned artwork, and the spells he knows. In the margins, I keep track of his sorcery points and jot down how much he has spent and how much he has earned during each session.

In this section, I look at the character sheet as an extension of the player's biological memory, integrated into their cognitive system. For new players, however, the difficulty of learning to use the sheet contributes to the already heavy cognitive load of learning to play the game. For this reason, they can benefit from sheets designed specifically to reduce that burden. Sheet design is important not just because of *what* it remembers, but *how* it remembers, how it structures the way that we think about, approach, and play the game.

Proficiency in History

Character sheets, containing both quantitative and qualitative information, are an essential part of play. Morningstar (2014) argues that the character sheet "serves many purposes, from state tracking, to space for note-taking, and is a focal point of player agency – a player's sense of ownership and control over the game world," noting that it is the "primary and very literal" – and material – "point of contact between player and character." Rients (2014) asserts that without it the character "doesn't exist," identifying the character sheet as "the one tangible, persistent object that uniquely connects the player to the game activity" (9). Adrian Hermann and Gerrit Reininghaus (2021) characterize the sheet as an "interface," that allows the player to interact with relevant information (33), while holding traces of previous sessions in the form of notes, stray marks, and eraser residue, which may explain why some players express "a feeling of remembrance and emotional significance towards it" (Leon, Lipuma, and Jimenez 2024). In a game known for its complexity, the character sheet helps players to keep track of a large amount of information. I don't remember how many spell slots Sildar has left or the amount of loot he got after the battle that ended our session two weeks ago. I don't have to remember it because the sheet remembers it for me.

But is that cognition? Clark and Chalmers (1998) argue that if

> as we confront some task, a part of the world functions as a process which, were it done in the head, we would have no hesitation in recognizing as part of the cognitive process, then that part of the world is...part of the cognitive process.
>
> (8)

If we recognize the act of remembering character stats and class features as a cognitive process, then by offloading onto environmental supports, like the character sheet, those supports become integrated into that process (Clark and Chalmers 1998, 8). The sheet takes the role of "biological memory" (12), extending the mind by remembering information about and changes in a character.

The character sheet, then, is not just a record of my thinking; it is thinking. There is, as Clark and Chalmers (1998) explain, "a two-way interaction" between player and sheet, "creating a *coupled system* that can be seen as a cognitive system in its own right" (9), through which the mental process of remembering is enacted. And if decoupling occurs and "we remove the external component the system's behavioural competence will drop, just as it would if we removed part of its brain" (Clark and Chalmers 1998, 9). Without the sheet's material extension of my memory, I can't recall all Sildar's spells or what his passive perception is, and, as a result, my behavioral competence when playing would decrease significantly. For this reason, Clark and Chalmers (1998) argue, access to these environmental structures needs to be "reliable" (11, emphasis in original). As we play, the character sheet has to be accessible – must be "in reach," as Bienia (2016) notes (76), because without the sheet, we lose the environmental support it provides.

For the sheet to effectively extend my cognitive system, a certain level of expertise is required. As Perkins (1993) reminds us, it is not enough to have access to environmental supports – for them to be effective, we need to understand how to use them (95). This need for expertise is why some existing players reacted negatively to the updated character sheet released by Wizards of the Coast in 2024 to accompany the new edition of *D&D*. u/ArtemisWingz (2024), for example, posted "I really dislike this character sheet. The Attributes not being symmetrical and the skills being grouped with specific stats annoys me." The new design feels less intuitive to this player, and others agree. u/Falbindan (2024) asserts that

> Sure, technically it's a Wisdom (Perception) check but nobody calls it that especially new players will have to do a lot of searching around at first. I do prefer alphabetical order but I guess that's because I'm used to that.

u/Falbindan is already an expert in reading the older version of the character sheet; to create an effective coupled cognitive system with the new one, veteran players will have to learn how to think with these new character sheets.

Perception Bonus

Veteran players will have an easier time learning to play with – to extend their cognition through – the 2024 character sheets than new players, because their experience with the game means that they already have a lighter cognitive load. u/Falbindan's (2024) concern for novice players is telling, because for those new to the game, character sheets can feel overwhelming. In fact, Rients (2014) observes that the character sheet is "baffling to new players" (11). Other players agree. In a thread on Reddit's r/DMAcademy subreddit, for example, a user asked "What do new players find most difficult when playing *D&D*?" (u/Otherwise_Lead3920 2024). One answer that came up multiple times in the thread was "knowing where to look on a character sheet for things" (u/S4R1N 2024) or as another user responded "Character sheets. It is the first biggest hurdle" (u/ostbythewatercooler 2024). Because these new players are not as adept at making use of the sheet as an environmental support, their cognitive load is higher and, as a result, playing the game is slowed.

It is not surprising, then, that there is no shortage of Reddit threads asking about character sheets for new players. These character sheets are designed to contain less information – enough for new players to play the game but not so much as to be overwhelmed. The information is also arranged differently. In a sheet designed for novice players recommended by u/jbecks (2019), for example, stats and information are arranged to facilitate combat. It reads "Battle has started" above the box for the character's initiative bonus, which is used to determine the order of combat. The next line is broken into the sections "It's my turn I want to: Move: Attack: Use an Item:" with boxes corresponding to each section, including information about movement speed and attack options. Another section reads, "I am being attacked!" with information about characters' AC and HP, which determines how hard they are to hit and how much damage they can take. The last set of boxes says, "I need to heal" with information about their hit dice and death saves. The last section is labeled "I want to try and do..." with a list of the characters, stats, skills, and proficiencies. This sheet functions as scaffolding designed to help new players learn not only their stats and abilities but also how to use them within the context of the game, thereby easing their cognitive load.

However, it is worth noting that design is important because it teaches us not just how to play the game mechanically but how to approach playing it. Konzack (2013) argues that "character sheets are not neutral, but allow for a certain range of player behavior" (86), though their design encourages some modes of play while discouraging others. Analyzing the layout of the sheet, Rients (2014) suggests that the focus on equipment and treasure encourages players to orient play toward obtaining material wealth for their characters (11). Beginner sheets, like the one described above, that focus on teaching players combat procedures might exacerbate that problem, suggesting to new players that in-game challenges and conflicts are best resolved through force. Or as Rients puts it, the "emphasis on combat abilities on the front side of the sheet sends the wrong message about *D&D*, encouraging players to see their characters as hammers and all the world as a nail" (11). He argues that there is an imbalance between the representation of quantitative and qualitative aspects of the character – primacy given to the latter – so that it might encourage players to see their characters as a series of stats (Rients 2014, 11). While that might work well for some approaches to the game, there are other ways of playing, other ways of thinking. We should consider not just how the design of character sheets eases the cognitive load of play, but what they teach us about how to think about play, what to prioritize, and how to deal with challenges.

Character sheets are a powerful way of offloading information that would otherwise present an inhibitory cognitive load on players. They play a role in both *how* and *what* we think during the game. Educators and students should think about the importance of design when developing worksheets and notetaking guides. Do these designs encourage students to think in a specific way? Do they prioritize certain kinds of problem-solving? The design of the environmental and learning supports should not only consider what students need to know but also how they encourage students to think. For example, educators might consider the levels of Bloom's taxonomy that worksheets and notetaking guides engage and what that communicates to students about what it means to know or understand material in class.

DICE, DICE, BABY

Dice are perhaps the most iconic material elements of *D&D*. Almost every table has at least one dice goblin – a player who collects multiple sets of dice – and some players buy or make formal "jails" for dice that produce a string of low rolls. In one of the earliest studies of *D&D*, Fine (1983) discusses the superstitions that emerge around lucky dice and players' false sense of control over the outcome of rolls (93–98). Superstitions pervade player interactions with dice because of the integral role they play in the game, both mechanical and narrative elements depending on them. Whether or not your attack lands, what you notice, how persuasive you are, your ability to avoid the negative effects of a trap – all depend on the roll of a die. The d20, a 20-sided dice, is the most commonly used throughout play to decide character success and failure; other dice d12s, d10s, d8s, d6s, and d4s are used less frequently, often to determine the damage from weapon attacks and spell effects.

In this section, I argue that dice play an important role in not just the game's narrative and mechanical operation but also within the cognitive ecology of the game. New players often find differentiating the different dice difficult; I examine how "accidental" but "locally effective features" of the dice can be used to structure the environment by having players focus on characteristics that are "computationally cheap" to identify (Clark 1997, 149). Then, I consider how the physical dice are manipulated to reduce the cognitive burden of the arithmetic the game requires.

Getting Dicey

For new players, learning to differentiate dice can be a difficult task. As u/TradReulo (2024) notes in a Reddit thread, "As for the dice thing, it's always been an issue for new players going back decades in my experience." Although iconic within the community, the shapes of the dice look similar to new players and telling the difference between a d20 from a d12, a d10 from a d8 can be challenging, especially for those already feeling overwhelmed by the game's intrinsic cognitive load.

Users on Reddit suggest ways to reduce the cognitive load on players by offloading some of the mental work of learning the difference between dice onto the environment. For example, u/TradReulo (2024) explains that

> The trick I've always used is making sure the players keep their dice on the max number so that they all look for. Keeping a d8 on 8 helps make it easy to quickly id until they learn what is what.

Another player, u/asilvahalo (2024) suggests helping new players by

> having color-coded dice instead of a matching set. 'Roll a d20' 'Which one is that?' 'The red one.' 'Roll a d10' 'Which one is that?' 'the blue one' or whatever. It obviously breaks down if your player is colorblind, but otherwise, I think it helps new players get used to the die shapes.

These methods take advantage of what players already know and can easily recognize – numbers and colors – to develop an understanding of what they don't know – the different dice shapes.

As these suggestions reveal, new players do not need to develop an abstracted mental representation of the dice because, as Clark (1997) notes, humans "use the representations of idiosyncratic, locally effective features to guide behaviors" rather than abstracted mental representations (149). For example, you might direct someone to find your coffee cup – or a d4 – by saying that it is yellow. The classical systems of computation and representation tend to dismiss these kinds of incidental or "accidental features" in favor of those considered more ontologically essential (Clark 1997, 150). For dice, these properties would include the shape or the number of sides, rather than the color or the number that happens to be facing up. However, as Clark (1997) explains,

The classical emphasis neglects the pervasive tendency of human agents to *actively structure* their environments in ways that will reduce subsequent cognitive loads. Thus, it is plausible to suppose that some of us use brightly colored coffee mugs [or different colored dice] partly because this enables us to rely on simple, personalized representations to guide search and identification.

(150)

For new players, the problem that needs to be solved is how to distinguish the different dice from each other. Learning the different shapes – the essential features of the dice – can be challenging, so u/TradReulo and u/asilvahalo suggest ways for new players to "*actively* structure their environments" – by manipulating or color-coding dice – to ease the cognitive load of identification by focusing on "computationally cheap" features (Clark 1997, 149). By encouraging new players to work from "simple, personalized representations" of the dice, the thinking they must do to find the dice they need for a particular roll is offloaded onto and guided by the environment, supporting them as they learn.

Shiny Math Rocks Go Click-Clack

Once you locate your dice, the next cognitive challenge is adding up your roll. As a general rule, the higher your character level, the more dice you are required to roll to determine things like attack damage. This means more math for players as they add up the individual dice – often without the aid of a calculator – as quickly as possible so as not to slow down the game. Doing this sort of math on the fly can be challenging for veteran players but can be really daunting for new players. Fortunately, I argue, players are often not doing the math "in their heads" because their computation is extended into the world as they interact with their dice to think with and through them.

Players manipulate and make use of their environment, offloading some of the cognitive burden of computation onto the dice themselves. For example, when Sildar flings a fireball at those pesky frost worms, I roll 13 d6. That means that in order to figure out how much damage the worm takes, I add up $3 + 4 + 4 + 6 + 2 + 3 + 4 + 6 + 5 + 5 + 3 + 2 + 4$ to get 51. It's not hard math, but the long string of computation creates a heavier cognitive load. For a large number of dice like this, I find myself physically moving them in my tray, grouping them together into tens. So, instead of adding a long string of numbers, I simply count my groups of ten, multiply them by how many there are, and add what remains. Repositioning my dice and restructuring my environment lessens the cognitive load of computation. I am dealing with fewer numbers, so the math is easier to do "in my head," because of all the math I'm doing with my dice. Clark and Chalmers (1998) discuss moving titles on a Scrabble tray to generate words, arguing that "in a very real sense, the rearrangement [...] on the tray is not part of action; it is part of thought" (10). And that's what's happening in my dice tray as well; it is not that I am acting on and physically manipulating the environment and then thinking about the numbers, the physical manipulation is thinking.

In one thread on Reddit, a user asked for advice about how to quickly add up dice rolls. One player suggested a similar strategy to the one I outlined above, "find multiples of 5s and 10s. Move the dice into these 5s and 10s" (u/WestCoastHippy 2018). Another response urges the initial poster to

> Drop the calculator and start doing it in your head. DnD math isn't very hard, and even if you have difficulty with math or numbers practicing will help get you to the point of being able to add up dice quicker...and you'll find your own short cuts. For me when I'm rolling large pools I move dice back towards me that I've already added so I know not to add them again.[5]

By physically moving the dice that have already been counted, the player offloads the cognitive task of remembering which dice have been added and instead can focus on the arithmetic. While this player refers to this math as being done "in your head," this computation is not being done by just his brain, but is extended into the physical environment, which functions as an external support that enables it.

This approach to adding up numbers is not so different from how we learn basic addition or subtraction. At first, we interact with manipulatable objects of the environment; beginning with a group of five blocks, we physically add three to a group, counting the result to learn that $5 + 3 = 8$. We might not yet be capable of doing this math "in our head," but we are able to do it "in our world" by thinking with and through environmental supports. Eventually, we switch to another environmental support: pencil and paper. When learning to add larger numbers, for example, we are taught to include a notation for the numbers we "carry" when adding 89 and 53 to reduce the "cognitive load" of our calculations. As we develop our skills and become more expert, we might rely less on environmental supports, while returning to them when necessary – like when trying to add numbers while distracted by something else or adding large numbers like 946572803+620842 or, as have seen, adding a long string of numbers. In these cases, we might quickly jot down numbers on a piece of paper, gesture as though we were working through the problem in the air in front of us – or physically move the dice in our try. We learn to manipulate our world to provide scaffolding for our mental processes and by doing so, we are able to think, learn, and play in ways that we might not otherwise be able to. As educators, we might have our students engage in more meta-cognition about the ways that they extend their cognition to help them consciously structure their environment for more effective learning.

AND THAT'S WHERE WE'LL END FOR TODAY

Cognition is not something that happens in the individual mind locked away within our skulls; it is porous and diffuse, seeping and leaky as it extends throughout and is distributed across the environments that we think in and with. When playing a complex tabletop RPG, like D&D, we offload some of the cognitive burden onto material supports, so that we don't need to memorize all the rules or remember the HP or spell slots that our characters had left at the end of the previous session or add up a long string of numbers in our head. Learning to play the game, and learning in general, entails learning how to structure your environment to support cognition and how to use the cognitive supports that it provides.

NOTES

1 There are numerous subreddits dedicated to discussions about D&D and other tabletop role playing games. Comments included in this paper are from r/DMAcademy, r/DnD, r/DungeonsandDragons, r/onednd, and r/3d6.
2 There are many digital tools that can replace or supplement the material components of the game, for the purposes of this chapter, I will be focusing on the analogue experience of the game.
3 Rather than a unified theory of the mind, the term 4-E cognition refers to a cluster of theories of cognition. These theories agree that the mind is not abstract or disembodied but may disagree about the extent to which it is embodied, extended, embedded, and enacted.
4 Posted under username u/DrTenochtitlan.
5 This user's account has been deleted since this 2018 comment was posted to r/DND.

REFERENCES

Armor Class (@armorclassco). "🎲Master D&D with the Player's Cheat Sheet🎲." October 24, 2024. https://www.instagram.com/p/DBg72rgAF-c/

Banks, Jamie, Nicholas David Bowman, and Joe A. Wasserman. "A Bard in Hand: The Role of Materiality in Player-Character Relationships." *Imagination, Cognition and Personality: Consciousness in Theory, Research, and Clinical Practice* 38, no. 2 (2017): 1–21.

Bienia, Rafael. "Role Playing Materials." PhD diss., Maastricht University, 2016.

Clark, Andy. *Being There: Putting Brain, Body, and World Together Again.* The MIT Press, 1997.

Clark, Andy, and David Chalmers. "The Extended Mind." *Analysis* 58, no. 1 (1998): 7–19.

Eyler, Joshua R. *How Humans Learn: The Science and Stories behind Effective College Teaching.* West Virginia University Press, 2018.

Fine, Gary Alan. *Shared Fantasy: Role Playing Games as Social Worlds.* University of Chicago Press, 1983.

Garcia, Antero. "Gaming Literacies: Spatiality, Materiality, and Analog Learning in a Digital Age." *Reading Research Quarterly* 55, no. 1 (2019): 9–27.

Hermann, Adria, and Gerrit Reininghaus. "Beyond the Character Sheet: 'Character Keepers' as Digital Play Aids in the Contemporary Indie Tabletop RPG Community." *Japanese Journal of Analog Role-Playing Game Studies* 2 (2021): 31–50. https://repository.kulib.kyoto-u.ac.jp/dspace/bitstream/2433/266699/1/jarps_2_31.pdf

Hutchins, Edwin. *Cognition in the Wild.* The MIT Press, 1995.

Jennings, Thomas. "An Important Thing to Remember Is That While You'll Learn the Basics Relatively Fast." *Reddit*, posted under/DrTenochtitlan, December 5, 2023. https://www.reddit.com/r/DungeonsAndDragons/comments/18b6ktz/help_im_scared_of_getting_into_dd/.

Konzack, Lars. "Characterology in Tabletop RolePlaying Games: A Textual Analysis of Character Sheets." In *WyrdCon Companion Book*, edited by Sarah Lynne Bowman and Aaron Vanek, Wyrd Con, 2013: 86–93.

Leon, Christo, James Lipuma, and Mauricio Rangel Jimenez. "Tabletop and Digital Rituals in Dungeons & Dragons." *Analog Game Studies* 11, no. 3 (2024). https://analoggamestudies.org/2024/10/tabletop-and-digital-rituals-in-dungeons-dragons/

Malafouris, Lambros. *How Things Shape the Mind: A Theory of Material Engagement.* The MIT Press, 2016.

Morningstar, Jason. "Visual Design as Metaphor: The Evolution of a Character Sheet." *Analog Game Studies* 1, no. 5 (2014). https://analoggamestudies.org/2014/12/visual-design-as-metaphor-the-evolution-of-a-character-sheet/

Noë, Alva. *Out of Our Heads: Why You Are Not Your Brain, and Other Lessons from the Biology of Consciousness.* Hill and Wang, 2010.

Perkins, David N. "Person-Plus: A Distributed View of Thinking and Learning." In *Distributed Cognitions: Psychological and Educational Considerations*, edited by Gavriel Salomon. Cambridge University Press, 1993: 88–110.

Rients, Jeffrey. "The Elf That Is You: The Failure of the Character Sheet in *Dungeons & Dragons*." *GWRJ* 4, no. 2 (2014): 7–19.

Salomon, Gavriel. "Editor's Introduction." In *Distributed Cognitions: Psychological and Educational Considerations*, edited by Gavriel Salomon. Cambridge University Press, 1993: xi–xxi.

Scriven, Paul. "From Tabletop to Screen: Playing Dungeons and Dragons during Covid-19." *Societies* 11, no. 4 (2021). https://www.mdpi.com/2075-4698/11/4/125

u/ArtemisWingz. "I Really Dislike This Character Sheet." *Reddit*, September 3, 2024. https://www.reddit.com/r/onednd/comments/1f89kzu/2024_official_dd_character_sheet_pdf_available_now/

u/asilvahalo. "One Thing I've Found Helps New Players with 'What Die Is That?'" *Reddit*, March 7, 2024. https://www.reddit.com/r/DMAcademy/comments/1b978a9/what_do_new_players_find_most_difficult_when/

u/E-C-3. "(HELP) I'm Scared of Getting into *D&D*." *Reddit*, December 5, 2023. https://www.reddit.com/r/DungeonsAndDragons/comments/18b6ktz/help_im_scared_of_getting_into_dd/

u/Falbindan. "I'm Personally Not a Fan of Grouping Skills under Abilities." *Reddit*, September 3, 2024. https://www.reddit.com/r/onednd/comments/1f89kzu/2024_official_dd_character_sheet_pdf_available_now/

u/jbecks. "Try This One." *Reddit*, March 13, 2019. https://www.reddit.com/r/3d6/comments/b0gex8/comment/eiepchn/

u/lostbythewatercooler. "Character Sheets. It Is the First Biggest Hurdle." *Reddit*, March 7, 2024. https://www.reddit.com/r/DMAcademy/comments/1b978a9/what_do_new_players_find_most_difficult_when/

u/Otherwise_Lead3920. "What Do New Players Find Most Difficult When First Playing *D&D*?" *Reddit*, March 7, 20204. https://www.reddit.com/r/DMAcademy/comments/1b978a9/what_do_new_players_find_most_difficult_when/

u/S4R1N. "Knowing Where to Look on a Character Sheet for Things and What They Need to Add together." *Reddit*, March 7, 2024. https://www.reddit.com/r/DMAcademy/comments/1b978a9/what_do_new_players_find_most_difficult_when/

u/stirfriedpenguin. "For Most People, *D&D* Is the Most Complicated Game." *Reddit*, March 7, 2024. https://www.reddit.com/r/DMAcademy/comments/1b978a9/what_do_new_players_find_most_difficult_when/

u/TradReulo. "As for the Dice Thing." *Reddit*, March 7, 2024. https://www.reddit.com/r/DMAcademy/comments/1b978a9/what_do_new_players_find_most_difficult_when/

u/WestCoastHippy. "Find Multiples of 5s and 10s." *Reddit*, October 25, 2018. https://www.reddit.com/r/DnD/comments/9rdymj/is_there_something_i_can_use_to_add_up_physical/

u/Zohwithpie. "At the End of the Day, Every Player That Is on the Table (Including the DM) Will Have That They Don't Know." *Reddit*, 5 December 2023. https://www.reddit.com/r/DungeonsAndDragons/comments/18b6ktz/help_im_scared_of_getting_into_dd/

Vygotsky, Lev Semyonovich. *Mind in Society: The Development of Higher Psychological Processes*, edited by Michael Cole, Vera John-Steiner, Sylvia Scribner, and Ellen Souberman. Harvard University Press, 1978.

CHAPTER 3

From Diverse Roots to Dual Classing

Crystallizing the Role of Tabletop Role-Playing Games in Education, with Examples from Corporate Learning and Development

Mátyás Hartyándi

INTRODUCTION

In the 21st century, particularly in the last decade, the educational use of analog role-playing games (RPGs), including tabletop and live action role-playing games (larps), has significantly increased, accompanied by a growing body of related research (Henriksen 2004; Andresen 2012; Mochocki 2013, 2014; Bowman 2014; Bowman and Standiford 2015; Branc and Mochocki 2018; Westborg 2019; Bagès, Hoareau, and Guerrien 2021; Westborg 2023; Cullinan 2024; Hartyándi and van Bilsen 2024; Hixson and Eike 2024). This trend represents the latest wave of role-playing applications in education, uniquely rooted in leisure activities, despite role-playing being a staple learning method for educators for decades (Bolton and Heathcote 1999).

Role-playing may appear too whimsical for the serious world of adulthood and business, but it has been applied in business and management

 DOI: 10.1201/9781003641353-5

education since the 1940s. As early as 1943, Ronald Lippitt, a colleague of Kurt Lewin, wrote that role-playing can address the classic challenges of leadership development:

> One of the most effective techniques the writer has discovered [...] is the utilization of several variations of the role-playing or psychodramatic situation which Moreno has developed most fully in the areas of individual diagnosis and therapy in psychiatric cases.

> *(Lippitt 1943, 287)*

The renowned organization researcher and one of the fathers of organization development, Chris Argyris, also noted in an early paper: "Management and union officials have both found it extremely useful to role-play their points before presenting them in final bargaining sessions" (Argyris 1951, 7). Or, as another author stated, "[s]tudents role-play some of the situations they will meet on the job" (Argyle 1964, 133). These early sources confirm that role-playing has been used for diagnosing, informing, and training in corporate and educational settings and has been researched widely (Corsini, Shaw, and Blake 1961; Craig 1979; Hartyándi and van Bilsen 2024, 146–148). Moreover, contrary to popular belief, the phrase "role-playing game" has been used in human resource development since the 1950s, referring to psychodramatic contests and crisis-playing political simulations (Driver 1954; Guetzkow 1963).

Meanwhile, hobby RPGs trace their origin back to *Dungeons & Dragons* (D&D) in 1974. Fifty years later, its 2024 edition remains the world's most popular tabletop RPG. However, few realize that the original D&D did not identify as an RPG (Gygax and Arneson 1974; Gygax 1975; Peterson 2022; Peterson 2024). This background exposes a highly complicated context where

- Role-playing is a natural form of learning that has long been utilized in education.

- Before D&D, RPG-labeled cases were all serious, education-oriented games.

- Modern analog RPGs, rooted in D&D-style hobby play, are now transitioning from leisure into the realm of education.

In this situation, the question arises about what real added value hobby RPGs can bring to education. This study aims to clarify the educational potential of tabletop RPGs for adult education. The examples used are from corporate learning and development (L&D) programs because they are substantial settings for non-formal learning, often characterized by bold, creative, and well-financed initiatives.

Tabletop RPGs integrate a wide range of game genres and playstyles (Arjoranta 2011). These diverse roots require detailed analysis to clarify their educational potential. This rich context provides a foundation to crystallize the actual value of tabletop RPGs in education. Through a comparative analysis, the study highlights functional combinations of RPG elements, forms of "dual classing" in D&D terms, that excel when contrasted with long-standing role-playing methodologies.

DIFFERENTIATING ROLE-PLAYING FROM OTHER FORMS OF PRETENSE

The educational potential of role-playing is based on the observation that "[p]laying in the fictional context of x is advantageous for actions in the real context of y" (Kapitany, Hampejs, and Goldstein 2022, 8). In this sense, role-playing is a form of pretense that can be utilized as an action method to collect first-person experiences under safe laboratory environment to

- explore and better understand past situations;

- put the present in a different light; and

- explore possible futures, thus preparing and rehearsing for future situations.

Shaun Nichols and Stephen Stich (2000) identified four key components of pretense:

1. Setting initial premise: Establishing an imaginary situation's foundational premise and shared assumptions.

2. Inferential elaboration: Expanding the imaginary situation by logically deducing additional elements that align with the initial premise.

3. Embellishment (non-inferential elaboration): Adding aesthetic or creative details to enrich the imaginary situation beyond logical deductions.

4. Production of appropriate pretend behavior: Engaging in actions that align with the imagined scenario, such as pretending to be in a different time or place or adopting someone else's persona.

These four key components alone can demarcate certain interactive intervention types. *Case studies*, for example, engage participants with a real or fictional case, where setting an initial premise and inferential elaboration is necessary for case analysis and hypothetical problem-solving (Harland 2014). Embellishment might also make the case more personal and easier to imagine, indirectly contributing to learning. However, in case studies, participants do not start behaving as if they were in that situation, or if they are, it is no longer only a case study but some kind of complex activity involving a case. This is similar to *scenario planning* and similar acts, where exploring future situations remains hypothetical at a cognitive level (Coates 2000). Thus, the behavioral factor alone can delimit cognitive methods that operate at a hypothetical level.

All four of the above components apply to role-playing, as well as other activities such as educational simulations and games. Unfortunately, the use of the terms *simulation*, *game*, and *role-playing* is inconsistent in the literature and can lead to many misunderstandings (Hallinger and Wang 2020). Based on David Crookall and Danny Saunders (1989), we define these terms in the following way:

- Simulations attempt to authentically model and represent some segment of consensus reality (Tuson 1994; Kriz 2022). Simulations prompt us to behave *as if* we were in a different situation.

- Games, by their rules, allow for more and less successful strategies (Hallinger and Wang 2020, 12). Games prompt us to behave *as if* their arbitrary rules were binding.

- When role-playing, we attempt to behave *as if* we were different.

Since these categories are not mutually exclusive, mixing them in the same activity is highly possible, leading to the conceptual confusion indicated above. Interactive *business simulations* often involve (digitally or physically) modeled organizational environments where participants must make decisions according to rules, similar to a game (Avolio, Waldman, and Einstein 1988; Klabbers 2009). Augusto Boal's *Image theater* has been utilized in industry teambuilding, where coworkers created three still images with their bodies to represent their group dynamics: first, revealing their current situation, then envisioning an ideal future, and finally forming a transitional image to guide the group from the present to the ideal (Ferris 2001). Morenian dramatic techniques involving modeling and role-play have been used to uncover employees' hidden assumptions and unconscious beliefs about organizational AI acceptance and to diagnose what went wrong with the process (Hartyándi 2025).

Other analog *situational exercises* and *skill drills* place individuals in a hypothetical scenario, requiring them to act according to specific social or professional roles, focusing on appropriate responses and behavior (Guenthner and Moore 2005). For example, they can practice communicating with different types of customers. *In-basket exercises* put participants in managerial or administrative roles, focusing on task management and decision-making within organizational structures (Bass 1985).

As an even more specific example, situational leadership theory divides subordinates into four categories based on their level of skill and motivation and, in parallel, into four matching leadership styles according to their degree of task and relationship orientation (Hersey and Blanchard 1969). In *situational leadership training,* participants are often given exercises where they can only behave according to one of the above styles or alternate between them in a fixed sequence. In all these cases, however, participants only assume social or psychological roles. They act as themselves in a specific role and do not have to think and behave *as if* they were a different person or, in RPG terms, a character (Peterson 2022). In this way, it is possible to distinguish, somewhat artificially, between two senses of role-playing: *simple* or *social-psychological role-playing,* where simulation and/or game aspects are more substantial and *complex,* or *character role-playing* that requires the enactment of a specific personality, which includes hobby RPGs (Harviainen 2011).

DIFFERENTIATING RPGS FROM OTHER FORMS OF COMPLEX ROLE-PLAYING

In addition to a detailed description of the situation, complex role-playing exercises utilized in various *action methods* and *applied drama* often offer much information for role-taking and impersonation. The most common of these elements are

- Name

- Demographics such as gender, age, etc.

- Background information

- Personality traits

- Relationships with the other roles

- Opinions on the subject matter, personal goals

- Proposed actions

The psycho-social descriptions seen in complex role-playing setups can be categorized as a mix of inferential elaborations of the initial premise and simple embellishments. Most of these role descriptions are qualitative and lack attached rules. Even the most detailed and complex role-playing simulation will lack a game element distinguishing RPGs from other forms of complex role-playing.

The model used to support this claim originates from one of the earliest academic analyses of RPG, sociologist Gary Alan Fine (1983). His three-layered approach has been revisited and refined through multiple authors, creating a model that can be used to analyze the educational potential of RPGs compared to other forms of RPGs (Baker 2005; Montola 2008; Cullinan and Genova 2023; Hartyándi and van Bilsen 2024; Stenros and Montola 2024). According to this, each RPG activity has three parallel, simultaneous layers (see Table 3.1):

TABLE 3.1   The three-layered model of role-playing game activities

Layer	Space	Presence	Framework
Social	Physical and social consensus reality	As a person	Personal purpose and social contract
Ludic	Set design and game materials	As a player	Game objectives and rules
Diegetic	Pretense and shared imagination	As a character	Character goals and diegetic fate/laws

Source: By author, based on Fine (1983), Baker (2005), Montola (2008), and Cullinan and Genova (2023), replicated from Hartyándi and van Bilsen (2024).

1. The primary, social, exogenous, or contextual layer is situated in the participating individuals' physical and social consensus reality and is mediated by personal needs, goals, and an implicit or explicit social contract, and in the broader context, by cultural norms and legal regulations.

2. The secondary, ludic, or endogenous frame is inhabited by players and game materials, regulated by formal game rules and objectives, and the dynamic impact of game elements.

3. The third, diegetic, or imagined frame is populated by fictional characters, influenced by character goals, diegetic laws, and the power of fate, mirroring the first layer of our reality.

What makes RPGs unique is the interplay between the three layers present in them. RPGs can be understood both as role-playing within a game framework or as a gamification of role assumption.

DIFFERENTIATING EDUCATIONAL RPGS FROM HOBBY RPGS

Many RPG fans have shared anecdotes about how much they owe to their hobby. From these accounts, it can be inferred that long-term engagement in hobby RPGs creates an excellent foundation for organic personal development. Moreover, in an informal sense, every game is educational, even if its only lesson is how to play itself (Gee and Hayes 2009; Gadamer 2004, 106). However, these do not make RPGs an *effective* and/or *efficient* educational tool. As autotelic activities pursued for their intrinsic enjoyment, hobby RPGs could be considered playful party experiences (Masek and Stenros 2024). Moreover, they do not distinguish developmental and non-developmental elements.

To highlight the potential misconceptions, let's use the paradox of the domino as a metaphor. In a domino run, artists arrange tiles in sequence, knock over the first, and if the setup is well designed, a cascading chain reaction follows. That is where the term domino effect comes from. Few realize that this spectacle has almost nothing to do with the original Italian tile game of Dominoes or its rules. In fact, only one characteristic, the physical proportions of the tiles, matters in a domino run, and even that has only an indirect connection to how the traditional game is played. Similarly, when applying tabletop RPGs in education, we need to be careful with apparent continuity. Just as a domino tile does not carry the rules of Dominoes into a domino run, not every element of tabletop RPGs necessarily supports learning. Thus, the educational potential of tabletop RPGs warrants further exploration.

Regarding the three-layered model, RPGs can be educational in at least three ways:

1. **Educational through Application**: Many leisure RPGs can be directly applied in formal or informal educational settings without altering their game (ludic) or narrative (diegetic) layers. In these cases, their educational value emerges in the social layer, where a shared learning goal is established through a social contract among players.

2. **Educational by Game Design**: RPGs can be designed with education in mind, shaping their game rules and materials to prioritize learning outcomes rather than pure entertainment, directly impacting the game layer.

3. **Educational in Content**: The diegetic layer of an RPG, in other words, the fictional content, scenarios, and settings, can be intentionally crafted to deliver educational value, fostering learning through the narrative itself.

According to Josefin Westborg (2023, 22), educational RPGs must incorporate educational elements in their framing and gameplay designs. In our model, all three layers (social, ludic, and diegetic) must be explicitly educational. In contrast, the broader term "edu-larp" encompasses a wide range of RPGs, including those that are educational only in their application, as described in the first sense (Bowman 2014). Westborg (2023, 21–22) labels this category as RPGs in education and contrasts them with stand-alone educational RPGs with an educational gameplay design but played for leisure. Compared to Westborg's four categories, the sets in our model indicate eight distinct categories, allowing for a more nuanced comparison.

1. Not explicitly educational: A hobby RPG played for leisure.

2. Educational only in Content: A hobby RPG played for leisure, with educational value in their content.

3. Educational only through Application: A hobby RPG applied in education.

4. Educational only by Design: An RPG designed to be educational, but without educational content, played for leisure.

5. Educational through Application and in Content, but not by Design: A hobby RPG with educational value in their content, applied in education.

6. Educational through Application and by Design, but not in Content: An educational RPG applied in education, where the content contradicts or clashes with its educational design, weakening or derailing the educational purpose, as a form of ludonarrative dissonance (Grabarczyk and Walther 2022).

7. Educational by Design and in Content, but not through Application: An educational RPG played for leisure.

8. Educational in Content, by Design and through Application: A truly educational RPG.

We can further distinguish tabletop RPGs from larp and computer-based formats (Zagal and Deterding 2018). Some authors argue that pretense varies across two major, relatively independent factors: physical embodiment and cognitive engagement (Kapitany, Hampejs, and Goldstein 2022, 9). While all RPG formats demand significant cognitive engagement, tabletop RPGs emphasize verbal expression and upper-body movement to a lesser extent. This places them midway between computer RPGs, which primarily involve manual input, and larps, which require full-body movement in terms of physical embodiment. Due to their focus on verbal interaction, tabletop RPGs offer a less physically intense experience than larps but stand out for their flexibility. This makes them particularly well-suited for oral reflection and fostering cognitive insights.

THE EDUCATIONAL POTENTIAL OF THE SOCIAL LAYER

Being part of a group inherently offers numerous factors that can both facilitate and hinder learning. Positive aspects include information exchange, cooperation, competition, advice, support, role modeling, imitation, and social and interpersonal learning. Additionally, experiencing group cohesion and a sense of belonging can enhance learning as individuals realize that others face similar challenges. Huizinga (1955) highlights that play encourages the creation of social groups. In this regard, leisure tabletop RPG environments are usually affinity spaces (Gee 2005) where participants are brought together with shared interests, activities, or goals that further encourage socialization, sharing, and learning.

Traditional play theories define play as voluntary and unproductive (Caillois 1961). However, corporate learning and development (L&D) programs are typically mandatory, performance-evaluated, and framed as work, which appears to contradict the nature of play. Participants frequently mention they were "sent here," indicating a lack of voluntary engagement. This issue isn't unique to (non-)formal education; it extends to any activity involving make-believe and playfulness, as such activities inherently disrupt and "breach" established social norms (Garfinkel 1967). The expectation to (role)play can lead to reluctance, resistance, or subversive behaviors, even in voluntary settings (Carnes 2014).

Structured activities, such as corporate training, mitigate this challenge by warming up participants to secure their buy-in. Moreover, Jacob L. Moreno (1949) asserts that any activity not entirely scripted contains spontaneity, proving that constraints and expectations do not eliminate play. Every environment enables and restricts playful behaviors simultaneously, and every game has an implied player (Aarseth 2014; Stenros and Montola 2024), making the gap between leisure gaming and structured training a matter of degree rather than a fundamental difference. While play is typically voluntary, it can be nudged, encouraged, or even enforced, much like the social pressures and structured expectations that shape behavior in any context.

THE EDUCATIONAL POTENTIAL OF THE DIEGETIC LAYER

Part of what makes role-playing different from other group-based learning methods lies in its diegetic layer. As we saw earlier, pretense can cover many things within the diegetic layer of the imaginary world, including the setting, specific situations, etc. These types of content could be all educational. Here and now, we will focus only on complex role-playing, a distinctive feature of RPGs.

Psychology has long recognized the impact of imitating role models relevant to us, such as the "Batman Effect" (White et al. 2017), or behaving in ways contrary to our professed self-image, such as in anti-role-playing

(Huncik 2006). Similarly, as psychodrama (Moreno 1962), Internal Family Systems (Carlisle 2015), or Avatar therapy (Ward et al. 2020) demonstrates, interacting with inner ego functions or parts of the self through role-playing can be beneficial. While some aspects of hobby RPGs can align with these, it remains unclear whether other character-playing elements have any learning potential and, if so, to what extent.

We lack clear evidence on the educational impact of attempting to portray a fully individualized personality that is theoretically very different from our own. Behaving as someone else, in other words, complex role-playing, might allow for identity exploration and transformation by embodying different personas, contributing to personal development. However, the educational potential of the non-inferential elaboration in complex role-playing is challenging to assess. Excessive decorative details may hinder learning by adding unnecessary ballast or diverting attention from the activity's educational focus (Imlig-Iten and Petko 2018). On the other hand, some argue that including pomp and circumstance can foster a sense of permission to play, ultimately enhancing the learning experience (Lasley and Rahn 2024).

It is also questionable what added value uninterrupted, long-term complex role-playing has, particularly in learning and development. Action methods like psychodrama primarily view the role-playing activity as a catalyst with cathartic potential, emphasizing the importance of subsequent processing and integration phases as equal, if not more crucial learning spaces (Moreno 1949), consistent with the experiential learning process (Kolb 1984). In sociodrama or educational drama, a continuous 30-minute role-playing scene is considered a significantly long event. By contrast, leisure tabletop RPG sessions require hours, and they are typically envisioned as half-to-full-day gaming marathon sessions played through years-long campaigns. There is no evidence to verify that this extreme duration of complex role-play is advantageous from an educational perspective.

Complex role portrayal may be an essential criterion for RPGs, but there is more anecdote than evidence about its educational potential (Harviainen 2011; Hartyándi van Bilsen 2024). Extended, uninterrupted, complex role-playing in RPGs may hold some unknown complex developmental potential. However, it may primarily serve as ballast regarding educational impact. Longitudinal research is needed to determine whether complex role-playing is complicating learning.

THE EDUCATIONAL POTENTIAL OF THE LUDIC LAYER

RPGs' educational potential may come from mixing the diegetic role-playing layer with the ludic rule-playing layer. Players voluntarily accept rules, even those making tasks uneasy, because doing so enables meaningful play. This lusory attitude (Suits 1978) is mirrored by the interpretation that game rules "force" desired behaviors and outcomes that mutual agreement alone cannot sustain (Baker 2008). However, the rules of most RPGs are not only meant to entertain but also to model reality. In other words, as the famous RPG designer Vincent D. Baker described: "[W]e create games to examine, explore, understand, or explain dynamic systems" (Baker 2017).

Tabletop RPGs have their origins in conflict-simulating war games, and a significant portion of tabletop RPG rules still focus on overcoming external challenges, mainly modeling melee combat, sometimes in a highly abstract manner that prioritizes entertainment over realism (Peterson 2022). This raises serious questions about how transferable and applicable the specific lessons and skills learned through such simulations are to real-life situations. Of course, this tradition does not exclude the possibility of creating serious educational RPGs that simulate other aspects of real-life situations by design and game rules (Duke 1974; Crookall and Saunders 1989).

A particular advantage of traditional tabletop RPGs compared to other forms of role-playing is the way they incorporate quantified randomness in their procedures. Participants use dice rolls, card draws, or other random number generators (RNG) to determine the outcomes of certain situations. The resulting dopamine release makes the experience more tense. While many games, such as video and board games, contain quantitative uncertainty (Costikyan 2015), most other role-playing forms lack these elements. RPGs are thus better at modeling stochastic, random processes than other role-playing forms. When role-playing combined with RNG is used for educational purposes, we can design educational RPGs that promote probabilistic thinking, risk management, and ownership, which are especially beneficial for developing decision-making and leadership skills in complex, chaotic, and turbulent environments (Lawrence 2013; Snowden and Rancati 2021; Hartyándi and van Bilsen 2024).

Both extreme positions about the ludic layer of RPGs have some educational potential, and both directions align with different schools of gaming simulations. One approach lies in hiding the complex set of rules from the participants. This leaves the entire ludic layer management up to a referee, while the participants can concentrate solely on the fictional situation and their character. This can be done to reduce cognitive load for players or, if the rules of the game also simulate real-world aspects, to teach these principles through play and experience. This can result in a situation almost indistinguishable from other complex role-playing forms from the player's point of view. Still, the outcome of the situations does not depend on the participants' will but on expert decisions, often influenced by randomness.

The root of this approach lies in German educational wargaming. Baron Georg von Reiswitz's *Kriegsspiel* (1824), reviving his father's 1812 initiative, developed a training game for cadets that abandoned moving miniatures or game tokens on a board. Instead, players simulated actual military exercises by issuing written commands to a referee. The referee would compare these commands against each other and predefined rules, resolving outcomes with dice rolls when necessary. The aim was to teach participants how to issue effective commands and handle the uncertainty of battlefield conditions (Peterson 2022). This experience became even more fluid and flexible in the *Free Kriegsspiel* formula proposed by General Julius von Verdy du Vernois (1884), where players verbally interacted with the referee, who used their military expertise to make decisions.

The combination or "dual classing" of role-playing with a hidden ludic layer managed by a referee comes from the *Braunstein* games (Wesely 1969–1970), a precursor to D&D. The author, Dave Wesely, a prominent figure in the wargaming community, was familiar with the *Free Kriegsspiel* tradition through the wargame *Strategos* (Totten 1880) and mixed it with *Diplomacy* style (Calhamer 1959) strategy gaming (Peterson 2024). In his one-session games, players represented different sides of a complex conflict, negotiating with one another while issuing secret orders that the referee compared and resolved.

While this combination is simulation-based, unlike in other gaming simulations, the rules do not restrict learners, and the process remains highly flexible, or in Totten's words, "Anything can be attempted" (Totten 1880, 105; Peterson 2024, 97–101). For example, experiencing the consequences of our behavior firsthand in a safe, simulated environment can be far more impactful than simply being told what to watch for, especially in the context of intercultural awareness and Diversity, Equity, and Inclusion (DEI) sensitization. Such experiences allow participants to recognize when they may have unintentionally caused offense. Another application could be practicing recognizing and managing different personality types through NPC interactions based on pre-established personality typologies such as DISC, MBTI, PCM, Enneagram, and others. The disadvantage of this type of "dual classing" is the heavy burden on the referee.

The other extreme approach might also be valuable from an educational perspective. In this case, the ludic layer is transparent to the players, or in different terms, player-facing, and they are expected to embrace it over time. The better the rules simulate the educational topic being addressed, the more transferable knowledge can be acquired through game mastery. The rules, in this case, of course, limit the participants and put a cognitive load on them, but ideally, they draw attention to the hidden contexts and limiting laws of reality that they seek to represent. This also means that any game rule element that does not represent learning content or promote learning hinders the educational potential of this "dual classing" that mixes role-playing with complex gameplay. Moreover, the weight and finality of dice rolls, their *alea iacta est* quality, create a point of no return that makes fictional scenarios feel more like real-life high-stakes situations.

Two key areas naturally lend themselves to these. The first is learning to navigate turbulent environments and complex problem spaces (Snowden and Rancati 2021). Situations characterized by volatility, uncertainty, complexity, and ambiguity (VUCA) can be effectively modeled using traditional tabletop RPG mechanics such as dice rolls and probability systems (Lawrence 2013). By making these challenges transparent and interactive, players can develop practical decision-making heuristics that translate into real-world problem-solving. Another valuable application is enhancing role-playing exercises in communication training where success is often binary; if the participant identifies the correct approach, they succeed. However, reality is rarely so straightforward. In tabletop RPGs, having the right approach isn't always enough; you also need a bit of luck. Introducing randomized outcomes through dice rolls can teach patience, resilience, and the understanding that even well-chosen strategies don't always guarantee immediate success. Instead, players learn the value of persistence, adaptability, and long-term problem-solving.

In addition to all of the above, considering the long-term complex role-playing in RPGs, their educational utility may not lie in prolonged role assumption itself but instead in two other aspects. First, simulating and navigating complex, intricate decision-making scenarios can be time-consuming, as seen in days-long crisis-playing RPGs run in the 50s

(Guetzkow 1963). Secondly, long-term processes are relevant for tracking progress, such as quantifying development over time. Gathering experience, gaining new levels, and becoming more powerful are standard features of tabletop RPGs (Peterson 2024). Parallelly, cognitive behavioral therapy has long employed development quantification to facilitate enduring changes in thought and behavior (Williams and Garland 2002). While hobby RPG game systems and character sheets are ill-suited for this purpose, educational RPGs might incorporate gamified functions like these to enhance their educational potential.

CONCLUSION

Role-playing distinguishes itself from other imagination-based cognitive methods by incorporating behavior in addition to hypothetical scenarios. Among various forms of pretense, RPGs stand out by combining complex role-playing, requiring the enactment of specific personalities, with a strong ludic layer. Tabletop RPGs, in particular, strike a balance between moderate physical embodiment and significant cognitive engagement, making them especially suitable for educational purposes that require cognitive exploration.

Although the educational value of complex role-playing remains uncertain due to a lack of longitudinal research, the ludic aspects of RPGs appear more promising. When combined with an all-knowing referee, complex role-playing offers a highly flexible gaming experience, allowing players to freely experiment with their decisions in ways that many fixed educational simulations do not. Alternatively, integrating complex role-playing with player-facing rules can be highly effective if the rules model the dynamics of the educational subject matter and reinforce cognitive and behavioral changes through measurable development. These two "dual classing" approaches represent the ends of a spectrum that can be explored and tailored to specific educational goals (Bowman 2022). This study highlights the multifaceted educational potential of tabletop RPGs, advocating for more comprehensive comparisons and deeper investigation, especially in the context of adult and corporate education.

REFERENCES

Aarseth, Espen. "I Fought the Law: Transgressive Play and the Implied Player." In *From Literature to Cultural Literacy*, edited by Naomi Segal and Daniela Koleva. London: Palgrave Macmillan, 2014. https://doi.org/10.1057/9781137429704_13.

Andresen, Martin Eckhoff, ed. *Playing the Learning Game: A Practical Introduction to Educational Roleplaying*. Oslo: Fantasiforbundet, 2012.

Argyle, Michael. *Psychology and Social Problems*. London: Routledge, 1964. https://doi.org/10.4324/9780203785744.

Argyris, Chris. "Role-Playing in Action." In *New York State School of Industrial and Labor Relations, Bulletin* 16, edited by France P. Eagan, 1–23. Ithaca, NY: Cornell University, 1951.

Arjoranta, Jonne. "Defining Role-Playing Games as Language-Games." *International Journal of Role-Playing*, no. 2 (2011): 3–17. https://doi.org/10.33063/ijrp.vi2.190.

Avolio, Bruce J., David A. Waldman, and Walter O. Einstein. "Transformational Leadership in a Management Game Simulation: Impacting the Bottom Line." *Group & Organization Studies* 13, no. 1 (1988): 59–80. https://doi.org/10.1177/105960118801300109.

Bagès, Céline, Natacha Hoareau, and Alain Guerrien. "Play to Reduce Bullying! Role-Playing Games Are a Useful Tool for Therapists and Teachers." *Journal of Research in Childhood Education* 35, no. 4 (2021): 631–641. https://doi.org/10.1080/02568543.2020.1810834.

Baker, Vincent David. "How RPG Rules Work." *Anyway*, January 18, 2005. https://www.lumpley.com/archive/156.html.

Baker, Vincent David. "Rules vs Vigorous Creative Agreement." *Anyway*, April 9, 2008. lumpley.com/index.php/anyway/thread/360.

Baker, Vincent David. "Systems in Miniature." *Anyway*, September 1, 2017. lumpley.com/index.php/anyway/thread/856.

Bass, Bernard M. *Leadership and Performance beyond Expectations*. New York: Free Press, 1985.

Bolton, Gavin M., and Dorothy Heathcote. *So You Want to Use Role-Play? A New Approach in How to Plan*. Stoke-on-Trent: Trentham, 1999.

Bowman, Sarah Lynne. "Educational Live Action Role-Playing Games: A Secondary Literature Review." In *Wyrd Con Companion Book 2014*, edited by Sarah Lynne Bowman, 112–131. Los Angeles, CA: Wyrd Con., 2014.

Bowman, Sarah Lynne. "The Mixing Desk of Edu-Larp." *Transformative Play Initiative*. YouTube video, 1:01:27. July 21, 2022. https://www.youtube.com/watch?v=aR4CQ2vhFus.

Bowman, Sarah Lynne, and Andhe Standiford. "Educational Larp in the Middle School Classroom: A Mixed Method Case Study." *International Journal of Role-Playing* 5 (2015): 4–25. https://doi.org/10.33063/ijrp.vi5.233.

Branc, Blaž, and Michał Mochocki. "Imagine This." In *Imagine This: The Transformative Power of Edu-Larp in Corporate Training and Assessment*, edited by Michał Mochocki, 8–19. Copenhagen: Rollespilsakademiet, 2018.

Caillois, Roger. *Man, Play, and Games*. New York: Free Press of Glencoe, 1961.

Calhamer, Allan. *Diplomacy*. Cambridge: Self-published, 1959.

Carlisle, Robert M. "Internal Family Systems Model." In *The SAGE Encyclopedia of Theory in Counseling and Psychotherapy*, edited by Edward S. Neukrug, 567–569. Los Angeles, CA: SAGE Publications, 2015.

Carnes, Mark C. *Minds on Fire: How Role-Immersion Games Transform College.* Cambridge: Harvard University Press, 2014. https://doi.org/10.4159/harvard. 9780674735606.

Coates, Joseph F. "Scenario Planning." *Technological Forecasting and Social Change* 65, no. 1 (2000): 115–123. https://doi.org/10.1016/j.techfore.2016.10.043.

Corsini, Raymond J., Malcolm E. Shaw, and Robert R. Blake. *Roleplaying in Business and Industry.* New York: Free Press of Glencoe, 1961.

Costikyan, Greg. *Uncertainty in Games.* Cambridge: MIT Press, 2015.

Craig, Robert L. *Training and Development Handbook: A Guide to Human Resource Development.* New York: McGraw-Hill, 1979.

Crookall, David, and Danny Saunders. "Towards an Integration of Communication and Simulation." In *Communication and Simulation: From Two Fields to One Theme,* edited by David Crookall and Danny Saunders, 3–29. Philadelphia, PA: Multilingual Matters, 1989.

Cullinan, Maryanne. "Surveying the Perspectives of Middle and High School Educators Who Use Role-Playing Games as Pedagogy." *International Journal of Role-Playing* 15 (June, 2024): 127–141. https://doi.org/10.33063/ijrp.vi15.335.

Cullinan, Maryanne, and Jennifer Genova. "Gaming the Systems: A Component Analysis Framework for the Classroom Use of RPGs." *International Journal of Role-Playing* 13 (May, 2023): 7–17. https://doi.org/10.33063/ijrp.vi13.305.

Driver, Helen Irene. "Effective Participation in Small-Group Discussion and Role-Playing." In *Multiple Counseling: A Small-Group Discussion Method for Personal Growth,* 79–88. Monona Publications, 1954. https://doi.org/10.1037/14487-005.

Duke, Richard D. *Gaming: The Future's Language.* New York: Sage, 1974.

Ferris, William P. "An Innovative Technique to Enhance Teambuilding: The Impact of Image Theatre." *Academy of Management Proceedings* 2001, no. 1 (2001): 1–6. https://doi.org/10.5465/apbpp.2001.6133575.

Fine, Gary Allen. *Shared Fantasy: Role-Playing Games as Social Worlds.* Chicago, IL: University of Chicago Press, 1983.

Gadamer, Hans-Georg. *Truth and Method.* London: Sheed and Ward, 2004.

Garfinkel, Harold. *Studies in Ethnomethodology.* Englewood Cliffs, NJ: Prentice-Hall, 1967.

Gee, James Paul. "Semiotic Social Spaces and Affinity Spaces: From the Age of Mythology to Today's Schools." In *Beyond Communities of Practice: Language, Power and Social Context,* edited by David Barton and Karin Tusting, 214–232. Cambridge: Cambridge University Press, 2005.

Gee, James Paul, and Elisabeth Hayes. "Public Pedagogy through Video Games: Design, Resources & Affinity Spaces." *Game Based Learning,* 2009. https://web.archive.org/web/20100820191022/https://www.gamebasedlearning.org.uk/content/view/59.

Grabarczyk, Piotr, and Bo Kampmann Walther. "A Game of Twisted Shouting: Ludo-Narrative Dissonance Revisited." *Eludamos: Journal for Computer Game Culture* 13, no. 1 (2022): 7–27. https://doi.org/10.7557/23.6506.

Guenthner, Joseph F., and Lori L. Moore. "Role Playing as a Leadership Development Tool." *Journal of Leadership Education* 4, no. 2 (2005): 59–65. https://doi.org/10.12806/V4/I2/AB1

Guetzkow, Harold Steere. *Simulation in International Relations: Developments for Research and Teaching.* Englewood Cliffs, NJ: Prentice-Hall, 1963.

Gygax, Gary. "EXchange (Commentary) Readership." *Europe* 9 (1975): 5–7.

Gygax, Gary, and Dave Arneson. *Dungeons & Dragons: Rules for Fantastic Medieval Wargames Campaigns Playable with Paper and Pencil and Miniature Figures.* Lake Geneva, WI: TSR Inc., 1974.

Hallinger, Philip, and Ray Wang. "The Evolution of Simulation-Based Learning across the Disciplines, 1965–2018: A Science Map of the Literature." *Simulation & Gaming* 51, no. 1 (2020): 9–32. https://doi.org/10.1177/1046878119888246.

Harland, Tony. "Learning about Case Study Methodology to Research Higher Education." *Higher Education Research & Development* 33, no. 6 (2014): 1113–1122. https://doi.org/10.1080/07294360.2014.911253.

Hartyándi, Mátyás. "Distrust and Disillusionment toward Generative Artificial Intelligence: Psychodramatic Exploration of Employee Trust in Organizational Technology Acceptance." *Society & Economy* 47, no. 2 (2025): Online first. https://doi.org/10.1556/204.2025.00002.

Hartyándi, Mátyás, and Gijs van Bilsen. "Playing with Leadership: A Multiple Case Study of Leadership Development Larps." *International Journal of Role-Playing* 15 (June, 2024): 142–177. https://doi.org/10.33063/ijrp.vi15.327.

Harviainen, J. Tuomas. "The Larping That Is Not Larp." In *Think Larp: Academic Writings from KP2011*, edited by Thomas Duus Henriksen, Christian Bierlich, Kasper Friis Hansen, and Valdemar Kølle, 172–193. Copenhagen: Rollespilsakademiet, 2011.

Henriksen, Thomas D. 2004. "On the Transmutation of Educational Role-Play: A Critical Reframing to the Role-Play in Order to Meet the Educational Demands." In *Beyond Role and Play: Tools, Toys and Theory for Harnessing the Imagination*, edited by Markus Montola and Jaakko Stenros, 107–130. Helsinki: Ropecon.

Hersey, Paul, and Kenneth H. Blanchard. *Management of Organizational Behavior: Utilizing Human Resources.* Englewood Cliffs, NJ: Prentice-Hall, 1969.

Hixson, Sarah West, and Rachel J. Eike. 2024. "Mixed-Methods Assessment of an Apparel Edu-Larp Rooted in Self-Determination Theory." *International Journal of Fashion Design, Technology and Education* 1–13. https://doi.org/10.1080/17543266.2024.2339240.

Huizinga, Johan. *Homo Ludens: A Study of the Play-Element in Culture.* Boston, MA: Beacon Press, 1955.

Huncik, Peter. "Inter-Ethnic Training with Psychodrama Methods." *International Journal of Healing and Caring* 6, no. 3 (2006): 1–14.

Imlig-Iten, Nina, and Dominik Petko. "Comparing Serious Games and Educational Simulations: Effects on Enjoyment, Deep Thinking, Interest, and Cognitive Learning Gains." *Simulation & Gaming* 49, no. 4 (2018): 401–422.

Kapitany, Rohan, Tomas Hampejs, and Thalia R. Goldstein. "Pretensive Shared Reality: From Childhood Pretense to Adult Imaginative Play." *Frontiers in Psychology* 13 (2022): 19. https://doi.org/10.3389/fpsyg.2022.774085.

Klabbers, Jan H. G. *The Magic Circle: Principles of Gaming & Simulation.* 3rd and rev. ed. Rotterdam: Sense Publishers, 2009.

Kolb, David A. *Experiential Learning: Experience as the Source of Learning and Development.* Englewood Cliffs, NJ: Prentice-Hall, 1984.

Kriz, Willy Christian. "Knowledge from the Great Ancestors: The 'Cone of Abstraction'—Revisiting a Key Concept Through Interviews with Gaming Simulation Veterans." In *Gaming as a Cultural Commons,* edited by Toshiko Kikkawa, Willy Christian Kriz, and Junkichi Sugiura, 25–41. Translational Systems Sciences 28. Singapore: Springer, 2022. https://doi.org/10.1007/978-981-19-0348-9_2.

Lasley, Joe, and Cosmo Rahn. "LeadRPG: A Quest for Creative Leadership in a Role-Playing Adventure." *Presentation at the International Leadership Association (ILA) Global Conference,* Chicago, IL, November 8, 2024.

Lawrence, Kirk. *Developing Leaders in a VUCA Environment.* Chapel Hill: UNC Kenan-Flagler Business School, 2013.

Lippitt, Ronald. "The Psychodrama in Leadership Training." *Sociometry* 6, no. 3 (1943): 286–292. https://doi.org/10.2307/2785182.

Masek, Leland, and Jaakko Stenros. "Parties as Playful Experiences: Why Game Studies Should Study Partying." *Eludamos: Journal for Computer Game Culture* 15, no. 1 (2024): 75–96. https://doi.org/10.7557/23.7562.

Mochocki, Michał. "Edu-Larp as Revision of Subject-Matter Knowledge." *International Journal of Role-Playing* 4 (2013): 55–75. https://doi.org/10.33063/ijrp.vi4.229.

Mochocki, Michał. "Larping the Past: Research Report on High-School Edu-Larp." In *The Wyrd Con Companion Book 2014,* edited by Sarah Lynne Bowman, 132–149. Los Angeles, CA: Wyrd Con., 2014.

Montola, Markus. "The Invisible Rules of Role-Playing: The Social Framework of Role-Playing Process." *International Journal of Role-Playing* 1 (2008): 22–36. https://doi.org/10.33063/ijrp.vi1.184.

Moreno, Jacob Levy. *Psychodrama.* Vol. 1. New York: Beacon, 1949.

Moreno, Jacob Levy. "Role Theory and the Emergence of the Self." *Group Psychotherapy* 15 (1962): 114–117.

Nichols, Shaun, and Stephen Stich. "A Cognitive Theory of Pretense." *Cognition* 74 (2000): 115–147. https://doi.org/10.1016/S0010-0277(99)00070-0.

Peterson, Jon. *The Elusive Shift: How Role-Playing Games Forged Their Identity.* London: The MIT Press, 2022.

Peterson, Jon. *Playing at the World 2E: The Invention of Dungeons & Dragons.* London: The MIT Press, 2024.

Snowden, Dave, and Alessandro Rancati. *Managing Complexity (and Chaos) in Times of Crisis: A Field Guide for Decision Makers Inspired by the Cynefin Framework.* Luxembourg: Publications Office of the European Union, 2021.

Stenros, Jaakko, and Markus Montola. *The Rule Book: The Building Blocks of Games.* Cambridge: MIT Press, 2024. https://doi.org/10.7551/mitpress/14730.001.0001.

Suits, Bernard. *The Grasshopper: Games, Life and Utopia.* Toronto: University of Toronto Press, 1978.

Totten, Charles A. L. *Strategos: The American Game of War.* New York: D. Appleton, 1880.

Tuson, Mark. *Outdoor Training for Employee Effectiveness.* New York: Hyperion Books, 1994.

Verdy du Vernois, Julius von. *Beitrag zum Kriegsspiel.* London: William Clowes, 1884.

von Reiswitz, Georg Heinrich Rudolf Johann. *Anleitung zur Darstellung militairischer Manöver mit dem Apparat des Kriegs-Spieles.* Berlin: Trowitzsch, 1824.

Ward, Thomas, Mar Rus-Calafell, Zeyana Ramadhan, Olga Soumelidou, Miriam Fornells-Ambrojo, Philippa Garety, and Tom K. J. Craig. "AVATAR Therapy for Distressing Voices: A Comprehensive Account of Therapeutic Targets." *Schizophrenia Bulletin* 46, no. 5 (2020): 1038–1044. https://doi.org/10.1093/schbul/sbaa061.

Wesely, David. *Braunstein.* St. Paul, MN: Midwest Military Simulation Association, 1969–1970.

Westborg, Josefin. "How to Run Edularp." In *Larp Design: Creating Role-Play Experiences,* edited by Johanna Koljonen, Jaakko Stenros, Anne Serup Grove, Aina D. Skjønsfjell, and Elin Nilsen, 355–360. Copenhagen: Landsforeningen Bifrost, 2019.

Westborg, Josefin. "The Educational Role-Playing Game Design Matrix: Mapping Design Components onto Types of Education," *International Journal of Role-Playing* 13 (2023): 18–30. https://doi.org/10.33063/ijrp.vi13.306

White, Rachel E., Emily O. Prager, Catherine Schaefer, Ethan Kross, Angela L. Duckworth, and Stephanie M. Carlson. "The 'Batman Effect': Improving Perseverance in Young Children." *Child Development* 88, no. 5 (2017): 1563–1571. https://doi.org/10.1111/cdev.12695

Williams, Chris, and Anne Garland. "A Cognitive–Behavioural Therapy Assessment Model for Use in Everyday Clinical Practice." *Advances in Psychiatric Treatment* 8, no. 3 (2002): 172–179. https://doi.org/10.1192/apt.8.3.172.

Zagal, José P., and Sebastian Deterding, eds. *Role-Playing Game Studies: A Transmedia Approach.* New York: Routledge, 2018.

CHAPTER 4

Edu-larp

The Promises and Pitfalls of the Method

Josefin Westborg

BACKGROUND

The idea of embodied role-playing is not new in education. It has been used thoroughly, for example, as model UN (Muldoon 1995) in the simulation tradition, as Komtemåtta at Foglestad (Gothenburg University Library n.d.) in the civic training tradition, and by Dorothy Heathcote (Wagner 1992; Bolton and Heathcote 1999) in the drama tradition. A more recent development is the use of larps, live action role-playing games, for educational purposes. The big difference between modern edu-larps and traditional role-playing in educational settings is that modern edu-larps have developed from the tradition of games rather than drama and theater. This connection to games can be seen in things such as character sheets, puzzles, and other game-like elements that are often included in the design (even if this is not always the case). Edu-larps are larps created with clear learning goals. They are becoming increasingly accepted and used as a teaching method. The method is used in many different areas, such as science teaching (McSharry and Jones 2000), German literature (Torner 2016), and conflict transformation (Taraghi, Bowman, and Khosrospour 2022). The games can be anything from short scenes to week-long sessions in character, and they can be run as one-offs or in a more campaign-like arrangement. Today, there are schools

DOI: 10.1201/9781003641353-6

and organizations that specialize in working with the method, among others, the Danish boarding school Efterskolen Epos (2024), the Swedish company LajvVerkstaden (n.d.), and the American organization Reacting to the Past (n.d.). In higher education, there are now national courses for teachers (Stockholms Universitet n.d.), international programs such as the Master's program in Transformative Game Design (Uppsala University n.d.), and coordinating units giving out edu-larps for researchers in interdisciplinary research projects (Bowman and Westborg 2024).

How edu-larp is used as a method can vary greatly, but to give you an idea, I will share a short description from my own professional career. I have worked with edu-larp for 15 years in both primary schools and higher education and could meet and play with over a thousand students in a year. Often, when running an edu-larp, my colleagues and I would visit a school as an external actor for one day. In the first part, we informed about what larps are and what world we would play in to introduce the method and setting. Everyone would get a character, and we had workshops to help everyone get into their characters and become comfortable. The second part was the actual game, where participants played their characters. Finally, we concluded with a debrief, discussing the experience, what was learned, and what could be taken away from it. Often, there was also extra material for the teachers on how to keep working with what we had done after we left.

Even though there is a considerable amount of research on edu-larp as a method today (Bowman 2014; Transformative Play n.d.a), much of it focuses on what edu-larp is good for. In this chapter, I would like to talk a bit about the pitfalls of the method: what needs to be taken into consideration when working with it, what it might not be as good for, what the risks are, and how to mitigate some of this. I will base this chapter on the insights gained from my interviews as part of my master's thesis (Westborg 2024), previous research in the field, and my own professional experience. For my master's thesis, I did a critical discourse analysis that focused on ideas about learning. I conducted hour-long interviews with ten experienced practitioners whom I would call experts. They come from six countries in North America, Middle and Eastern Europe, and the Nordic countries. The participants had between 7 and 25 years of experience using edu-larp when working with groups. They had different primary target audiences spanning from 6- to 40-year-olds. Six of the ten primarily worked with edu-larp within formal educational settings, two in non-formal educational settings, and two within both.

Analog role-playing games, as a field, encompass both hobbyist and academic approaches, with significant overlaps in authors and citations between the two. Hence, it is not doable to completely separate hobbyist and scholarly works because they influence each other through a dialectic interplay (Teilmann and Qvortrup 2021). This can also be seen in the references used in this chapter.

PITFALLS

In this section, I will discuss the different pitfalls of using edu-larp as a method. These pitfalls build on what came up in the interviews and are supported by references from other research. I will sometimes illustrate the pitfalls with examples from my own experience.

Practical Considerations

The first thing you, as an educator, might encounter when wanting to use the method is the problem that play is often seen as frivolous, which can make it hard to get buy-in from superiors, colleagues, and students. This is not unique to larps or even role-playing games; games, in general, are often seen as more frivolous and only for entertainment (Deterding 2014, 2017; Euteneuer 2019). However, role-playing games get an extra layer since they are connected to playing make-believe as children, and larps, with their embodiment aspect, even more so. Getting buy-in from superiors is not only a "nice to have"; for many, it is a "must have" since they are not free to use any method of choice in the classroom without approval. This means having to justify using the method and needing to show how it connects to the curriculum and the learning objectives. In his interview, Steve (in Westborg 2024, 131) talked about how educators had brought this up at an international conference and that, for some, it might even mean they could get fired. That is a lot of risk to take instead of just going along with something already established. There can also be resistance from colleagues. When talking to Bill, he mentions three things that his colleagues at other institutions have gotten push-back about from their colleagues:

> Where people assume that if the class is being directed by students it's going to be silly and unproductive. And that, if I'm sitting in the back of the classroom, I'm not really doing my job, because my job is to be in the front of the classroom directing things.
>
> *(Bill in Westborg 2024, 91)*

In other words, it is seen as frivolous that the students will not learn anything and that you are unprofessional. Working with a method that your colleagues understand and where you get support from them makes life a lot easier, not just on an emotional level but, I would like to add, also if you get sick and need someone to step in for you. Dealing with resistance from both superiors and colleagues takes time and energy that could have been used for other things. The final group that might be skeptical is the students. Here, my experience is that the resistance differs a lot depending on the age of students, with younger students being more motivated than teenagers while adults are more of a mix. I was workshopping to run a larp with a class of 14-year-olds, and I remember them saying, "We do not play; we are not children." This clearly highlights the idea that play is something children do and that to become an adult is to distance oneself from that (Deterding 2017). Tarjei (in Westborg 2024, 102) brings this up when he talks about how, when working with larp at confirmation camps, he always would get a group that felt they were too cool to participate in the larp. This type of resistance is more common in certain parts of the teenage years and with some adults (and sometimes even among preadolescents), especially if it is a group with strong hierarchies and they are afraid to lose face or status.

If you have buy-in (or do not need it) and are ready to start, the next hurdle is about finding a game and preparing for it. This takes time. Finding ready-made edu-larps that match your learning objectives might be really hard, especially if you do not already know where to look. Even if you find a game, it can be hard to understand how it will play out if you have not seen it played, played it yourself, or at least know someone who has played it that you can ask. An alternative can be to write a game of your own, but this requires some skill and a lot of time. A final version might be to take an existing non-educational larp you know of and then just design the framing around the game (such as the workshops before and the debrief after) to your learning objectives. This might be a more viable option for the general teacher, but it still comes with the problem of finding a game, and it also takes a lot of time to design the framing.

On top of that, you have a lot of preparation, which can include things like printing material, planning how to run it, creating props, finding or creating a suitable environment to fit the theme, and so on. The time needed to prep was mentioned as a con with the method not only in my interviews but also has been highlighted by Geneuss (2022) in her work with teachers trying to use the method, and time just is not something teachers have a lot of. Time is not just an issue when it comes to preparation, but it is also relevant when it comes to actually running the game. Even if there are short larps, most larps are not written to be run in one hour. That means you either have to break up the process into different parts or borrow scheduled time from colleagues' classes, which is not always possible. And when you actually manage to run a short larp, a lot of the time, when the larp is finished, both teachers and students wish they had more time (Geneuss 2022). In a formal educational setting, you usually only have a specific amount of hours to get through a certain amount of content. larps take much time compared to giving a lecture you have given before. The time aspect can make it hard to add an edu-larp to your planning since that means you might need to cut out a number of other things in order to make the larp fit into the schedule.

The final thing I want to highlight regarding the more practical obstacles is facilitation. To run an edu-larp, you need to have facilitation skills. The emergent and co-creative process of a larp builds on improvisation, which means you must be able to improvise yourself and steer the gameplay while in character and trying to keep up with the overarching learning objectives and the story.

WHAT DO PARTICIPANTS LEARN?

Moving on to learning in relation to edu-larp, I first want to highlight something that was brought up by all the experts I interviewed: edu-larp is not the magic tool that works for everyone. This might seem obvious from an educational point of view, but many people I have talked to within the hobby seem genuinely surprised that there are both children and grown-ups who do not like edu-larp and would prefer a traditional lecture instead. The students might become overwhelmed, feel unsafe, or just not feel very motivated by all the extra fluff, and since cognitive overload, safety, and motivation are all very important for learning, this will have a negative impact on those students' learning.

Since edu-larp is very focused on interaction between players, this brings a focus on personal and social skills in relation to learning. These are very important skills, but, as mentioned in the practical considerations, many educators also need to be able to show the connections between the learning goals and the curriculum, which often focuses on more theoretical content. Basic subject-specific knowledge, such as facts, is an important part of more content-focused learning, and here, edu-larp seems to be not as strong. Because of this, learning this type of material is often done before or after the edu-larp and not so much during. The larp can work as a motivator and is good at putting the knowledge into context and making students apply it, but not as good for learning it in the first place (Mochocki 2013). Valdemar describes it like this in my interview with him:

> Edu-larp can sometimes be not so strong, or good, a method to learn pure academics and some very specific skills, like punctuation and grammar... or very specific skills for mathematics.

(Valdemar in Westborg 2024, 206)

This does not mean you cannot use edu-larp to teach basic knowledge, but there are other methods that probably will work better, especially going back to the time aspect. This is an area where more research is needed, especially effect studies looking at learning specific basic content through edu-larp compared to other teaching methods.

Even if role-playing games and larps are becoming more known to the general public, they are still unknown to many people, or they have a very vague idea about it. Lina describes it like this in my interview

> Everyone in Sweden have at some point played football. So if your teacher is saying, 'today we're going to play football', or if there's a football cup, everyone will know what is expected. But at a larp, at an edu-larp, it's very uncertain for a lot of the participants what it means. And even if we would do the *best* video of it, you still wouldn't understand it, because you have to try it.

(Lina in Westborg 2024, 177)

In other words, the students lack larp literacy, and you must teach them about larp: what it is, how it works, and how to do it. Understanding larp includes a lot of skills, such as what a player can and cannot do, how to read the game, and what creates interesting gameplay. Even if you have students with previous experience with larp, they often have not played it in an educational context. Thereby, you need to teach students not only the learning content but also larp literacy and how to combine those and draw conclusions from it. This is a lot to handle at once. When I was out in primary schools running edu-larps, one of the most common answers I got from students to the questions "What have you learned today?" was that they had learned how to larp. To be able to participate in a larp, the player needs to try to understand how it works, which will take precedence over the content at the start.

A larp is a different experience for every participant, while if you have them watch a movie, everyone will have the same experience. A movie can, of course, lead to different associations and emotional reactions, but to a large extent, there will be an aligned view of what happened. In a larp, every player will see different things, have different types of interactions, and play characters with different approaches. The experiences differ to a much higher degree (Henriksen 2004). Many larps are designed around conflict, with the characters being on different sides, meaning the participants usually only get to play one side of the conflict. This makes things complicated when it comes to learning since, in an educational context, you usually have one specific learning outcome that you want all the students to take away. One example of this is when I, for my bachelor's thesis, interviewed a university student who had played an edu-larp with me six months earlier. The game was written to focus on what it means to be brave, how bravery is very complex, and that sticking up for personal values can mean different things in different situations. This student had played the game in a course about game design, so the focus on the original learning objective of the game was not as strong. When I asked her about the experience, she had found it very engaging and interesting to play a character that tried to vocally stand up for their values against the majority. She found that tough and learned that if she ever ended up in a situation like that, she would make sure to stay quiet and not speak up. That was not the takeaway I was going for in a larp about being brave.

In relation to what can be learned, there is also the problem of measuring what was learned: assessment. Since edu-larp tends to be chaotic and emergent, it is hard to do assessments during the game. Moreover, what would you assess? Do the participants get to show knowledge and skills during the larp that you then assess? What happens if someone plays a character that is supposed to be very bad at those skills? Or are you assessing the performance of the character portrayal? Then, it is very easy to focus on those who take on a very extroverted character, while someone playing a shy and introverted character might have done an even stronger performance, but it is harder to see. Being judged while playing also risks the participants becoming self-aware instead of being able to focus on the game and the learning content. In my interviews, Steve reflects on the assessment:

> I know around assessment there are lots of discussions happening with edu-larp. But for me, edu-larp really is using these tools we know from larp, again, giving people characters as a dramatic situation, relationships between the characters with the sort of goal in mind, and then also that we as educators have an educational goal lurking there. And I think without the educational goal, there isn't an edu-larp, but that then *assessing* that goal, with respect to the larp, is always a problem. Because I, you, I don't, you can't pin people's experiences down or it may not go the way you thought it did. And that's fine. Maybe it's not fine for, you know, administrators, or assessors, who are trying to see about the viability of your program, right? So I'm always very cagey about what edu-larp does or doesn't actually accomplish, because serious bureaucrats can call it into question. They *can*. But I can also say, well, how can you pin down human experience? You can't, so sorry.
>
> *(Steve in Westborg 2024, 120)*

This points to the problem with validity in edu-larp. It becomes very hard to pin down what to measure and whether it can be measured well. Since every run of a game is different, and all students get different experiences, there will also be problems with reliability.

WHEN THE STRENGTHS BECOME WEAKNESSES

A practical reality about running an edu-larp is that it is very chaotic. As a teacher, having control over what is going on can be hard. This is a side effect of one of the main strengths of edu-larp: it distributes power to the students, giving them agency (Westborg 2024). For some educators, this can be a very uncomfortable situation in itself, as educators often are used to a different set-up in the classroom. You also have to run the game not as yourself but while playing a character for most of the time. On top of all of this, you also have your more formal tasks related to being a teacher to perform, such as keeping time, trying to observe what is going on in relation to learning for each student, and reading the social dynamics of the group. Trying to keep all of this together while giving away control to the students can be enough to keep educators from applying the method (Geneuss 2022).

Since larp is an embodied experience, our bodies become tools to use as part of the method. This can bring up a lot of dimensions of inclusion. There are considerations to be made regarding the players' physical and mental abilities. Can all your players participate in the game, or are they excluded or feel unwelcome because of the design? A practical example of inclusion is if you are going to have costumes as part of the larp, then you need to consider if the students are making them themselves or if you are providing them. If they make them themselves, is that something everyone can do and afford? If you are providing them, do you have enough in a variety of sizes so everyone can find one that fits their body?

An embodied experience also connects stronger to feelings and emotions, which means you, as the educator, will need to be able to handle and connect with the students in that situation. As Steve put it:

> it actually takes to get emotional involvement with one students. If you're kind of rushed for time or don't really have a good trust relationship with them, it's not gonna work as well, right?
>
> *(Steve in Westborg, 126)*

Having emotions involved in the learning process can be positive, but it can also be tricky. A strong emotional experience can help with remembering things better, but it seems like it might also strengthen confirmation biases. Tarjei (in Westborg 2024, 103–104) found this when doing a small survey for the Red Cross, where they studied teenagers' relations to myths about refugees. They had two groups, one playing an edu-larp and one doing more classic methods with seminars and such. They did a survey before and after where the participants got to answer questions about refugees in the world today and also rate their confidence in the answers. What Tarjei found out was that in the survey, the group that did not do the larp were more unsure about if they were right on the questions they got wrong, while the group that played the larp were more sure about their answers, no matter if they were right or wrong. This is an area where more research is needed to find out why this happens, if it is generalizable, and if/how to design around it.

Edu-larp is engaging and can get students really immersed. But is immersion always a good thing? Deeper learning often requires us to take a step back to be able to reflect, while being immersed (immersed as absorbed in, rather than present) into something is the opposite of that. Leni brings this up in our interview, where she describes it:

> We notice that the more cognitive learning goals we included, in maths for example, or in natural science, social science, whatever, the more fact-based learning goals we included, the more difficult it was for the kids, and the teachers, to take on and interpret their characters. There seem to be like a block, blocking situation, that when you work with your brain and focus.

(Leni in Westborg, 232)

That the student is immersed in the game also doesn't mean that they are immersed in the learning content (Whitton 2014, 81). This has been seen, for example, in educational wargaming where players have been focusing on goals optimal for winning the game but suboptimal for the learning objectives (Frank 2012) and in digital games with competitive elements (Harviainen, Lainema, and Saarinen 2014). This gets even more relevant when dealing with role-playing and larps, where there often are conflicting agendas between the characters, making it hard to have everyone align with the learning goals while also creating dynamics between the characters. One of the participants in the study, outside of the interview, mentioned how they had heard their students reflecting on how hard it was to focus on the learning content when they were supposed to play characters who did not care about the things that related to the learning content. The students then felt they could either be true to their character or focus on learning, but that doing both was not doable.

In a larp, the character provides an alibi to act in a way a player normally would not and explore things in a new way (Deterding 2017; Montola 2010). This can also be used by some players as a shield to not take responsibility for their actions by saying, "It was not me; it was my character." This hurts the safety and the social contract of play, risking that the game will not work.

The alibi is not just created by playing a character but also by being in another world. By adding an extra layer of reality, students get the opportunity to approach specific content in a different way. It might even work against biases and resistance against learning (Westborg 2022). However, adding an extra layer also means separating the content from everyday life. This leads us to the transfer problem. The transfer problem is a well-known problem in pedagogy and one that is tricky to solve (Illeris 2015, 71; Woolfolk and Karlberg 2015, 331). Transfer is the concept of taking knowledge from one area and being able to use it in another area. Knowledge is, to a large extent, situated; it is bound to the specific environment and social situation where the knowledge was acquired (Woolfolk and Karlberg 2015; Lave and Wenger 1991). It is already hard for students to take what they learn in one subject and then apply it in another, and even harder to take something they learned in one subject and then apply it in another while also being outside the context of school. By adding one extra step of a fictional world, this can get even harder, and the students might leave the new knowledge and skill sets bound within the context of the game (Whitton 2014, 135).

This was absent in the interviews, where participants instead expressed ideas about high transfer, the idea that there are generalizable skills and that these skills can be transferred between different contexts (Woolford and Karlberg 2015, 332; Aarkrog 2011, 4). However, since there were some mentions in the direction of alibi as adding an extra layer working against transfer, making it a potential pitfall, I mention it here. It is also something I witnessed in my own work. For example, when my colleagues and I were in another location than the students' classroom and asked them if they had learned anything, most of them said yes, but if we asked them if they could use what they learned in their ordinary school work, most of them said no. They could not see how to transfer their knowledge and skills to another context. This also adds another layer of complexity when it comes to assessment; if there is no way of knowing if the knowledge was transferred out of the game, then what is being assessed?

HOW TO HANDLE THE PITFALLS

Based on the interview data, I have discussed the pitfalls and weaknesses of using edu-larp as a method for learning. Now, I would like to focus on how to mitigate some of these and what parts are difficult to address. Based on what was presented as pitfalls, I will share my opinions and ideas about mitigation as well as solutions from the participants in the interviews.

General Problems

Some of the problems mentioned are the same for all educational methods. The first is that they will not work for all students. No educational method will work perfectly for every student, and edu-larp is no exception. You cannot mitigate this in itself, but instead, you can ensure that you use different methods to reach more students.

Next, there is the problem of not being familiar with the method, where the students will have to learn the method before they can look beyond that to other content. They have to get a certain level of literacy (in this case, larp literacy) to be able to use it. This is also something you cannot really mitigate in itself outside of having a large number of experienced players participate, but the good news is that larp is very close to playing make-believe, which most (but not all) children have done before, meaning most participants can pick it up pretty fast.

After that, there is the matter of getting approval from others when introducing a new method. Regarding colleagues and superiors, research can support your case and show that it is used by others. For yourself, it can be good to have a network with other teachers using the method to get support and have others you can ask when there is a tricky situation. When it comes to buy-in from students, you can help this along by having proper pre-work to frame the game and build safety (Mochocki 2013). By helping the students take it step by step, you make it easier for them to participate. Another way to lower the bar for participating is by having characters with different degrees of participation that you can offer the students. Then, you can make sure everybody participates and has a character, but some of them might be focused on more practical parts or play a character that is not expected to take as much social space.

Facilitation

Edu-larp also requires facilitation skills. The good news is that most educators are already very skilled at this. This skill can also be improved by practising it, such as running activities outside of school for friends or starting small by having the students make short scenes instead of full-length scenarios.

Time

The time issue is not something you can simply ignore; the method is very time-consuming. Using something pre-written can help to a certain extent, but other than that, all you can do is think about what you want to teach and when this method can give you enough to make it worth that time investment. Bill makes a reflection about when he tends to use it:

I think for edu-larp, I tend to lean into that when it's a part of the course that I've never figured out how to teach it effectively using other methods. *chuckle* And those are usually moments where there are a lot of different perspectives and they're all pulling in different directions. And these tend to be the games that I've written, are things that I've tried all kinds of different ways to teach and in the end I'm like, 'Well, I guess I have to have a game, to teach this thing'.

(Bill in Westborg 2024, 93)

Subject-Specific Content

Edu-larp seems to be less strong regarding basic subject-specific content than it is regarding social and personal aspects. Even if this is not something that cannot be mitigated in itself, it can still, as Bill mentioned in the last quote, be good for other complex learning. It can also be very good for putting knowledge into context and applying it. Having a tool like this can also be very important for creating a good group dynamic and a functioning classroom, thereby making other types of learning easier and mitigating many other problems.

CONTROL, DIFFERENT EXPERIENCES, TAKEAWAYS, AND TRANSFER

There are two tools that can be used to mitigate several pitfalls with edu-larp. These two tools are taking short breaks and debriefing. By taking short breaks during the game, you can help the students get back on track if they start to run away with the story. It is a way of taking back some control while still giving a lot of freedom. During the break, you can work with steering the game by having the students reflect on where the game is at, help them (and yourself) get an overview of what is going on in other parts of the game, think about where their characters are in relation to the character's goal, what they feel they need to do to move forward, and, if absolutely necessary, you can step in and retcon something to get back on track. You can also use this break to start helping them with transfer and keeping focus on the learning outcomes by making them reflect on questions or prompts that bring their focus to what this could be in the real world and how it connects to the subject. The second tool is the debrief. By running a structured debrief after the game is finished, you can mitigate the problem of having different experiences or getting the wrong takeaways (Crookall, Moseley, and Whitton 2014; Mochocki 2013). It becomes a way to get some control back over the story and focus on the learning objectives. In my interviews, Kolos describes it like this:

> And debriefing or structured reflection is very important because sometimes people have very weird or strange conclusions in their head about their experiences. So it's very important. So when I use it for educational purposes, it's very important that *I* can influence the reflection part and don't let them do their own conclusions on their own.
>
> *(Kolos in Westborg 2024, 193)*

This becomes very clear in the example I described with the player who had participated in a game about being brave and came out with a takeaway that was not at all aligned with the game's learning goals. The run that player participated in was focused on how to run a larp and not on the main content of the game (being brave). Because of this, the debrief was more or less skipped since there were other learning goals in that situation, which led to the takeaways from the content of the edu-larp becoming something other than planned. This starkly contrasts with when my colleagues and I ran a larp about norm criticism for all 14-year-olds in a large municipality in Sweden. In this sci-fi game, their characters get sorted into a sort of cast system with two casts: one extremely privileged and one oppressed by the system (Westborg 2016).

When the larp was done, we asked the students who thought this was a world they thought would be nice to live in. All who said yes were the students who had played characters that got sorted into the privileged cast. After having a structured debrief, they realized they would not get to decide what cast they would get sorted into. Hearing the other students talk about their characters' perspectives, they could see that the system was built on arbitrary sorting and only worked because it oppressed large parts of the population, making them reconsider their opinions. It also helped with bringing their different perspectives together to an overarching narrative while still having the personal experience of their part in it. Without the debrief, the students would have very different takeaways from that game depending on what cast their character got sorted into. The debrief is also a place to work with transfer. Here, you can help the students make connections between what they did in the game, how it connects to their ordinary school work, and what it can mean in other contexts outside of school. By referring back to the larp later, working with making the connections over time and integration processes, the students get a deeper understanding that is not as bound to the game, thereby increasing the chance for transfer to happen (Aarebrot and Nielsen 2012).

Assessment

Many problems around assessment in relation to edu-larp are the same for other games. For example, when it comes to in-game assessment, it might be worth considering if it is worth it. I would recommend using in-game actions for formative assessment and for students to show things they have not had the chance to do before. I was contacted by a teacher amazed at how this student, who usually was very quiet, suddenly went up holding a speech using advanced technical language in their second language in front of 60 other students. The reason the students gave for this was that they were playing a scientist, and "That is what scientists do even if I wouldn't." This prompted the teacher to adjust the student's grade to a higher one, as the student had demonstrated skills and knowledge that they had not previously shown in the ordinary classroom. Therefore, the larp became a way to get a better idea of the student's level. For out-of-game assessment, materials created in relation to the larp, both before and after, can be used. Having other out-of-game activities that are assessed is more manageable and takes the pressure off the larp itself. It also makes it easier to handle situations where students missed out on the larp for some reason. Bill takes this approach, which is one way to go:

> The way that I assess the game is 'how engaged in the game were you', is part of it, and then the second part is 'how good was your paper that you wrote', which I can assess using pretty traditional means.
>
> *(Bill in Westborg 2024, 86)*

More research is needed in this area. While there is some good literature on assessment and digital games (Whitton 2014, 104), more research is needed to examine assessment in relation to edu-larps with its added components of character and embodiment.

EMBODIMENT, IMMERSION, AND EMOTIONS

Embodiment is a part you do not want to mitigate since it is an important part of the method. However, you might want to think through what problems can arise in relation to the content of your specific game. For example, one simple thing about costumes is to work with more neutral and simple pieces such as headgear. They make it easy to differentiate between groups and are easier to fit than full-on clothes. It will not give an immersive experience, but as mentioned in the pitfalls, too much immersion might not be a good thing. In larps, there is a tension between creating a realistic illusion and using fantasy as representation. This is actively discussed, and inclusion in larp design and facilitation is a big topic in and of itself (Transformative Play n.d.b). There is no one easy answer to all these questions. What you can do is try to think of the needs of your players beforehand, be open to adjusting on the fly, and listen to your players.

One of the pitfalls with immersion and emotions is finding the right balance between immersion and separation. If the players get too immersed in the game or the character, that might work against learning, and they can also momentarily lose focus on consent. Here, taking short breaks is a valuable tool to help keep the balance. The breaks can also be made as a type of meta space where you pause the game and ask a player to give a short monologue on what their character is thinking at the moment or just have the players do a silent reflection on what is going on and how this relates to the learning content.

Emotions are not something that, in general, should be mitigated (even the balance should be kept), but rather something to hold space for. The most important part about this is to work with safety: have safety mechanics, be available for your students, and listen to them (Bowman 2022a, 2022b, 2022c, 2022d, 2022e). Working with emotions as part of the debrief is also important to help them put words to their emotions and experiences to move on to the more intellectual parts thereafter (Westborg and Bowman 2025). Giving the students tasks to write post-game reflections in the form of journaling can also be a way to follow their process and see where they are emotionally. To keep students feeling safe also during the game it is important to be able to communicate with them as players as well as in character. What I have found to work well is to have a mechanic for this. I usually use the phrase "I would like to talk to you alone." I inform the students before the game that when they hear this, they need to come with me to the side, or maybe even out of the room, to talk privately.

They can, in turn, also use this phrase to ask about anything they feel is important that cannot be handled in-game. When they are taken to the side, this can mean that they will be asked about doing things related to the game, for example, if there is a special scene to be played and you want to ask if they are interested in playing a major part in it. By doing this, the students know that being taken to the side is nothing weird and that it can be a positive thing where you get offered fun things. This makes it easier for them to step away without them or the other students, seeing it as some kind of punishment. I use this mechanic to steer the game, check in with students emotionally, and handle students who are using their alibi in a way that disrupts the game. It is important here that you also use it to give gameplay offers and not just to talk to students who might be disrupting the game somehow.

FINAL WORDS

Edu-larp, like all educational methods, comes with pros and cons. It is good for some things and not as good for others. No single method is the perfect tool to teach everything to everyone. Having more tools means you can reach more students and find more joy in your work as an educator. Understanding your tools better and knowing what they are good or not as good for makes it easier to make an informed decision about what to use and when. I hope this chapter has given you a better understanding of edu-larp as a tool and how to handle some of the pitfalls that come with it in relation to your own subject. I enjoy working with this method and hope it can bring joy to many more educators and students.

REFERENCES

Aarebrot Erik, and Martin Nielsen. 2012. "Prisoner for a Day." In *Playing the Learning Game*, edited by Martin Eckhoff Andresen, 24–29. Fantasiforbundet and Education Center POST.

Aarkrog, Vibe. 2011. "A Taxonomy for Teaching Transfer Skills in the Danish VET System". *Nordic Journal of Vocational Education and Training* 1 (1): 1–13. https://doi.org/10.3384/njvet.2242-458X.11v1i1a5

Bolton, Gavin M., and Heathcote Dorothy. 1999. *So You Want to Use Role Play?: A New Approach in How to Plan*. Trentham Books Ltd.

Bowman, Sarah Lynne. 2014. "Educational Live Action Role-Playing Games: A Secondary Literature Review." In *Wyrd Con Companion Book 2014*, edited by Sarah Lynne Bowman, 112–131. Wyrd Con.

Bowman, Sarah Bowman. 2022a. "Safety in Role-Playing Games I: Introduction – Sarah Lynne Bowman." YouTube. Video, 20:15. Transformative Play Initiative, February 4. https://youtu.be/zpzDXV7By48?si=c4Br83JR5toLleY1

Bowman, Sarah Bowman. 2022b. "Safety in Role-Playing Games II: Before the Game – Sarah Lynne Bowman." YouTube. Video, 27:20. Transformative Play Initiative, February 4. https://youtu.be/TzBkbzKd-ck?si=H5fDCUBo4MA7XyvU

Bowman, Sarah Bowman. 2022c. "Safety in Role-Playing Games Part III: During the Game – Sarah Lynne Bowman." YouTube. Video, 23:01. Transformative Play Initiative, February 4. https://youtu.be/i_h_WCgXrHY?si=vHgsNmZ1Ew_2pPsj

Bowman, Sarah Bowman. 2022d. "Safety in Role-Playing Games Part IV: After the Game—Sarah Lynne Bowman." YouTube. Video, 12:41. Transformative Play Initiative, February 4. https://youtu.be/bIhMlGXNF50?si=IvZd7htMeda_3IR4

Bowman, Sarah Bowman. 2022e. "Safety in Role Playing Games Part V: Cultivating Safer Communities – Sarah Lynne Bowman." YouTube. Video, 13:54. Transformative Play Initiative, February 4. https://youtu.be/MwHkRlnb1tk?si=u-c_sVNOE77nfFGE

Bowman, Sarah Lynne, and Josefin Westborg, eds. 2024. *Role-Playing Games for Interdisciplinary Research Collaborations.* CIRCUS Interdisciplinary Insights, Uppsala University.

Crookall, David, Alex Moseley, and Nicola Whitton. 2014. "Engaging (in) Gameplay and (in) Debriefing". *Simulation & Gaming* 45 (4–5): 416–427.

Deterding, Sebastian. 2014. "The Ambiguity of Games: Histories and Discourses of a Gameful World." In *The Gameful World: Approaches, Issues, Applications,* edited by Steffen P. Walz, and Sebastian Deterding, 23–64. MIT Press.

Deterding, Sebastian. 2017. "Alibis for Adult Play: A Goffmanian Account of Escaping Embarrassment in Adult Play." *Games and Culture* 13 (3): 260–279.

Efterskolen Epos. 2024. Last Modified September 12. https://efterskolen-epos.dk/

Euteneuer, Jacob. 2019. "Defining Games, Designing Identity, and Developing Toxicity: Future Trends in Game Studies." *New Media & Society* 21 (3): 786–790.

Frank, Anders. 2012. "Gaming the Game: A Study of the Gamer Mode in Educational Wargaming." *Simulation & Gaming* 43 (1): 118–132.

Geneuss, Katrin. 2022. "To Play or Not to Play: Edu-Larp in Curricular Settings – Katrin Geneuss." YouTube. Video, 1:30:49. Transformative Play Initiative, April 8. https://youtu.be/Afz712_o2n4?si=N0hftpq5bfuCu5rZ

Gothenburg University Library. n.d. "Göteborgs Universitetsbibliotek: Kvinnliga Medborgarskolan Vid Fogelstad." https://www2.ub.gu.se/kvinn/portaler/kunskap/fogelstad/

Harviainen, J. Tuomas, Timo Lainema, and Eeli Saarinen. 2014 "Player-Reported Impediments to Game-Based Learning." *Transactions of the Digital Games Research Association* 1(2), 55–83.

Henriksen Thomas. 2004. "Transmutation of Educational Role-Play – A Critical Reframing to the Role-Play in Order to Meet the Educational Demands." In *Beyond Role and Play – Tools, Toys and Theory for Harnessing the Imagination,* edited by Markus Montola and Jaakko Stenros, 107–130. Ropecon ry.

Illeris, Knud. 2015. *Lärande.* Studentlitteratur.

Lajvverkstaden. n.d. Accessed November 8, 2024. https://lajvverkstaden.se/

Lave, Jean, and Etienne Wenger. 1991. *Situated Learning: Legitimate Peripheral Participation*. Cambridge University Press.

McSharry, Gabrielle, and Sam Jones. 2000. "Role-Play in Science Teaching and Learning." *School Science Review* 82 (298): 73–82.

Mochocki, Michał. 2013. "Edu-Larp as Revision of Subject-Matter Knowledge." *The International Journal of Role-Playing* 4: 55–75.

Montola, Markus. 2010. "The Positive Negative Experience in Extreme Role-Playing." In *Proceedings of DiGRA Nordic 2010: Experiencing Games: Games, Play, and Players*. Stockholm, Sweden, August 16.

Muldoon Jr, James P. 1995. "The Model United Nations Revisited." *Simulation & Gaming* 26 (1): 27–35.

Reacting to the Past. n.d. Accessed November 8, 2024. https://reacting.barnard.edu/

Stockholms Universitet. n.d. "Berättelser och rollspel som pedagogiska verktyg i historie- och SO-undervisning." Accessed November 8, 2024. https://www.su.se/sok-kurser-och-program/hv2ran-1.602380

Taraghi, Laila, Sarah Lynne Bowman, and Shirin Khosrospour. 2022. "Teaching Conflict Transformation Through Roleplaying." Presentation at *10th Annual National Community College Peacebuilding Seminar*, October 28. Forage Center. YouTube. Video, 2:03:12. Forage Center. https://youtu.be/_YPgkm_psmE?si=4kzl4pOgp10-W_yj (0:11:47–1:08:34).

Teilmann, Rasmus, and Jakob T. Qvortrup. 2021. "Applied Role-Play – Reflections on Tabletop Role-Playing Games as Interventional Practice." Master's thesis, Educational Psychology. Danmarks Institut for Pædagogik og Uddannelse, DPU, Aarhus University.

Torner, Evan. 2016. "Teaching German Literature Through Larp: A Proposition." *International Journal of Role-Playing* 6: 55–59.

Transformative Play. n.d.a. "Role-Playing Games and Education Bibliography." Accessed November 8, 2024. https://docs.google.com/document/d/1lAPcKxRMiNZ3sAGIDkcSC7HVJM7yuzHpaYti_sL3vyI/edit?usp=sharing

Transformative Play. n.d.b. "Safety, Equity, Inclusion, and Accessibility Bibliography." Accessed March 6, 2025. https://docs.google.com/document/d/1OOqjIzDQwlP_D_k_yZ56P4cGlCzEtTkVuLK3gSndPPw/edit?usp=sharing

Uppsala University. n.d. "Master's Programme in Transformative Game Design." Accessed November 8, 2024. https://www.uu.se/en/study/programme/masters-programme-transformative-game-design

Wagner, Betty Jane. 1992. *Drama i undervisningen – En bok om Dorothy Heathcotes pedagogik*. Daidalos. English version: Wagner, Betty Jane. 1976. *Dorothy Heathcote – Drama as a Learning Medium*. Heinemann; Revised, Subsequent edition (June 1, 1999).

Westborg, Josefin. 2016. "Alfa/Omega: A Larp about Norm Criticism for 14-Year Old School Kids." In *Larp Realia: Analysis, Design, and Discussions of Nordic Larp*, edited by Jukka Särkijärvi, Mika Loponen, and Kaisa Kangas, 19–23. Ropecon ry.

Westborg, Josefin. 2022. "Learning and Transfer through Role-Playing and Edu-Larp: A Cognitive Perspective." Paper presented at *Popular Culture Association*, April 13. Available at: YouTube. Video, 14:57. Transformative Play Initiative. https://youtu.be/bjmfPOyPuqw?si=eh1IHGRR3JyukSF3

Westborg, Josefin. 2024. "Placing Edu-Larp on the Map of Educational Learning Theories: A Critical Discourse Analysis of Ideas about Learning in the Edu-larp Community." Master's thesis, Gothenburg University. https://gupea.ub.gu.se/handle/2077/81988

Westborg, Josefin, and Sarah Lynne Bowman. In press for 2025 publication. "GM Screen: The Didactic Potential of RPGs." In German: "Das didaktische Potential von Rollenspielen." In #eduRPG. Rollenspiel als Methode der Bildung, edited by Frank J. Robertz and Kathrin Fischer. Gelsenkirchen: SystemMatters Publ. Academia.edu: https://www.academia.edu/109659917/GM_Screen_The_Didactic_Potential_of_RPGs

Whitton, Nicola. 2014. *Digital Games and Learning*. Routledge.

Woolfolk, Anita, and Martin Karlberg. 2015. *Pedagogisk psykologi*. Pearson Education Limited. English version: Woolfolk, Anita. 2010. *Educational Psychology: Global Edition*. Pearson Education Limited.

II

A Place at the Table

Inclusive and Transformative Learning through Tabletop Role-Playing Game

CHAPTER 5

Storyworlding Together

Tabletop Role-Playing Games as Inclusive Becoming

Kari Gustafson

INTRODUCTION – IMAGINE WITH ME

You're an adventurer, on a high-stakes mission with the rest of your party. To reach your goal, you must sneak into a cave full of goblins. Crouching behind a nearby boulder, you can see that there are goblin guards stationed all around the entrance. It looks utterly hopeless. You will have to give up or risk a fight that you probably won't win. But then, one of your fellows gets an idea. "I'm gonna disguise myself as a hobgoblin and convince the guards that they need to go inside. And then I'm going to follow them."

There is a bit of skepticism from the group, but your teammate overcomes their hesitation. They perform the ritual to don a magical disguise, sneak out from behind the boulder, and saunter up to the goblin guards. You peer out from your hiding spot for a tense minute or two, while the goblin guards point their spears and shuffle back and forth. But, to everyone's astonishment, it works! It could be fading light, or your companion's clever speech, or perhaps the guards have been drinking all night. But for whatever reason, the goblins are convinced to return to the cave. Your friend gives the secret signal, and the rest of the group sneaks in behind.

You duck into the entrance of the cave and are surrounded by darkness. Your stomach clenches as you realize you are probably in big trouble – only

DOI: 10.1201/9781003641353-8

one person in your group can see in the dark! You hear the voices of the goblin guards slowly moving away into the cave.

You stand for a moment at the edge of the cave mouth, back pressed against the cold stone. And then you notice the snuffling and growling. There are dire wolves chained up in a nearby side passage! It seems the goblins have some extra security, and they have noticed you, barking and howling and lunging. There is a shout from one of the guards farther down the main passage. Before you know it, you're under attack! Now, everyone is grappling and groping around in the dark to draw weapons. You're fighting against vicious wolves on the one side and a mess of angry goblins on the other, exchanging blow for blow.

And *then*, the Ranger in the group, the only one who can see properly in the dark, steps up to the wolves with arms outstretched.

"Puppies!" they exclaim. And then croon in the silly sort of voice reserved for favorite canine pets,

"Hello buddies! Who's a good boy? Who's a good boy?"

_____

This story is from an interview participant who was part of my doctoral research a few years ago. "Nat" was describing some favorite in-game moments, through several decades of playing role-playing games (RPGs), and across many different genres and game systems. The context of this particular story is *Dungeons & Dragons* (D&D), the ubiquitous and well-known high-fantasy tabletop RPG published first by Gary Gygax in the 1970s (Crawford et al. 2014).

Nat continues, laughing:

"I'm like, 'I am shooting arrows for our lives here!'" she recalls thinking. Or maybe she even said it out loud to her fellow players. I laugh along, recalling similar situations in games I have been part of.

"*Animal Handling*?" I guess.

"Yes!" Nat confirms. "She rolled *Animal Handling* [a spell in D&D] and calmed them down and got them to stop snarling at us. It was like, *Oh my god, I love this!*" As Nat finishes, her voice is breathless with delight.

This simple, and somewhat silly, encounter was what Nat chose as one of her favorite moments in a lifetime of gaming. It might seem mundane, or uninspired, or maybe only interesting to the characters in her gaming group. However, I see moments like this as something more. I believe they can provide entry points to consider what RPGs might offer in inclusive educational spaces.

The Backstory

My introduction to RPGs came several years earlier, through my kids, who were part of a larp (live action role-playing) group for children. In conversations with parents, older youth, and group leaders, I discovered that among the 80 participants and 20 young adult leaders, a considerable number were, like my own children, neurodivergent. I was captured by the unique way this community, which included orcs and evil wizards, a large number of latex swords, and wild battle encounters, was able to pull off an astonishing level of inclusivity and low-barrier participation – oh yes, and plenty of neurodivergent joy! The reality was that it far exceeded the expectations many parents and caregivers have for inclusive settings, including classrooms. Thus began my journey to further and more deeply understand this magic.

RPGs are widely experienced by participants as spaces for personal transformation, insights, and learning (Bowman and Hugaas 2021; Daniau 2016; Transformative Play Initiative. 2021). Increasingly, they are also recognized as creating contexts for acquiring and inspiring academic learning (Gjedde 2013; Brave 2024; Bawa 2022) and moral development (Wright, Weissglass, and Casey 2020; Schrier 2019). RPGs are also growing as a form of therapeutic intervention within fields like counseling and psychology (Abbott, Stauss, and Burnett 2021; Henrich and Worthington 2021). In addition to the anecdotal reports of a resonance between neurodivergence and role-playing communities, there is also attention to social learning and competency building through RPGs (Kilmer et al. 2023; Fein 2015).

While important, many of these projects tend to focus on individual learning and transformation. In this chapter, I invite you to think with me about how RPGs might also help us transform our thinking and practices for *inclusive educational communities* and learning contexts. I argue that RPGs can be a site of experiential learning, through exploration of different identities, communities, and ways of being and *becoming otherwise together*.

Our path through this, as through any playful adventure, will not be linear, but rather winding, zig-zagging, sometimes doubling back, and covering the same territory, but differently. We will first wander through a couple of important concepts that can help reorient our thinking (St. Pierre 2019, 12). Further along, we will revisit and expand on the story begun at the opening of this chapter, to look for potentialities for inclusive pedagogical thinking that might be found through be/coming a role-player and thinking with RPGs. The main themes here are supporting the mechanics of diverse groups, challenging the "Hero's Journey" trajectory of education, and embracing radical power sharing. Along the way, we will consider the role of play and explore some of the ways in which be/coming a role-player, and exploring collaborative storytelling through multiple perspectives, might transform us as educators, as well as individuals.

Play and games may seem a frivolous context for understanding serious issues of social marginalization and oppression. But as Kuntz and Goyotte (2018) point out, that's a function of the role we assign to play:

> …elements of play, as a practice of living, often escape critical notice; like the playground, they exist on the periphery of legitimate expression. Play is positioned as excessive to normative processes of meaning-making.
>
> *(665)*

What if we took play more seriously as a process of meaning-making? What kinds of insights might we reach through play, playfulness, and experimentation? How might such experiences saturate how we approach in other contexts, in ways that support inclusive practices?

DIFFRACTIVE READING

Thinking with is important in this exploration. It captures the affirmative potentialities (Braidotti 2018) of layering multiple perspectives into and within such an inquiry. I offer a *diffractive reading*, or exploration (Murris and Bozalek 2019; Bozalek and Zembylas 2017; Engman, Ennser-Kananen, and Saarinen 2023; Jonker 2024) of multiple contexts: neuroatypicality (Manning 2020), inclusive education, and RPGs.

Diffractive reading is a practice that has emerged through scholarship and practices of relationality, such as critical posthumanism (Braidotti 2019b) and new materialism (Barad 2007; Haraway 2016). To read or understand through diffraction is a "metaphor and a strategy" that breaks with epistemologies of "reductionist thinking about things and words" (Bozalek and Zembylas 2017, 1). It is a step back from self-reflection, and from that embraces and attempts to capture the multiplicity and complexity of becoming-together, in relation, and the *entanglements* (Barad 2007) of matter, practice, and understanding.

By dwelling in these different worlds together, and reading them with and through one another, we might tease out new understandings in the way that wave patterns diffract one another on the surface of a pond. Diffraction is a way to "[pay] attention to the differences that matter without creating oppositions" (Murris and Bozalek 2019, 11); a generative and affirmative practice rather than a critique of that seeks to contradict or replace (Braidotti 2018).

This chapter is not about how RPGs might be implemented in educational contexts. It is likewise not about how to create game-based learning experiences, although both of these are worthy and exciting educational endeavors. Rather, I invite you to accompany me on a pathway through exploring, playing, and *thinking with* RPGs, as an inclusive postsecondary educator, researcher, family member in a multiply-neurodivergent family, and not least a role-playing gamer. I will explore how these many experiences, taken together, create a more complex and further-reaching ripple pattern than any one of them alone.

"Practices of knowing," writes Barad (2007), "are specific material engagements that participate in (re)configuring the world" (91). This chapter engages not only text but also the materiality of games, bodyminds, dice, and classrooms, all diffracted through one another, into a *practice of knowing*.

Diffraction offers a path that "helps us understand the narrative of ourselves … as well as the device doing the diffracting" (Engman, Ennser-Kananen, and Saarinen 2023). In this spirit, exploring disparate storyworlds, like disability, education, and RPGs together, offers a possibility to re/examine the ways in which we create and embody educational spaces. It is a practice of knowing that shows where disability, particularly neurodivergence, bumps up against barriers in our systems of care, like schools, that embody an "assumption that neurotypicality is the neutral ground from which difference asserts itself" (Manning 2020, 2). Diffraction can help cast shadows on the blank whiteness of that "neutral ground" and reveal a contoured and porous surface.

STORYWORLDING

Let us turn our attention back to the erstwhile companions, trying to work their way through the dangers of the goblin cave. Their plight – and the ways they move through it – can help us understand another idea that is important to this chapter: *storyworlding*. When I joined a D&D game for the first time, I was astonished to discover that it isn't a *game* so much as a collaborative storytelling *practice*. RPGs of all types invite player participants to enact characters of their making into a collaboratively imagined story, with different levels of immersion and embodiment. In D&D and other tabletop RPGs, the action in the story is mostly carried through a collaboratively created, spoken narrative.

Maps and minifigures act as surrogates for the characters, in an emergent cartographic practice that follows and supports the process. And importantly, there is often some mechanism to emulate the twists and turns of chance, which in many tabletop games is dice. I think, in fact, the dice are key to what gives tabletop role-playing the feel of a "game," although they function more as a narrative device. The layers of story and suggestion, the push and pull of the gamemaster's and the players' ideas, and the outcome of the dice, are all part of the emergent, deeply collaborative, storytelling practice I call *storyworlding*. A storyworld is something recognizable, from RPGs and world-building heavy literature, such as science fiction and fantasy. It is both a story and a world; a world imagined into being for a story to inhabit. But it has a permanence that doesn't fully capture what is, in my experience, the slippery and ephemeral space that is RPGs.

Here, it can be helpful to reach for Haraway's concept of "relation, material-semiotic *worlding*" (2016, 13). In RPGs, characters, stories, and worlds "do not pre-exist their intertwined worldings" (14). Instead, a story and a world emerge, together, producing and produced by, shaping and shaped by, characters, players, gamemaster, maps, dice, and more. It is nonsensical to separate role-playing storyworlds from the processes that create them, and from the characters who inhabit, and players who enact them. There is magic and delight in that space, especially in its indeterminacy, adventurous uncertainty, and intense relationality. In the space of storyworlding, we are "in this together" (Braidotti 2019a, 36). We have the possibility of *becoming otherwise, together*, in ways that resist normativity and typicality, and which may even inform the way we approach out-of-game contexts.

Reciprocal becoming-together includes reimagining ways of communicating, interacting, and collaborating that are constantly negotiated, in community, and potentially in ways that challenge normative expectations. It might be a space that allows for the emergence of open-ended and accepting social interactions that resonate with ideas of "autistic sociality" (Caldwell-Harris and Schwartz 2023; Dunn et al. 2023; Ochs and Solomon 2010) and other non-normative (to us) experiences of relationality. It could nudge us to become familiar with difference, to lean in to awkwardness, and learn alternative ways of communicating, all of which support our ability to make connections with folks unlike ourselves in a variety of ways.

But how do they work? How do RPGs contain such slipperiness? Let's take a closer look by returning to the story. In the cave, the Ranger used a skill, *Animal Handling*, to communicate with and befriend the dire wolves. It was an imaginative use of the skill on the part of the player, and most likely a very high dice roll, that combined to allow for an unexpected twist in what the gamemaster perhaps planned for that scene. In that moment, it is apparent how the storyworld, along with all the characters in it, shifts and reconfigures through one simple action. There are a multiplicity of directions available for the story to go from there! The wolves, designed by the gamemaster to be a challenge, or perhaps a battle, have become something else entirely. They are friends, or allies, which perhaps tips the balance of that encounter with the goblins. Who knows, the fight may simply end, as the goblins realize the playing field is suddenly quite different.

Nat recalled that the Ranger character/player was transformed in the encounter, as well as the whole party of characters. From that moment, her tactic was to befriend any animals they encountered. The party now had a dire wolf trailing along behind them, living off their scraps. It may even be that the story would come to focus more on the wolf, and its growing relationship with the player/characters.

Stepping outside of the story, each of the players experienced another way of approaching an encounter, created and offered by their gamemaster, and will enter the game differently in the future. And they will take this with them into new campaigns, new encounters, new games, and perhaps into different contexts entirely. The story, the world, the players, and the gaming context have all been mutually transformed in a process of reciprocity.

Just as we imagine storyworlds into being, the real-life storyworlds with/ in we live also produce and shape what we can imagine. Tressie McMillan Cottom asks the question "why me, not her?" in exploring her life and her grandmother's. She describes how the two of them are quite alike, but had very different life trajectories, based on living as Black women in two different social and political contexts in the United States. Cottom tells us, "I am always limited by how well other people can imagine the possibility of me" (Klein n.d.).

Could RPGs offer important transformational learning beyond the individual's experience? Could they be a model for us as educators, as peers, and as classmates, in relationship? We can only become what those around us are able to imagine for us, and we would do well to create spaces where that happens collaboratively. Storyworlding together encourages us to expand the repertoire of potentialities we can imagine for other people.

DIVERSITY AS STRENGTH

There are sadly too few examples of how diversity of interest and ability is encouraged through the systems and institutions of schooling. There are, of course, many individual attempts to welcome and celebrate diversity; however, these are often working against the dominant ideologies and practices that shape our systemic experiences. As Roger Slee (2018) observes, "The mobilisation of exclusion through the structures, processes, programmes and ethos; that is, the cultures, of schooling is an embodiment of our social condition" (16). The underlying premise, or the "game mechanics" of schooling, if you will, centers certain experiences of the world as *typical*, and thereby produces its counterpart, *atypicality* (Manning 2020), which is rejected and excluded.

At times, the business of inclusion seems to be considered addressed, or even *settled*, by having opened the doors to all, and by perhaps increasing the availability of individual accommodations. As I once heard a colleague muse, *It's like we think schools are inclusive because we say they are.* However, as my research participants have pointed out through the years, merely placing someone in a classroom together with peers does not by any means ensure social or even academic inclusion. It's entirely possible to be a lonely island or an outlier planet.

RPG mechanics, on the other hand, tend to systemically encourage and support diversity of ability as a strength. Many game systems actively *require* different types of characters in order for a party to succeed, and a diverse group is certainly seen as a strength. To be clear, this is not to say that role-playing communities, or the published content or player materials, are always inclusive. It is important to acknowledge the deeply problematic ways in which many game systems and communities, including D&D in particular, reproduce racism (Garcia 2017; Trammell 2020) and colonialism (Eddy 2020; Flanagan and Jakobsson 2023; Trammell 2022), as well as deeply ableist paradigms. Disability is often present mostly as a punishment, or to enhance the villainy of the evil Non-Player Characters (NPCs) (Jones 2018). Most game systems rely on normative assumptions of ability, and can be inaccessible, as they require spoken language as their narrative vehicle and often include a complex world of dice, densely packed books, and pages of character stats in order to play (Heron 2024). Role-playing communities are often experienced as White and male-dominated. Sexism, heteronormativity, and anti-trans sentiments pop up with alarming frequency, both in and outside of game space.

These are all areas of deep concern, and justifiably the subject of substantial scholarship around games in the last decade and more. Somehow, despite these troubling and troublesome aspects, tabletop games *can* still be experienced as a context that feels inclusive by many folks who are marginalized, ignored, and unheard in other social and educational spaces. Part of understanding this paradox may be to focus on game mechanics that facilitate and support inclusive practices, and that welcome and support diversity in the collaborative storyworlding process, but which can be at odds with the "acts of gatekeeping" (Trammell 2023, 14) that hold marginalized and minoritized folks out of gaming spaces. As Trammell documents, "the politics of whiteness informed the politics of the hobby," (2023, 183) leaving us a legacy of deep and troubling roots in colonial structures, assumptions, and violence that often pervade storyworlds, player materials, and in-game experiences; and which are in tension with what are nonetheless inclusive and engaging aspects of game mechanics.

As an illustration of this tension, my own experiences with RPGs and inclusive mechanics have made me more sensitive to systems of exclusion as a postsecondary instructor. In my practice, game mechanics have served as a model for thinking about more inclusive classroom mechanics: assessments and classroom dynamics that offer more authentic engagement for a wider variety of ways of being or learning, that value different profiles of strengths, and reproduce expectations of student abilities that are less normative.

Back in the goblin cave, this aspect of game mechanics can be seen when we read between the lines just a bit. When a high-stakes situation like the goblin attack emerges in the story, characters will take turns. The in-game time slows at this point, while each player rolls a dice to determine what the turn order will be. Each character then has an opportunity to take their chosen action, in that order.

"Can I use *Animal Handling*?" I imagine the Ranger player asking the gamemaster.

There could be many reasons for this: Maybe they didn't have other options – perhaps they couldn't see in the dark, and knew they wouldn't be much help in attacking the goblins. Perhaps the player had a particular love of animals, or their character did. Perhaps it was a whim, or they were just looking to try out a new ability for fun. Regardless, it wasn't a choice that led toward the expected "outcome" of the encounter, and likely the gamemaster was surprised. (If they were what I have come to understand as a *good* gamemaster, they would also have been delighted, but we'll get back to that in the next section.) The rest of the players may have weighed in on the decision, as players' actions are always taken publicly. In most groups I've played in, there would have been great enthusiasm for such an unorthodox idea. And, when the player rolled a number high enough to win over the dire wolf, it would have been genuinely celebrated by everyone gathered.

In a world where those we revere are often individual action hero types than ensemble casts, it is refreshing to collectively imagine a storyworld within a system that elevates supporting characters and quirky decisions, which end up every bit as important as the heavy-hitting, archetypal heroes and their overpowered deeds. In classrooms, there are certain types of students, behaviors, and ways of being that are consistently noticed as non-normative and are generally *corrected*, or ignored, or marginalized. In contrast, an RPG actually requires that everyone have an equal stake and get a turn to contribute, and more ideas are heard and valued. In the end, the storyworld is richer and more rewarding for that inclusion! As Slee (2018) suggests, our schools and social organizations are "forged within the furnace of competitive individualism that shape their ethical framework" (Slee 2018, 16), discouraging this type of authentic collaboration that embraces and supports all students. Playing RPGs can help us to imagine otherwise.

CHALLENGING THE "HERO'S" LEARNING JOURNEY

RPGs are storyworlds that encourage the "fuck around and find out" approach to learning, as expressed by role-player, dancer, and storyteller Alan Turner (2021). Turner encourages us to throw off the oppressive expectation of the *Hero's Journey* (Gerringer n.d.) as a life or learning trajectory:

> For many of us, we don't have personally singular journeys. We explore and we molt like beetles, and do not just go from caterpillar to butterfly. We move and recover, we do it over and over, so many times that we lose count. Each pass brings us closer and

closer to the truth of us in our expression, and we find that voice. We find the thing that makes the world take notice.

(Transformative Play Initiative 2021, 24:50)

Although they are a context where players often embody "heroes," RPGs also fundamentally challenge the narrative template of the Hero's Journey, and offer space for disruption, reinvention, and constant, ongoing transformation.

This is especially relevant for including students with non-normative learning and developmental trajectories. Classrooms tend to be planned to encompass a similar, pre-established, mostly linear, trajectory of progres. A typical semester or school year includes the *call of adventure* in the form of a syllabus or schedule of topics. There is some expectation that students might *resist the call* or demonstrate some reluctance to engage with new or difficult ideas, but there is also an expectation that they will overcome this and move on to accept the *mentorship* of their instructor. I reflect that passing the "final date for withdrawal" might be akin to *crossing the threshold to the point of no return* for older students. Younger children, I would argue, have far less agency in this process.

There most certainly follows a series of *tests, allies, and enemies*, including the *ordeal* of the final exam or major project, which is presented in terms of life/pass or death/fail stakes. A similar trajectory is repeated at scale across a K-12 arc, a certificate, or a university degree. The treasure at the end is the much sought-after golden "A," which unfortunately (as per statistical expectations and zero-sum educational structures) is designed to only be achievable to a certain small percentage of the would-be heroes. Failure to complete this journey successfully is laid at the feet of the individual learner, with their lack of effort or will (or perhaps our old nemesis "ability") as the widely accepted, and ableist explanation.

Being constantly held to this sort of standardized, time-restricted, normative measure of learning is exhausting for many people, but for those who consistently come up as lacking, it can be soul-crushing. In one of my courses, I experimented with a role-playing-based syllabus, where students chose their own *adventures* (assessments) and completed different *quests* to accumulate XP (experience points) for their grade. What was notable was the enthusiastic response it created in certain students, as they realized, with incredulity, that "*even I* could get an A plus." I'll be honest, I've backed away from this model to rethink it because it was too effective. I observed that it encouraged students to work much harder than they needed to, even beyond what was healthy or balanced with other demands, once that reward seemed in reach. I was once again reminded of the ways that "neoliberalism provides an ethical framework for the organization and operation of our social institutions including schooling" (Slee 2018, 16), relying upon and centring normative examples of *ability, excellence, achievement,* and *typicality.*

In contrast, role-playing storyworlds allow for stretch and pull. They play with linear, forward-directed perceptions of time and story progression. In the moments of action, like the goblin cave encounter, in-game time is paused, or stretched out, while players get a chance to plan and describe their individual actions. They can even collaborate with one another on what characters will do, and how. That stretch allows for reflection and discussion, and gives the air needed to truly explore different courses of action.

When confronted with goblins and dire wolves, the Ranger wanted to try out a different pathway, offering something unexpected, whimsical, and creative. In my experience, Rangers are usually quite good with a bow and arrow, for instance, or several pointy spell options that would offer considerable damage to opponents. Another context might have pressured this character into reaching for the most powerful tool they had, facing the challenge head-on, as prescribed by the lead storyteller. "If the only tool you have is a hammer," as the saying goes, "everything starts to look like a nail." I must ask, are we encouraging our students to approach everything with a similar bludgeoning tactic? When we let them, RPGs offer a broader range of tools. In fact, some of them have nothing to do with fighting. As a gamemaster, one can encourage innovative ways of approaching a challenge and help support troubleshooting with players to find a path to success for their characters. Learning contexts should similarly allow for a breadth of approaches to topics and assignments, and facilitate students access to communication channels that allow them to question and propose alternatives.

At the end of the journey, the hero is, hopefully, transformed in some way. They return to the everyday world, but bring with them something new. I expect this is the way we like to conceptualize the educational journey. As educators, of course, we hope that our students experience something meaningful and come away different as a result of their time in our classroom communities. My experiences role-playing, and talking to role-players, have pointed out an important difference contrasting the way we engage when we know the outcome of the story as opposed to when we don't know; when we have a stake in storyworlding, and what emerges with/in it, and when we don't. The same is true for our students.

How might our students' experiences change if we were able to encourage and create space for stretching, exploring, even whimsy? As educators, this can mean stepping back, decentring ourselves as educators (Manning and Bozalek 2024), and welcoming the unexpected as we storyworld our classrooms in collaboration with our students.

In the goblin cave, the critical dice roll succeeded, and the Ranger was able to connect with the dire wolf. It changed everything. It's also possible that it would not have succeeded. RPG mechanics are intentionally shaped to allow for all shades of failure. Which is brilliant! Here again, time is stretched, and we are allowed to sift through the many other options that are available to our characters. The storyworlding happens just as richly through our characters' and players' failures as through our successes. Instead of a hero's journey, we end up with long, winding strings of moments of highs and lows for every character. Working through disappointment alongside one another, again and again, is uniquely instructive. And experiencing the unexpected nuance and depth that emerges through finding new ways to do things, or different directions forward, is even more enlightening. RPGs don't focus on a hero, but rather on *heroics*, reflected in our decisions and our actions and reactions. Heroics are something we all may be capable of, now and again, and experiencing this can be a powerful lesson.

The Hero's Journey also embodies normative learning and developmental trajectories that may be at odds with disability and neurodivergence. "We don't have a popular cultural narrative of chronic illness," Megan O'Rourke tells us in a discussion of her book *The Invisible Kingdom* (2022). "No one wants to listen to that…. It's a hard, chaotic story to hear" (Douthat 2021). Disability and neuroatypicality are similarly positioned at the edges of the map with regard to cultural awareness (although there have been some important shifts in recent years). Furthermore, the lived experience of disability tends to resist being pressed into the comfortable medical and developmental binaries within which it is generally understood, and challenges standard measures of health/wellness/typicality that pervade the clean arc of a Hero's Journey. The complex and zigzagging paths of atypical development push against the expectations of forward momentum that characterize expectations of typicality, around which the educational system is built. For those of us who dance in this grey, who both flourish and struggle in the indeterminate, life perpetually at odds with rigid systems can be exhausting.

I can't help but wonder, how, as teachers, we might also push back at the rigidity and expectations of typicality? How might we bring playfulness into the storyworlding that happens in our classrooms, in ways that subvert the race to learning outcomes and rigid expectations? This sometimes means resisting or refusing the expectations of those around us, on behalf of our students, as we work to transform the fabric of the multiverse. It is vital to find ways to refuse of normativity in our classrooms, making space for, welcoming, and valuing other ways of being.

The Hero's Journey isn't the only approach to storytelling – that particular view of conflict and resolution is related to a specific historical and cultural context (Alfieri 2021; Maa 2024). What would happen if we were to diminish the importance of this journey, and the focus on a central conflict and heroic arc? The characters' – or our students' – actions and reactions to the situations in which they find themselves, and their journey of self-discovery as they found a place in the world, would be more explicitly the focus, in a way which might look more like individualized and contextualized learning.

RADICAL POWER-SHARING

Let's return, one final time, to the goblin cave, thinking back to Nat's delight in their recollection. It reflects a common thread repeated in almost every story I heard from my participants about the best moments of role-playing, which is their freshness. It was the spontaneous, the unexpected, the emergent, when we're pushed off the map that delights us: when we're discovering and co-creating a storyworld together, and things arise in a way that no one expects.

It's when the gamemaster is no longer the *master*. Which brings us back to one place: All of these elements are held together through a practice of radical power-sharing and reciprocity. It was commonly agreed that a *good* role-playing experience is engaging, precisely because everyone, including the ostensible leader or director of the storyworld, lets go of controlling the narrative. In a previous section, I promised to return to the gamemaster's role in meeting the ideas of the other players with a spirit of *yes, and....*

"Can I use Animal Handling?" asks the Ranger, breathless. The player's eyes are sparkling as they look up from their character sheet. The gamemaster hesitates a moment. They think about all the time they spent creating stat blocks for dire wolves to be able to fight, and the complexity of adjudicating a request that is on the very edges of the map, and likely isn't clearly spelled out in the player's handbook.

"No, they are trained by the goblins, and are already looking at you as an enemy," the gamemaster could have answered. It would have been a way to direct players toward the planned outcome. But no one likes to be herded, as I learned decisively as a novice gamemaster. I had meticulously planned for a really cool dream sequence, and I tried to coerce my players to the *right conclusion*, so they would experience a specific realization at just the right moment. But that type of foolishness is doomed to failure.

Fortunately, that's not what happened with Nat's group. This is a *good* gamemaster, ready to follow their player's lead. Or maybe they think, *What are the chances? It would take a miracle.*

"Yes, you can try," the gamemaster responds.

The Ranger looks down at their character sheet. They wish this had happened a session or two later, when they would have had a higher level and better skills. But their character *really* wants to befriend a dire wolf, and this is an amazing opportunity. They take a deep breath and roll.

And a miracle occurs!

The whole table is transformed by this moment: players, storyworld, characters, and gamemaster. *This* is the moment that releases the magic.

"Hold lightly to your own ideas," is a piece of advice from a presentation by game designer Avery Alder (2019). It is something that is encouraged in game contexts, but much less comfortable in a classroom. And it most assuredly isn't someplace we get to by presenting our students with specific learning outcomes, and then expecting them to follow a singular roadmap, or story arc, to get there. The practice of the gamemaster is one of imagining potentialities and setting up spaces in which co-creation and collaborative understandings might be explored, together. The hope and aim is to collectively imagine and practice reciprocity in ways that allow a storyworld to emerge, with a "quality of existence that erupts in excess of any one individual" (Bozalek, Kuby, and Van Hove 2021).

RPGs offer participants a practice of knowing that supports *becoming something new together*; to engage in storywordling in ways that are different, perhaps non-normative, and that include a wide range of ideas, perspectives, and abilities. They might help us see ways to take up an ethic of power-sharing in the classroom, and decenter ourselves and our rigid, normative, expectations. It would certainly transform the experience of students who tend to be described in contrast to an idea of "typicality." If we take play seriously, as a way of unsettling our expectations, it might support us in embracing a wider range of ways of being.

A few weeks ago, my own role-playing group gathered to mark our seventh year in the same campaign. Most of the celebration was an extra-long session, because, who are we kidding? The storyworlding is the party! But we did share memories of our favorite times in the campaign. And those were almost without exception when things had taken on a life of their own, and allowed transformation of ourselves, our storyworld, and one another. How might we draw from the lessons of *storyworlding together* to create classroom communities where all our students emerge with similar experiences of becoming, belonging, and transformation?

REFERENCES

Abbott, Matthew S., Kimberly A. Stauss, and Allen F. Burnett. 2021. "Table-Top Role-Playing Games as a Therapeutic Intervention with Adults to Increase Social Connectedness." *Social Work with Groups* 0 (0): 1–16. https://doi.org/10.1080/01609513.2021.1932014.

Alder, Avery. 2019. "Halcon – Hosting Roleplaying Sessions." *Presented at the HalCon*. October. https://docs.google.com/presentation/d/1PLtQE41x3nN8uydD95y9LRwqF_OJHXtJ1UW90o6JTi8.

Alfieri, Louis. 2021. "Storytelling & Culture: East Meets West, Part 2." Blooloop. August 25, 2021. https://blooloop.com/theme-park/opinion/culture-and-storytelling/.

Barad, Karen Michelle. 2007. *Meeting the Universe Halfway: Quantum Physics and the Entanglement of Matter and Meaning*. Durham, NC: Duke University Press.

Bawa, Arpit. 2022. "The Quest for Motivation: Tabletop Role Playing Games in the Educational Arena." *International Journal of Game-Based Learning* 12 (1): 1–12. https://doi.org/10.4018/IJGBL.287825.

Bowman, Sarah Lynne, and Kjell Hedgard Hugaas. 2021. "Magic Is Real: How Role-Playing Can Transform Our Identities, Our Communities, and Our Lives." *Nordic Larp* (blog). March 9, 2021. https://nordiclarp.org/2021/03/09/magic-is-real-how-role-playing-can-transform-our-identities-our-communities-and-our-lives/.

Bozalek, Vivienne, Candice Kuby, and Geert Van Hove, dirs. 2021. *Doing Higher Education Differently: In Conversation with Neuroatypicality – Session 3, Erin Manning*. Vol. 3. Doing Higher Education Differently. https://www.youtube.com/watch?v=dcaCx83aj-0.

Bozalek, Vivienne, and Michalinos Zembylas. 2017. "Diffraction or Reflection? Sketching the Contours of Two Methodologies in Educational Research." *International Journal of Qualitative Studies in Education* 30 (2): 111–127. https://doi.org/10.1080/09518398.2016.1201166.

Braidotti, Rosi. 2018. "Affirmative Ethics, Posthuman Subjectivity, and Intimate Scholarship: A Conversation with Rosi Braidotti." In *Decentering the Researcher in Intimate Scholarship.* Vol. 31, 179–188. Emerald Publishing Limited. https://doi.org/10.1108/S1479-368720180000031014.

Braidotti, Rosi. 2019a. "A Theoretical FramSework for the Critical Posthumanities." *Theory, Culture & Society* 36 (6): 31–61. https://doi.org/10.1177/0263276418771486.

Braidotti, Rosi. 2019b. *Posthuman Knowledge*. Medford, MA: Polity.

Brave, Luka. 2024. "Play as Learning: TTRPGs in the Classroom." *Rascal News.* November 7, 2024. https://www.rascal.news/play-as-learning-ttrpgs-in-the-classroom/.

Caldwell-Harris, Catherine L., and Anna M. Schwartz. 2023. "Why Autistic Sociality Is Different: Reduced Interest in Competing for Social Status." *Ought: The Journal of Autistic Culture* 5 (1). https://doi.org/10.9707/2833-1508.1145.

Crawford, Jeremy, James Wyatt, Robert J. Schwalb, and Bruce R. Cordell. 2014. *Player's Handbook*. Dungeons & Dragons. Renton, WA: Wizards of the Coast LLC.

Daniau, Stéphane. 2016. "The Transformative Potential of Role-Playing Games—: From Play Skills to Human Skills." *Simulation & Gaming* 47 (4): 423–444.

Douthat, Ross. 2021. "What Living 'At the Edge of Medical Knowledge' Reveals about American Healthcare." *New York Times.* October 26, 2021, sec. The Ezra Klein Show. https://www.nytimes.com/2021/10/26/opinion/ezra-klein-podcast-meghan-orourke.html.

Dunn, Danny, Jay D. de la Garza, Desiree R. Jones, and Noah J. Sasson. 2023. "Awkward but so What: Differences in Social Trait Preferences between Autistic and Non-Autistic Adults." *Neurodiversity* 1 (January): 27546330231203833. https://doi.org/10.1177/27546330231203833.

Eddy, Zoë Antoinette. 2020. "Playing at the Margins: Colonizing Fictions in New England Larp." *Humanities* 9 (4): 143. https://doi.org/10.3390/h9040143.

Engman, Mel, Johanna Ennser-Kananen, and Taina Saarinen. 2023. "A Diffractive Reading." In *New Materialist Explorations into Language Education*, edited by Johanna Ennser-Kananen and Taina Saarinen, 175–186. Cham: Springer International Publishing. https://doi.org/10.1007/978-3-031-13847-8_10.

Fein, Elizabeth. 2015. "Making Meaningful Worlds: Role-Playing Subcultures and the Autism Spectrum." *Culture, Medicine, and Psychiatry* 39 (2): 299–321. https://doi.org/10.1007/s11013-015-9443-x.

Flanagan, Mary, and Mikael Jakobsson. 2023. *Playing Oppression: The Legacy of Conquest and Empire in Colonialist Board Games.* Cambridge, MA: The MIT Press.

Garcia, Antero. 2017. "Privilege, Power, and Dungeons & Dragons: How Systems Shape Racial and Gender Identities in Tabletop Role-Playing Games." *Mind, Culture, and Activity* 24 (3): 232–246. https://doi.org/10.1080/10749039.2017.1293691.

Gerringer. n.d. "Joseph Campbell and the Hero's Journey." *JCF*. November 8, 2024. https://www.jcf.org/learn/joseph-campbell-heros-journey.

Gjedde, Lisa. 2013. "Role Game Playing as a Platform for Creative and Collaborative Learning." InProceedings of the 7th European Conference on Game Based Learning , edited by Paula Escudeiro and Carlos Vaz de Car Valho, 190-199. Reading, UK: Academic Conferences International Limited.

Haraway, Donna J. 2016. *Staying with the Trouble: Making Kin in the Chthulucene*. Duke University Press. https://doi.org/10.1215/9780822373780.

Henrich, Sören, and Rachel Worthington. 2021. "Let Your Clients Fight Dragons: A Rapid Evidence Assessment Regarding the Therapeutic Utility of 'Dungeons & Dragons.'" *Journal of Creativity in Mental Health* 0 (0): 1–19. https://doi.org/10.1080/15401383.2021.1987367.

Heron, James Michael. 2024. *Tabletop Game Accessibility: Meeple Centred Design*. Boca Raton, FL: CRC Press.

Jones, Shelly. 2018. "Blinded by the Roll: The Critical Fail of Disability in D&D | Analog Game Studies." March 5, 2018. https://analoggamestudies.org/2018/03/blinded-by-the-roll-the-critical-fail-of-disability-in-dd/.

Jonker, Francois. 2024. "Cripqueering Method in Posthuman Educational Research: Diffractive Reading/Writing-With Autistic Perception and Expression." *Qualitative Inquiry*. June, 10778004241253251. https://doi.org/10.1177/10778004241253251.

Kilmer, Elizabeth D., Adam D. Davis, Jared N. Kilmer, and Adam R. Johns. 2023. *Therapeutically Applied Role-Playing Games: The Game to Grow Method*. 1st ed. New York: Routledge. https://doi.org/10.4324/9781003281962.

Klein, Ezra. n.d. "Ezra Klein Interviews Tressie McMillan Cottom." *The Ezra Klein Show*. June 12, 2022. https://www.nytimes.com/2021/04/13/podcasts/ezra-klein-podcast-tressie-mcmillan-cottom-transcript.html.

Kuntz, Aaron M., and Kelly W. Guyotte. 2018. "Inquiry on the Sly: Playful Intervention as Philosophical Action." *Qualitative Inquiry* 24 (9): 664–671. https://doi.org/10.1177/1077800417734566.

Maa, Devin. 2024. "What Does the Next Evolution in Storytelling Look Like?" *Substack Newsletter. Overpowered Games* (blog). January 2, 2024. https://opgaming.substack.com/p/what-does-the-next-evolution-in-storytelling.

Manning, Erin. 2020. *For a Pragmatics of the Useless*. Durham, NC: Duke University Press. https://doi.org/10.1215/9781478012597.

Manning, Erin, and Vivienne Grace Bozalek. 2024. "In Conversation With Erin Manning: A Refusal of Neurotypicality Through Attunements to Learning Otherwise." *Qualitative Inquiry*. May, 10778004241254397. https://doi.org/10.1177/10778004241254397.

Murris, Karin, and Vivienne Bozalek. 2019. "Diffracting Diffractive Readings of Texts as Methodology: Some Propositions." *Educational Philosophy and Theory* 51 (14): 1504–1517. https://doi.org/10.1080/00131857.2019.1570843.

Ochs, Elinor, and Olga Solomon. 2010. "Autistic Sociality." *Ethos* 38 (1): 69–92. https://doi.org/10.1111/j.1548-1352.2009.01082.x.

O'Rourke, Meghan. 2022. *The Invisible Kingdom: Reimagining Chronic Illness*. New York City, NY: Riverhead Books.

Schrier, Karen. 2019. "Designing Games for Moral Learning and Knowledge Building." *Games and Culture* 14 (4): 306–343. https://doi.org/10.1177/1555412017711514.

Slee, Roger. 2018. *Inclusive Education Isn't Dead, It Just Smells Funny*. London: Routledge. https://doi.org/10.4324/9780429486869.

St. Pierre, Elizabeth A. 2019. "Post Qualitative Inquiry in an Ontology of Immanence." *Qualitative Inquiry* 25 (1): 3–16. https://doi.org/10.1177/1077800418772634.

Trammell, Aaron. 2020. "Torture, Play, and the Black Experience." *G|A|M|E Games as Art, Media, Entertainment* 1 (9). https://www.gamejournal.it/torture-play/.

Trammell, Aaron. 2022. "Decolonizing Play." *Critical Studies in Media Communication* 39 (3): 239–246. https://doi.org/10.1080/15295036.2022.2080844.

Trammell, Aaron. 2023. *The Privilege of Play: A History of Hobby Games, Race, and Geek Culture*. New York University Press. https://nyupress.org/9781479818433/the-privilege-of-play.

Transformative Play Initiative, dir. 2021. *"Disrupting Monkey, Laughing Raven: The Magic of the Tricksters' Dance" by Allen Turner*. https://www.youtube.com/watch?v=sLLFTM6Wysg.

Wright, Jennifer Cole, Daniel E. Weissglass, and Vanessa Casey. 2020. "Imaginative Role-Playing as a Medium for Moral Development: Dungeons & Dragons Provides Moral Training." *Journal of Humanistic Psychology* 60 (1): 99–129. https://doi.org/10.1177/0022167816686263.

Transforming Crisis into Growth

Neurodivergence, Bleed, and Care Ethics in RPGs

Albert R. Spencer

INTRODUCTION

One year into an excellent homebrew *Dungeons & Dragons* campaign, an unanticipated emotional crisis unfolded at the gaming table. As a neurodivergent player navigating the unique challenges of attention-deficit/hyperactivity disorder (ADHD) and flare-ups of rejection sensitivity, I experienced an intense episode of bleed – the emotional spillover between my in-game character and my real-life psyche. My character, Reaper, a Warforged Cleric with an enigmatic past, had unknowingly evolved from a philosophical experiment into a deeply personal vehicle for my identity, buried trauma, and purpose. Over several months, frustration accumulated as Reaper's backstory stagnated due to failed dice rolls and narrative dead ends. While consent-based safety tools were used by my game master (GM) and me to ameliorate these frustrations, they ultimately could not prevent them from escalating into a crisis during play. This rupture disrupted not only the game's momentum but also the trust between me and the GM. Fortunately, through reflective dialogue and collaborative adjustments to gameplay, the crisis became an opportunity for transformative growth.

 DOI: 10.1201/9781003641353-9

This experience builds upon the insights from my previous essay, "Beyond Consent: Care Ethics in Horror Role-Playing Games" (2025), which argued that while consent-based practices are vital, they have inherent limitations when it comes to addressing the complexities of emotional dynamics in role-playing games (RPGs). That work proposed that consent-based practices be situated within a broader framework grounded in Maurice Hamington's care ethics model of humble inquiry, inclusive connection, and responsive action. In this chapter, I extend these insights beyond horror RPGs to general role-playing contexts and focus on how care ethics can support neurodivergent players confronting intense emotional bleed and crises, particularly when unrecognized trauma or unknown triggers are involved. Indeed, this chapter illustrates how consent-based practices should be grounded within a care-based culture to effectively manage negative bleed. Especially for neurodivergent players whose disabilities may inhibit their ability to recognize the triggers and sources of their intense emotions, integrating care ethics into RPG facilitation ensures that facilitators are better equipped to address immediate conflicts and foster long-term emotional and social development. This experience underscores the necessity of placing relational dynamics at the heart of RPG safety practices.

This chapter builds upon the previous piece by exploring the intersection of neurodivergence, emotional bleed, and the pedagogical potential of RPGs. It is well established that neurodivergent players unknowingly gravitate toward RPGs for their structured yet imaginative environments, because they provide vital opportunities for identity exploration, creativity, and social connection (Kilmer et al. 2023; Walsh & Linehan 2024). However, the heightened emotional intensity and interpersonal challenges associated with traits like RSD can exacerbate bleed, leading to moments of crisis that traditional safety tools may not fully address (Hugaas 2024; Leonard & Thurman 2018). This paper argues that intentional care practices, rooted in empathy, communication, and collaboration, are essential for fostering a supportive RPG environment that enables neurodivergent players to thrive. The key concepts guiding this analysis include *neurodivergence*, *bleed*, and *care ethics*. Neurodivergence refers to variations in cognitive functioning, including ADHD and autism, that shape individuals' experiences and interactions with the world (Walsh & Linehan 2024). Bleed, a term from RPG studies, describes the crossover of emotions, behaviors, and thoughts between a player and their character, which can be either enriching or destabilizing depending on context (Hugaas 2024). Finally, care ethics emphasizes the moral and relational responsibility to address the holistic needs of others, going beyond procedural safeguards, like consent, to nurture trust and mutual understanding (Hammington 2024).

Thus, this chapter explores the transformative potential of RPGs for neurodivergent players, emphasizing how moments of emotional bleed – when in-game and real-life emotions overlap – can lead to both crises and growth (Hugaas, 2024; Leonard & Thurman, 2018). Through my personal case study of playing Reaper, a Warforged Cleric, the analysis highlights how traditional consent-based safety tools often fall short in addressing the deeper emotional needs of neurodivergent participants, particularly in the face of rejection sensitivity and trauma that is unknown or unresolved (Connell, 2023; Walsh & Linehan, 2024). It argues that RPGs, whether recreational, pedagogical, or therapeutic, should be embedded within a care-based framework that emphasizes empathy, communication, and collaborative problem-solving, rather than relying solely on the current widespread consent-based approach that requires an unrealistic degree of self-knowledge and the ability to communicate boundaries prior to play (Hammington, 2024). Indeed, the skills necessary for informed consent are frequently the very skills that pedagogical and therapeutic applications of RPGs hope to develop (Atwater & Rowland, 2018). Therefore, this chapter will survey the current literature on therapeutic gaming with an emphasis on meeting the needs of neurodivergent players, use the Reaper case study to demonstrate why care must take priority over consent, and outline practical strategies such as narrative scaffolding, structured debriefing, and relational processing to foster emotional resilience and identity exploration (Kilmer et al., 2023; Bowman, 2018). Ultimately, this chapter illustrates how RPGs, when facilitated with intentional care, can transform crises into opportunities for personal growth, social connection, and the development of inclusive gaming communities (Diakolambrianou & Bowman, 2023; Connell, 2023).

THE PSYCHOLOGY OF RPGS, THERAPEUTIC PLAY, AND NEURODIVERGENCE

Within the past five years, scholarly interest in the therapeutic and educational potential of RPGs has grown exponentially and in tandem with the rising popularity of RPGs and high-quality amateur theorizing about the hobby by designers and enthusiasts. Examples of the latter include, Matthew Colville's video "Different Kinds of Players"[1] in which he discusses how to incorporate the player typologies developed by Glenn Blacow and Robin Laws at the table, multiple videos by Ginny D that discuss the experience of Players and GMs with ADHD,[2] and the free pamphlet *Consent in Gaming* (2019) in which Sean K. Reynolds and Shanna Germain share a dragon's horde of safety tools. Indeed, the most popular subgenre of RPG social media uploads pertains to either dealing with problem players and/or RPG horror stories of transgressive behavior that occurred at or away from the table. These anecdotes reflect truths about the hobby that every player who has ever played RPGs knows: because RPGs occur primarily in the participants imagination they are inherently psychological, neurodivergent players are drawn to this hobby because they instinctively recognize it as an opportunity for self-expression and exploration, and the primary rewards of the hobby are powerfully immersive shared experiences and the deep social bonds they create amongst play-groups. Of course, any activity with the potential for social and psychological benefits also has the potential for social and psychological harm.

Indeed, reflection and concern regarding the psychology of RPGs has been present since the beginning of the hobby. In *The Elusive Shift* (2020), Jon Peterson examines how early RPG communities grappled with the psychological and philosophical implications of their games, particularly their capacity to blur the boundaries between player and character, as well as between reality and fiction. Designers, players, and theorists of the 1970s and 1980s engaged in debates over the very nature of RPGs, questioning whether they were primarily rule-based games, collaborative storytelling endeavors, or immersive psychological simulations. Peterson identifies two dominant philosophical currents within these debates: one emphasizing RPGs as structured, rule-governed systems rooted in wargaming traditions, and the other highlighting their narrative and emotional potential for exploring character and story. These differing perspectives laid the foundation for modern RPG playstyles, such as the strategic, system-focused "dungeon crawl" and the character-driven "theater of the mind." Importantly, Peterson notes how early discussions anticipated contemporary concepts like "bleed," as players theorized about the immersive qualities of role-playing and the emotional impacts of inhabiting fictional personas. By situating these debates within the cultural context of the 1970s and 1980s – marked by the rise of postmodernism and shifting leisure practices – Peterson demonstrates how RPGs challenged conventional notions of authorship and agency. They empowered players to collaboratively create meaning in shared imaginary spaces, reflecting broader societal trends of individualism and participatory culture. In tracing the psychological and philosophical roots of RPGs, Peterson reveals how the medium evolved into a unique platform for self-expression, community building, and problem-solving. His analysis underscores the enduring interplay between RPGs' historical origins and their contemporary potential as tools for exploring identity and fostering emotional growth.

Fortunately, the current generation of scholars and researchers who grew up playing these games (a.k.a., *acafans*) have done the heavy lifting of consolidating, confirming, and falsifying these informal anecdotal insights gathered by millions of players through 50 years of the hobby. Clearly, RPGs offer unique avenues for identity exploration and emotional growth, especially for neurodivergent individuals, and the scholarly literature reveals how these games promote self-awareness, social development, and therapeutic benefits through structured narratives and immersive play. This literature can be organized around five major subtopics based upon my own analysis of existing scholarship, although any typology is likely to be obsolete by the time it goes to print due to the rate of new scholarship: (1) identity exploration, (2) therapeutic play, (3) social benefits, (4) safety practices, and (5) transformative potential.

First, RPGs are a powerful tool for exploring identity, especially for neurodivergent players who often grapple with heightened emotional experiences. For example, Hugaas (2024) introduces the concept of "identity bleed," describing how the emotions and traits of in-game characters spill over into the player's real-world sense of self. This phenomenon allows players to experiment with identity and integrate new aspects into their self-concept. Such explorations align with psychological theories like Erikson's stages of psychosocial development and Goffman's self-presentation theory (McLeod 2018, 2019). Similarly, Leonard and Thurman (2018) emphasize the neuropsychological underpinnings of bleed, noting that neurodivergent players may be particularly vulnerable to intensified emotional spillover due to heightened sensitivity and cognitive resource depletion. Structured debriefing, as discussed by Atwater (2016), is critical for helping players transition from the immersive narrative space back into social reality, mitigating potential negative effects of emotional spillover; and in a subsequent article, Atwater and Rowland (2018) further underscore the importance of structured support during gameplay, proposing the role of live action role-playing (larp) counselors to address emotional challenges and facilitate safe, empowering transitions, emphasizing that these practices can enhance both the therapeutic and communal benefits of RPGs.

Second, the collaborative nature of RPGs fosters strong interpersonal bonds and enhances social skills. Walsh and Linehan (2024) identify five core themes that contribute to positive mental health outcomes in Dungeons & Dragons players: escapism, self-exploration, creative expression, social support, and routine. These elements are particularly beneficial for neurodivergent individuals, offering stability and a sense of belonging within a supportive community. Lehto (2021) echoes these findings, highlighting how the imaginative and participatory aspects of RPGs improve social connection and self-expression while offering low-stakes environments for navigating complex interpersonal dynamics.

Third, RPGs serve as "transformational containers" where players can safely re-author personal narratives and rehearse new behaviors. Diakolambrianou and Bowman (2023) argue that the dual consciousness inherent in RPGs – the interplay between player and character – enables neurodivergent individuals to experiment with aspects of identity and navigate social challenges. This aligns with therapeutic practices like narrative therapy and Gestalt therapy, emphasizing RPGs' potential for fostering personal growth and emotional resilience.

Fourth, given this emotional intensity and psychological depth of RPGs, safety tools and structured facilitation are essential. Connell (2023) underscores the importance of Session Zero as a foundational practice for establishing informed consent, setting boundaries, and ensuring player safety. Tools like the X-Card and Lines and Veils provide players with mechanisms to manage discomfort and maintain emotional well-being during gameplay. Atwater and Rowland (2018) expand on this by advocating for the role of larp counselors, who address players' emotional needs during larp events without disrupting the game's structure. These practices are particularly important for neurodivergent players, who may face unique challenges in articulating boundaries or processing emotional spillover.

Finally, tabletop RPGs have shown immense potential as therapeutic tools, particularly for neurodivergent individuals. Connell (2023) highlights how RPGs can be adapted to address conditions like autism spectrum disorder (ASD) and ADHD. For individuals with ASD, these games offer a safe space for practicing social interactions, meta-communication skills, and relationship-building. For players with ADHD, RPGs provide an engaging platform for developing planning, task initiation, and emotional regulation. These therapeutic interventions are especially effective because they build on the inherent strengths of neurodivergent participants, such as creativity and quick thinking, within a structured narrative framework. Likewise, Kilmer et al. (2023) expand these insights, noting that tabletop RPGs' collaborative and creative nature fosters skill development in social-emotional areas while also promoting personal growth. Therapeutic GMs guide players through narrative-driven challenges that encourage teamwork, self-exploration, and the application of problem-solving skills. This interactive environment helps participants engage with complex social scenarios in a way that traditional therapy often cannot, increasing their comfort and confidence in real-world interactions. By aligning game mechanics with therapeutic goals, tabletop RPGs harness the creativity and quick thinking of neurodivergent players, transforming these characteristics into assets that support both personal and social development. Indeed, Connell (2023) and Kilmer et al. (2023) offer complementary yet distinct perspectives on the therapeutic use of tabletop RPGs, each emphasizing unique methodologies and considerations tailored to specific neurodivergent populations. Both approaches recognize tabletop RPGs as flexible and collaborative tools for fostering social, emotional, and cognitive growth, but their therapeutic strategies and focus areas diverge in significant ways.

Connell emphasizes a highly adaptive and client-centered approach, leveraging game mechanics, storytelling, and character development to create a structured yet imaginative environment for participants. For neurodivergent individuals, Connell highlights tailored interventions: players with ASD can use tabletop RPGs to practice social skills and meta-communication in a safe, low-stakes environment, while those with ADHD benefit from structured gameplay that fosters planning, task management, and emotional regulation. Connell also explores the phenomenon of "bleed," wherein players experience emotional spillovers between their characters and real life, framing it as both an opportunity for self-reflection and a challenge requiring careful facilitation to maintain participant safety.

Kilmer et al., by contrast, advocate for a framework rooted in therapeutic GM practices that align with established psychotherapeutic modalities, such as acceptance and commitment therapy (ACT), cognitive-behavioral therapy (CBT), and narrative therapy. Their approach emphasizes using tabletop RPGs as structured interventions to promote psychological flexibility, adaptive strategies, and narrative reframing. While Kilmer et al. also address neurodivergent populations, their commentary is broader, noting how tabletop RPGs engage intrinsic motivation and offer aesthetic distance for participants to explore behaviors and emotions safely. For individuals with ASD, they highlight tabletop RPGs' capacity to foster a sense of social belonging and self-discovery. Similarly, for ADHD, they emphasize the games' validation of creativity and quick thinking as strengths. Ultimately, while both Connell and Kilmer et al. celebrate tabletop RPGs' versatility as therapeutic tools, Connell's work foregrounds personalized, diagnostic-specific interventions, whereas Kilmer et al. integrate tabletop RPGs into broader, evidence-based therapeutic frameworks, showcasing their adaptability across diverse mental health contexts.

As can be seen, there is wide agreement that RPGs can be powerful tools for personal growth and therapeutic intervention, particularly among neurodivergent individuals. Across diverse frameworks, from Connell's (2023) diagnostic-specific adaptations to Kilmer et al.'s (2023) evidence-based integration of tabletop RPGs into established psychotherapeutic modalities, the recurring theme is the unique ability of these games to engage participants in creative, collaborative, and structured exploration of self and relationships. For neurodivergent players, they provide opportunities to develop social and emotional competencies, navigate complex interpersonal scenarios, and reframe challenges through narrative immersion. However, as the literature reveals, even with robust frameworks for safety and inclusion, moments of crisis and emotional intensity are inevitable within the dynamic interplay of character and player. Furthermore, these crises can be especially challenging for neurodivergent individuals to navigate, particularly if a specific trigger, complex, or trauma is unknown to the player. While this observation is based on my own experience and anecdotal evidence, it is not uncommon for individuals to gain insights related to their identities through RPGs. In some cases, long-term engagement with RPGs may help players notice patterns in their behavior and how it compares to others, potentially revealing aspects of their neurodivergence that were previously unrecognized.

Thus, the following section delves into a recent personal play experience in which unrecognized traumas and triggers were reflected through my character Reaper and the events of a campaign. Not only did the experience inspire this chapter, but also through the lens of one player's journey, we can see how these theoretical insights translate into practice and how similar crises can become opportunities for meaningful growth and reflection. The narrative also reveals how the real-world application of safety tools, therapeutic frameworks, and the relational dynamics central to effective role-playing might be insufficient to resolve instances of intense bleed unless they are rooted in care ethics. Care ethics is a moral theory that emphasizes the importance of interpersonal relationships, empathy, and the responsibility to meet others' needs through compassionate action (Internet Encyclopedia of Philosophy). In this context, grounding play, safety tools, and consent-based practices within care ethics ensure that participants are supported through a dynamic, trust-based approach that prioritizes ongoing communication, understanding, and collaborative problem-solving. This is particularly vital in cases where neurodivergent players confront an unknown-unknown trauma during play.

REAPER'S EVOLUTION THROUGH TRANSFORMATIVE BLEED

The crisis emerged when my brewing insecurity crossed with the unfolding of my character's backstory. My character, Reaper, is a Warforged (i.e., an android) with amnesia. He does not know his origin, but he was clearly created to be a weapon of destruction because he is a Cleric who worships Death. Consequently, he has an ambivalent attitude toward learning more about his secret origin. He wants to know, but he is afraid of what he might find. He has met one of his siblings who provided some clues, but coincidentally, most of the bad dice rolls and conversation failures have involved this subplot. Of course, my bleed had little to do with the choices of my GM or my dice rolls. We were unknowingly playing with traumas deep in my Shadow.

During the *genesis phase* of character creation, I believed Reaper would be an *experimental self*, i.e. "a character created as an experiment in order to explore a bizarre concept, challenge the participant's role-playing abilities, highlighting interesting themes in the game, or test the boundaries of the game experience" (Bowman & Schrier 2018, 404). For years, the possibility of a Warforged Cleric has fascinated me. I liked that the inclusion of these androids as a playable race created an opportunity to play what futurist Ray Kurtzweil calls a "spiritual machine." This character concept seemed pleasantly paradoxical, and I thought it would be fun and illuminating philosophical experiment to explore this contradiction in game.

Does an android have a soul? Is their will less free than a biological being because they are an artificial being? Or are they freer because they "see the strings that are pulling them," whereas biological beings tend to be in denial about their motivations?

During the *development stage*, more and more of my interests and experiences informed the concept. First, I chose them to be a Cleric of the Death domain because of my adolescent love of classic hard rock and heavy metal (e.g. Blue Oyster Cult, Judas Priest, and Metallica). In fact, his amnesia was inspired by the lyrics of Black Sabbath's song "Iron Man" which suggests that who the robot becomes is not whom they were designed to be. Likewise, I decided Reaper should resemble the skeletal T-800 from the *Terminator* franchise, a vivid and terrifying image from my childhood in the 80s. Furthermore, I have also been a fan of the humane robots that appear throughout literature: Pinocchio, the Tin Man, the Gunslinger, Marvin the Paranoid Android, Johnny-5, Optimus Prime, Data, BMO, Vision, etc. Even Roy Batty from *Bladerunner* is a favorite android anti-hero, which introduces another important theme: rebelling against one's creator. This list includes other automatons, such as Milton's Lucifer (a spiritual automaton), Frankenstein's Monster (a biological automaton), and Tony Stark's Ultron (a digital automaton). Initially, it was also fun and comedic to play a character that was socially awkward and either feared or shunned by NPCs who could not see beyond his grim visage.

The trouble began as Reaper progressed through the *interaction stage,* i.e., nine months of weekly play. Two turning points occurred when (1) Reaper devoted himself to a specific deity of death, the Ravenqueen, instead of his original worship of death as an un-personified force and (2) a new PC was introduced to the campaign whose character had previously been enslaved and abused. Converting to the Ravenqueen represented a shift toward death as an expression of fate and the poignant coda to life that gives it meaning. What is a life, but a collection of ephemeral memories made painful and precious because eventually they will fade into nothingness? However, proselytizing was difficult because (1) most mortals are in denial of this truth and (2) they would not want to discuss this already terrifying topic face to face with the Grim Reaper. Likewise, Reaper and the new character, as well as me and their player, quickly became friends, and their backstories complimented each other. Reaper was afraid of nothing, not even death, except for the memories he could not remember. Meanwhile, the new character was constantly tortured by memories he could not forget. This dynamic was very inspiring and compelling, until the new character confronted Reaper regarding his binding of an extraplanar creature: a succubus whom Reaper defeated in a high-stakes game of "Two Truths and a Lie." It disgusted the new character that Reaper would deliberately subvert the will of another creature, even if that creature was a fiend.

Thus, Reaper realized two transformative insights, one external and the other internal. Externally, he lacked the social abilities necessary to succeed as a Herald of the Ravenqueen. He was built to be a weapon of war and destruction, not a servant of peace and healing. Internally, his friend's admonishment led to an anomalous experience for Reaper: the feeling of shame. In that moment, he developed a conscience because he witnessed the pain that could be caused by domination and recognized that he too had suffered as an agent of another master's will. Out of character, I made development choices that expanded Reaper's suite of social abilities, and in character, Reaper freed his thralls and himself of any debts. At first, the challenge of these agendas enhanced their sense of merit, but after several failed dice rolls across multiple sessions, Reaper failed to make progress on his subplot. I began to feel these goals were hopeless, and because of bleed, I could not separate my frustrations with failure in game from my friendship with the GM. In-game, it felt like fate or the Ravenqueen was toying with Reaper, and out-of-game, my GM was toying with me. Eventually, this triggered transgressive behavior at the table. I channeled my frustrations into Reaper's dialogue with an NPC which deeply confused my GM, especially since it occurred in the scene where Reaper's creator, Niv'Mizzt, an ancient and legendary dragon artificer, was revealed.

Objectively, there is nothing wrong with the ludic and narrative choices made by the DM with regard to my character's backstory. If anything, the difficulty of gaining this information made it even more tantalizing. Unfortunately, every attempt to uncover my origins ended in failure or red herrings, creating mounting frustration. Although I communicated my desire for progress to the DM, I failed to express how this stagnation, compounded by unrelated frustrations, was affecting me, and that it was due to the DMs' performance of NPCs as well as bad dice rolls. In a pivotal session, an NPC suggested speaking with Dandreth, an extraplanar hotel owner, but the encounter yielded only speculation. Just as my frustration peaked, my character's sister, a fellow Warfrorged named Stryfe, dramatically returned from the Shadowfell. Initially, I was thrilled, believing this twist would align with my goals – advancing my backstory while exploring the Shadowfell. However, it became clear we wouldn't travel there, thus the reunion felt like a bait and switch. My frustration spilled over as I questioned Stryfe, whose inhibitors blocked meaningful answers. A fellow PC suggested casting *Knock*, a spell that should not affect memories, on her brain. Surprisingly, the DM allowed it, granting me a brief window to ask my sister anything, and finally offering a moment of catharsis and narrative advancement.

Even at the time, I recognized why my DM made that call. They could sense my growing frustration and bent the rules to allow a hair-brained solution to work. Unfortunately, this decision was the worst possible because after months of devoting much effort and brainstorming multiple strategies in hopes of making progress on my backstory, sigh, my fellow PC cut the Gordian Knot. It would be the equivalent of spending months trying to solve a Rubik's Cube only to have your friend peel the stickers off and put them back into the original order to win the prize you had patiently worked toward. Thanks to my questions, the DM did reveal the name of Reaper's creator, an ancient dragon named Niv'Mizzet renowned for their legendary intelligence and arrogance, but at that moment I could not have cared less. While Niv'Mizzet is a famous canonical character from *Magic: The Gathering*, I did not play that game. Thus, the revelation would have fallen flat regardless, but by this point, I was completely crestfallen and demoralized and everyone at the table could tell.

Stoically, I tried to take the moment in stride and move on to the next encounter when the PC who suggested the Knock spell asked in character, "You seem upset, how do you feel?" On the spot, I decided to channel my frustrations into my character's response and said something like the following:

> I tell you how I feel. I wish I had never sought to learn about my past. I like who I am now, and I enjoyed being able to devote myself to my deity and my companions, but every time I try to learn about my past, I experience only frustration and confusion. Perhaps I should abandon the search completely. Why should I care about this Niv'Mizzet? So, he is my creator, so what? We have greater concerns before us, and I do not want to waste any more time on this pointless diversion.

At the time I thought I was being creative and constructive, and planned to speak to my DM away from the table before our next session. I did not want to consume more time and attention because I was unhappy. I just wanted to move on with the game. Play continued for another hour or so, but the momentum had been squashed and the session ended early.

Due to a hectic work schedule, I could not address the incident with my DM immediately. A few days before the next session, they reached out, expressing confusion and upset over my behavior and asking me to skip the session to give them space. I was devastated that I had hurt my friend, but respected their boundaries and used the time to reflect. After a week, we debriefed at a coffee shop. My DM explained they were trying to advance my backstory, but my apparent dissatisfaction confused and hurt them. They were particularly upset by my channeling frustrations through in-character dialogue, which felt passive-aggressive and personally insulting. I apologized, validated their experience, and explained the situational and ongoing frustrations that had built up, including the lack of agency and progress for my character. Once they understood the full context, they empathized with my feelings and asked for feedback on improving the game experience. I suggested giving my character more agency, a sense of progress in their goals, and a minor rebuild to align their abilities with their objectives. They agreed these adjustments were reasonable, and together, we brainstormed creative in-game solutions to move forward positively.

What really happened was that we had stumbled onto an unresolved trauma I was unconsciously working through with this character. Shadow Theory contends that all characters are a manifestation of the player's psyche, thus even when we deliberately play a character far from home we still pull from our subconscious, our Shadow, as we perform the character. In retrospect, Reaper was an *experimental self* during the genesis stage, became a *fragmented self* in the development stage, and then became an avatar of my *repressed self* in the interaction stage. A fragmented self is a character who represents a "subdued fragment of the primary identity that becomes accentuated, magnified, or twisted into a distinctive feature of the character" and a repressed self is a character who represents a "regression into an earlier state of consciousness, such as an Inner Child character" (Bowman & Schrier, 2018, 404).

As my lifelong interests shaped Reaper's identity, he became a proxy for different aspects of my personality, specifically my neurodivergence. Although I was not diagnosed as neurodivergent until middle age, in hindsight there are obvious clues. I have learned that an appreciation for fictional robots is a common preoccupation amongst neurodivergent folks, specifically people on the Autism spectrum. For example, Lt. Commander Data who first appeared in *Star Trek: The Next Generation* is beloved by many neurodivergent fans because they easily relate to his challenges with fitting into the crew of the Enterprise and finding his place amongst the sentient species of the universe. Ina Rae Hark explores this affection at length in her essay "Autistic Android? The Curious Instance of Star Trek's Data" (2022). First, she notes Data's resemblance to two other fictional characters who present as being ASD: Christopher Boone from Mark Haddon's The Curious Incident of the Dog in the Night-Time (2003) and the legendary Sherlock Holmes whom, ironically, Data frequently role-plays on the holodeck of the Enterprise. Likewise, Temple Grandin, a livestock management expert with ASD and famous advocate for the ASD community, has explicitly stated that she identifies with Data (36).

While I have not been diagnosed with autism, I clearly remember a strong connection to Data throughout the show's original broadcasts, which overlapped my early adolescence. His social misunderstandings and his longing to bridge the gap between his unique nature and the expectations of others resonated deeply with my own struggles. At the time, I grappled with rejection sensitivity, a common symptom of ADHD, which amplifies one's fear of criticism or abandonment and makes even minor social missteps feel catastrophic. Data's portrayal of striving to understand and emulate human behavior while often feeling inadequate mirrored my feelings of isolation and self-doubt. Like Data, I often felt alien, striving to interpret and adapt to unspoken social cues while fearing rejection – a challenge further compounded by my undiagnosed ADHD and my fears of abandonment due to my father's inconsistent presence in my life.

Furthermore, Reaper's character was also deeply influenced by the song "Iron Man" by Black Sabbath, which holds significant personal meaning for me. Performing this song at my first high school talent show became a defining moment – it was my calling card among students who didn't know me personally. The song's themes of rejection and abandonment resonated deeply with me; it tells the story of a man transformed into steel, who, after being mocked and ignored by those he tries to save, turns to vengeance. This narrative functioned as an unconscious projection of my own frustrations and longing for acceptance. Like Iron Man, Reaper embodied a self-fulfilling prophecy, shaped by his isolation and the world's inability – or unwillingness – to understand his purpose. Unconsciously, by crafting Reaper as a Warforged abandoned by his creator, I was mirroring the narrative of "Iron Man" and projecting my own feelings of abandonment by my father onto my character. From a psychoanalytic perspective, Reaper's quest for identity and acceptance became an externalization of my inner struggles, allowing me to explore and process these emotions within the safe space of the game. Thus, the parallels between the song's tragic antihero and Reaper highlight how deeply RPG characters can tap into and reflect unresolved personal emotions, transforming play into a space for exploring and, ultimately, confronting inner conflicts.

RESOLUTION THROUGH CARE PRACTICES

The resolution of this crisis underscores the importance of care-centered practices in navigating moments of emotional bleed and conflict. Safety tools were used at the table to mitigate bleed in real time. Active listening played a pivotal role, as my DM sought to understand the root of the player's frustrations without judgment, creating a space where concerns could be aired and addressed. Empathy bridged the gap between mine and DM's perspectives, fostering mutual understanding of how the in-game narrative misaligned with my emotional needs and collaborative problem-solving was the cornerstone of our conversation. Together, we brainstormed actionable solutions that respected my narrative aspirations for Reaper while preserving the integrity of the DM's game. Thus, these care practices not only repaired trust but also restored group cohesion, reaffirming the centrality of communication and mutual respect in RPG settings. However, it is crucial to note that informed consent played little, if any, role in resolving this crisis.

In a previous article, I argued that informed consent, while essential, is insufficient as the foundational ethos for RPGs. This limitation is particularly evident in situations where long-term play uncovers "unknown unknowns" – traumas or emotional triggers that neither players nor GMs could foresee during the negotiation of consent during Session Zero. While participants can articulate and anticipate *some* of their boundaries, no one is aware of *all* their boundaries, nor can they predict how they might be crossed as the relational complexities of an RPG unfold. Instead, enthusiasts, designers, and theorists should adopt a care ethos, like Maurice Hamington's triadic framework of humble inquiry, inclusive connection, and responsive action, as a more adaptive and holistic approach. By emphasizing the ongoing relational engagement and adaptability, it enables participants to navigate crises that arise unpredictably during play. This framework not only addresses the epistemological gaps inherent in consent models but also fosters a dynamic, trust-based environment where players can process and integrate challenging experiences. In the context of this case study, informed consent could not have anticipated the emotional depth and personal history revealed through Reaper's narrative arc; however, a care-based approach allowed for flexible, empathetic responses that supported emotional resilience and group harmony. By prioritizing care over rigid consent frameworks, RPG communities can create safer, more inclusive spaces that embrace the transformative potential of play.

Hammington's insights are even more crucial when playing with neurodivergent players, which might be most of the time. For example, humble inquiry involves actively engaging with the player's unique experiences and aspirations for their character, ensuring that adjustments align with both their narrative goals and emotional comfort. For Reaper, this meant reallocating skills to better reflect his identity and granting him greater narrative agency through scaffolding techniques. For instance, integrating opportunities for Reaper to pursue his creator's trail and explore existential questions not only aligned with the player's goals but also gave them tools to feel more empowered during play. These changes mirror the therapeutic interventions described by Connell (2023), who highlights how structured game mechanics can foster planning and emotional regulation for neurodivergent players. By tailoring gameplay to the player's specific needs, these adjustments created an environment where personal growth and meaningful engagement could thrive, demonstrating how responsive action translates theoretical insights into practical, inclusive play.

More broadly, this crisis and its resolution provide pedagogical insights by demonstrating how care practices transform emotional challenges into opportunities for learning and growth. Through inclusive connection, the DM recognizes the relational dynamics at play, fostering trust and understanding that allowed the group to navigate the emotional intensity of the experience. This care-based approach aligns with Bowman's (2010) emphasis on relational processing in RPGs, as well as the structured debriefing techniques discussed by Atwater (2016). By addressing the emotional fallout collaboratively and empathetically, the group modeled resilience, turning a moment of vulnerability into a learning experience that deepened interpersonal bonds and reinforced group harmony. This process reflects Hammington's emphasis on the relational and adaptive aspects of care ethics, showcasing how crises in RPGs can catalyze emotional resilience and foster a sense of community. Ultimately, this experience underscores the value of a care-centered ethos, which not only mitigates the risks of bleed but also elevates RPGs as transformative tools for personal and collective growth.

Traditional consent-based safety tools should not be abandoned, but participants should recognize that they often address surface-level issues without engaging the deeper emotional needs of players, especially neurodivergent players. Tools like the "X-Card" or "Lines and Veils" are designed to react to immediate discomfort, but they do not ameliorate the nuanced, subconscious experiences that emerge during long-term play. Likewise, players whose emotional landscapes may include heightened sensitivity or rejection sensitivity need more care and patience both at the table during play, but also through debriefing out of the game and away from the table. As Connell (2023) highlights, neurodivergent players often experience emotional bleed more intensely, which can lead to unintended triggers that cannot be anticipated during pre-session consent discussions nor sufficiently resolved at the table, as in cases like the Reaper narrative, where unknown traumas surfaced unexpectedly, relying solely on consent frameworks failed to provide the relational depth necessary to navigate the crisis. Instead, a care-based approach that emphasizes understanding the player's emotional context and fostering ongoing dialogue becomes essential for addressing these deeper needs.

Naturally, these standards of care for recreational play should be even higher for therapeutic and educational play. While players in recreational RPGs typically participate by choice, this may not always be the case in educational or therapeutic contexts where participants are often required to attend or may feel a level of obligation. This creates an inherent power imbalance, as facilitators or GMs possess authority over the structure, goals, and outcomes of the game. This power dynamic influences consent practices, as it raises questions about the degree to which participants feel free to set boundaries or express discomfort. Therefore, in these contexts, care ethics becomes even more crucial. Care ethics emphasizes empathy, relational understanding, and meeting others' needs through compassionate action, making it a vital framework for ensuring participants' voices are heard and respected, even within these imbalanced dynamics. For example, scheduling debriefing sessions, such as structured one-on-one discussions after emotionally intense sessions, provides low-stakes opportunities for neurodivergent players to process emotional bleed and receive personalized support. Lesson plans and treatment plans should include narrative scaffolding, which incorporates player-driven goals and clear arcs into the game to enhance a player's sense of agency and alignment with the story. Likewise, awareness of co-morbid conditions, like rejection sensitivity, strengthens a group's culture of affirmation and creates an environment where players feel valued and supported even when conflicts arise.

Additionally, it's important to consider how discussions within the neurodiversity and disability community, particularly the autism community, have highlighted concerns around interventions that prioritize behavioral conformity over genuine self-expression. These concerns are relevant to RPGs as well, as facilitators must ensure that the transformative goals of educational and therapeutic play are grounded in participants' own values and priorities, rather than imposing external expectations. This means that the ethics of the GM role must prioritize ongoing consent and mutual collaboration, embedding care practices that ensure participants feel understood, supported, and empowered to navigate moments of crisis and growth on their own terms. By explicitly pursuing a care ethos, practitioners create a framework that prioritizes relationships and fosters trust, empathy, and transformative growth, ensuring neurodivergent players feel understood and supported. This approach enhances the pedagogical and therapeutic potential of RPGs, transforming them into platforms for personal growth, emotional resilience, and the development of an inclusive learning environment where risk-taking is encouraged and failure is seen as a natural part of the process.

In conclusion, RPGs offer unparalleled potential for personal growth, identity exploration, and emotional resilience, particularly for neurodivergent players. However, their transformative power depends on the facilitator's ability to navigate crises that arise from emotional bleed and unforeseen challenges. This chapter has demonstrated that while traditional consent-based safety tools are vital, they must be complemented by a care-centered ethos that emphasizes empathy, communication, and adaptability. Within the context of recreational RPGs, this approach helps foster an environment where neurodivergent players can feel understood and supported, enabling them to engage more fully and authentically in the game. By embedding care ethics into facilitation practices, GMs can create spaces that not only address immediate conflicts but also nurture ongoing trust, relational understanding, and deeper social connection among participants. Furthermore, these insights have broader implications for educational and therapeutic RPGs. In these contexts, where participation may not always be entirely voluntary and there are often specific goals for transformation, a care-centered approach becomes even more essential. It ensures that the well-being and agency of neurodivergent players remain central, prioritizing collaborative problem-solving and emotional resilience over rigid adherence to external objectives. Ultimately, the stories we tell in RPGs are not just about the characters we play but also about the relationships we build and the lessons we learn together. Through intentional care practices, RPGs can become safe, inclusive spaces where players of all neurotypes can thrive, transforming moments of crisis into opportunities for profound connection and growth.

NOTE

1 https://www.youtube.com/watch?v=LQsJSqn71Fw&t.
2 https://www.youtube.com/results?search_query=ginny+d%27s+adhd.

REFERENCES

Atwater, Brodie. "We Need to Talk: A Literature Review of Debrief," *International Journal of Role-Playing*. No. 6, Issue 6, 2016, 7-11.

Atwater, Brodie, and Alexis Rowland. "Developing a Framework of Larp Counseling," *International Journal of Role-Playing*. No. 9, Issue 9, 2018, 16-23

Bowman, Sarah Lynne. *The Functions of Role-Playing Games: How Participants Create Community, Solve Problems, and Explore Identity*. McFarland & Company, 2010.

Bowman, Sarah Lynne, and Karen Schrier. "Players and Their Characters in Role-Playing Games," in *Role-Playing Game Studies: A Transmedia Approach*, edited by José P. Zagal and Sebastian Deterding. Routledge, 2018, 395-410.

Colville, Matthew. "Different Kinds of Players," *YouTube*, uploaded by Matthew Colville, 5 September 2016, www.youtube.com/watch?v=LQsJSqn71Fw. Accessed 25 Feb. 2025.

Connell, Megan. *Tabletop Role-Playing Therapy: A Guide for the Clinician Game Master*. Routledge, 2023.

Diakolambrianou, Maria, and Sarah Lynne Bowman. "Dual Consciousness: What Psychology and Counseling Theories Can Teach and Learn Regarding Identity and the Role-Playing Game Experience," *Journal of Roleplaying Studies and STEAM*. Vol. 2, Issue 2, Article 4, 2023.

Ginny Di. "Videos about ADHD," *YouTube*, uploaded by Ginny Di, www.youtube.com/results?search_query=ginny+d%27s+adhd. Accessed 25 Feb. 2025.

Haddon, Mark. *The Curious Incident of the Dog in the Night-Time*. New York, NY: Vintage, 2003.

Hammington, Maurice. *Revolutionary Care: Commitment and Ethos*. Routledge, 2024.

Hark, Ina Rae. "Autistic Android? The Curious Instance of Star Trek's Data," *Autism in Film and Television*. University of Texas Press, 2022, 35-46.

Hugaas, Kjell Hedgard. "Bleed and Identity: A Conceptual Model of Bleed and How Bleed-out from Role-Playing Games Can Affect a Player's Sense of Self," *International Journal of Role-Playing*. No. 15, Issue 15, 2024, 9-35

Internet Encyclopedia of Philosophy. "Care Ethics," *Internet Encyclopedia of Philosophy*, https://iep.utm.edu/care-ethics/. Accessed Feb. 25, 2025.

Kilmer, Elizabeth D., Adam D. Davis, Jared N. Kilmer, and Adam R. Johns. *Therapeutically Applied Role-Playing Games: The Game to Grow Method*. Routledge, 2023.

Leonard, Diana, and Tessa Thurman. "Bleed-out on the Brain: The Neuroscience of Character-to-Player Spillover in Larp," *International Journal of Role-Playing*. Issue 9, 2018, 9-15

Lehto, Kerttu. "Role-Playing Games and Well-Being," *International Journal of Role-Playing*. Issue 11, 72-93, 2021

McLeod, Saul. "Erik Erikson's Stages of Psychosocial Development," *Simply Psychology*, 2018, www.simplypsychology.org/erik-erikson.html. Accessed 25 Feb. 2025.

McLeod, Saul. "Impression Management." *Simply Psychology*, 2019, www.simplypsychology.org/impression-management.html. Accessed 25 Feb. 2025.

Peterson, Jon. *The Elusive Shift: How Role-Playing Games Forged Their Identity*. MIT Press. 2020.

Reynolds, Sean K., and Shanna Germain. *Consent in Gaming*. MonteCook Games, 2019.

Walsh, Orla, and Conor Linehan. "Roll for Insight: Understanding How the Experience of Playing *Dungeons & Dragons* Impacts the Mental Health of an Average Player," *International Journal of Role-Playing*. Issue 15, 2024, 36-60.

CHAPTER 7

Collaboration and Empowerment

Reimagining Literacy in the Composition Classroom through Tabletop Role-Playing Games

David Brockway

INTRODUCTION

In August of 2023, as I prepared for my first year of graduate school, if someone had asked me to define "literacy," I would have probably said something along the lines of, "The ability to read and write." As it turns out, I *would* have people asking me that question within a month's time, and the narrowness of my definition would quickly be challenged. As a graduate teaching assistant teaching first-year composition classes, the first project I assigned my students was a literacy memoir. We had class discussions about the memoir genre, but I assumed most students would inherently understand what was meant by the term "literacy." As more students asked me for clarification on the term, I became less confident about my answer – I questioned it even more when I began to read my students' papers. While most students wrote about their childhood experiences with reading and writing, I noticed many students wrote about

DOI: 10.1201/9781003641353-10

other interests: sports, video games, family dynamics, and swim lessons. I let these students pursue their lines of thought without steering them back toward my (then-narrow) definition of literacy – I thought I was just being an "open-minded" teacher. A good instinct at the time, perhaps, but I came to realize these students were, in fact, writing about their own literacies just as much as the other students who had tapped into their memories of reading and writing. Much of this realization stemmed from my exposure to pedagogical theories from social constructivists, especially the groundbreaking work of Paulo Freire.

One of the most significant and well-documented changes in the field of composition was the shift from positivism to constructivism in the mid- to late-20th century (Nystrand 1993). Integral to this shift was Freire's work (heavily influenced by the work of Marx, Dewey, Fanon, and Gramsci) embracing collaborative, student-centered pedagogy. In recent years, discussions of student agency and collaborative learning have gained renewed urgency within composition pedagogy (and educative spaces as a whole), driven by shifting attitudes toward authority and inclusivity in the classroom. This evolving educational landscape increasingly favors frameworks that emphasize social engagement, the shared construction of knowledge, and the dismantling of traditional power hierarchies. In composition, as in other humanities disciplines, the theories of Freire and other social constructivists underscore the transformative potential of such approaches, advocating for pedagogies that foster critical engagement through dialogue and collaboration rather than mere rote learning or submission to authority. This shift reflects a broader movement within education to reimagine literacy beyond traditional reading and writing competencies, embracing a more expansive, inclusive view that accounts for diverse modes of knowledge-making and expression. By viewing the student as an equal contributor and expanding traditional definitions of literacy, teachers can battle the all-too-prevalent feeling of exclusion in students struggling to maintain agency in oppressive, homogenizing academic environments.

Similarly, communities in the realm of tabletop role-playing games (tabletop RPGs) often face an exclusion problem, stemming from the antagonistic nature between player and game master (GM) and gatekeeping from some sects of "traditional" hobbyists. Many tabletop RPG players, GMs, and designers are pushing for a more inclusive, welcoming atmosphere at the gaming table through an emphasis on open collaboration and experimental, flexible, or narrative mechanics that subvert the power dynamics between players and GMs.

By juxtaposing the dynamics of tabletop RPGs and social constructivist pedagogy, this chapter proposes a pedagogical approach that leverages role-playing games as both a mirror and a tool for thinking about classroom collaboration; it posits that just as tabletop RPGs can foster inclusive play spaces that reduce hierarchical divides, instructors can use similar collaborative structures to encourage student engagement and agency. Drawing on social constructivist theories and liberatory pedagogy, this chapter seeks to illustrate how tabletop RPGs and social constructivist pedagogy can mutually inform one another, offering a rich, innovative framework for creating empowered, literate participants both in and beyond the classroom.

SOCIAL CONSTRUCTIVISM AND AN EXPANDED DEFINITION OF LITERACY

Before connecting education and game theories directly, I'd like to briefly describe social constructivism from Freire's standpoint and connect this pedagogy to an expanded view of literacy. Educational theories that emphasize collaboration, social engagement, and inclusivity provide a vital framework for reimagining literacy and agency in the composition classroom. Social constructivism, a theory foundational to this chapter, posits that knowledge is not transmitted in isolation but constructed through interaction, dialogue, and shared experiences. Freire (1972) describes an oppressive school system in his banking model of education, where "knowledge is a gift bestowed by those who consider themselves knowledgeable upon those whom they consider to know nothing" (58). This establishes an inherent power imbalance; the teacher is the knower, the student is the receiver of information. Freire's solution to this problem is a dialogic classroom, where students and teacher alike are co-learners and co-creators of knowledge. More broadly, Freire's (2005) philosophy toward literacy is one that extends beyond grammar: "Acquiring literacy does not involve memorizing sentences, words, or syllables—lifeless objects unconnected to an existential universe—but rather an attitude of creation on re-creation, a self-transformation producing a stance of intervention in one's context" (43). Here, we can understand literacy as more than just reading and writing, but as a way of interpreting the world. A social constructivist view of literacy is not a static skillset, but a dynamic, adaptive practice shaped by context.

Emphasizing learning in context empowers students, while rote learning reinforces the status quo. In this way, a broadened definition of literacy is a tool for subverting the power dynamics of banking-style education by centering student experience and decentering the lens of the instructor.

This socially constructed literacy is reflected by the UNESCO definition of literacy, as stated by Cushman et al. (2020), in the introduction to *Literacies: A Critical Sourcebook*: "Most recent definitions pluralize literacy to *literacies*—those meaning-making practices demonstrated by fluency with a wide range of symbolic tools necessary for lifelong learning and the ongoing creation of societies that learn and grow" (1). It makes sense that any aspect of our lives with semiotic components – which, I would argue, includes nearly every aspect of our lives – *by definition* requires some level of interpretation. This may seem obvious to many education or games studies scholars, but the recognition of the difficult, interpretative work needed to parse the myriad symbols in our everyday lives (both in and out of academic settings) has become integral to my definition of literacy and how I view my own and my students' development. UNESCO's (2024) website now offers an updated definition of literacy that reinforces the need for an expansive view: "Beyond its conventional concept as a set of reading, writing and counting skills, literacy is now understood as a means of identification, understanding, interpretation, creation, and communication in an increasingly digital, text-mediated, information-rich and fast-changing world." When students participate in activities that require negotiation, collaboration, and critical engagement – qualities central to both composition pedagogy and tabletop RPGs – they are practicing literacies that extend beyond mere text comprehension.

Of course, there are those who point to the potential limitations of social constructivism. Some see constructivism, in an educational context and more broadly, as too idealistic. Critics of constructivism, like Richard Fox (2001), often see its framework to be too broad to be truly useful: "Yet it is perhaps as much a guiding myth as a testable psychological theory, a general view rather than a single clearly stated set of claims" (23). Because social constructivism considers knowledge to be contextual, there is concern that it doesn't allow students to directly apply the skills they are learning. This is sometimes referred to as "weak transfer" or "far transfer." Fox also positions constructivism as the degradation of academic rigor: "Constructivism seems to offer learning without tears" (33). While I do not assert this chapter can discredit these critiques, I do believe a position of social construction can help us reposition ourselves away from a mind-set of positivism, which is integral to viewing learning as more than the regurgitation of cognitive function. We can see this through the previously cited evolution of UNESCO's definitions of literacy; their definitions have only become more expansive over time. Does this broadening definition necessarily point to an inherent watering-down of literacy? The acknowledgment that our students enter our classrooms with diverse backgrounds, and that these idiosyncrasies should be reflected in the way we approach both curriculum design and assessment, does not diminish the quality of learning. Rather, socially constructed pedagogy can allow space for multiple layers of complex learning, encouraging students to find connections to the course material through the lens of their own lives and interests.

In fact, teaching only cognitive behaviors (reading and writing in standard, academic English) and ignoring the cultural elements of learning is insufficient. We can see this through what educator and researcher Carol Lee (2020) calls the "Social and Emotional Dimensions of Learning":

> Emotional demands include a willingness to wrestle with uncertainty, wrestle with integrating one's own short- and long-term goals with the demands of such rigorous reading, and wrestle with the grit required to persist when the reading gets hard... Reading is also a social experience...even if I am reading a book by myself, I am still in dialogue with the author and with the history of ideas that inform that text.
>
> (621)

Literacy reaches far beyond the cognitive abilities that allow us to read and write; I believe this is especially true for required classes (such as first-year composition), where students may need more investment in order to engage with the course content. This leads me to the conclusion that, as an educator, I need to be constantly searching for new vectors of social and emotional development that can introduce my students to unique ways of creating knowledge, exploring their identities, and expressing their ideas in creative ways.

The concepts put forth by Lee align with social constructivist theories from the compositionists who have influenced me the most as an educator: Janet Emig, Donald Murray, and Peter Elbow. All three of these educators focus their pedagogical goals on the *process* of writing, rather than the product, and believe learning occurs when students interact with each other. Once I allowed the philosophies of social constructivism to permeate the habits I picked up from years of receiving banking-style education, I became committed to centering my classroom activities around dialogue. Additionally, I looked for the values of social constructivism in all aspects of my life. I reflected on personal activities that encouraged the simultaneous development of my cognitive, social, and emotional abilities, and continuously returned to one of my oldest hobbies: tabletop RPGs. I wondered if perhaps the skills encouraged by tabletop RPGs overlapped with my goals as a teacher: to inspire my students' capacities, to encourage them to contextualize their knowledge, and to ultimately empower them with the confidence to make interesting, risky choices in both academic and non-academic endeavors. Upon this deliberation, what I found surprised me: not only is there significant overlap between constructivism and tabletop RPGs, but also the very act of synthesizing the ideas from each field allowed me to defamiliarize myself with my own pedagogical practices and avoid stagnation.

ROLE-PLAY PEDAGOGY

Role-play, in a general sense, has long been deployed in education. It should be noted that the role-play referred to in this section is that of role-play pedagogy – related to but distinct from the role-play of tabletop RPGs. While an exact definition of role-play is "notoriously difficult to define" and could include "everything from quick warm-up games to more extensive projects requiring weeks of preparation" (Shapiro and Leopold 2012). Essentially, in role-play pedagogy, teachers ask students to assume certain "roles," allowing them to play out real-world scenarios and practice language use while embodying various viewpoints. Role-play pedagogy has been deployed widely in the field of Teaching English to Speakers of Other Languages (TESOL) since the 1970s. Since the 1990s, role-play has seen a decreased usage in TESOL classrooms, but has seen increased usage in other disciplines, especially in the humanities: "Across the college curriculum, role-play is being used to facilitate a deeper and more critical understanding of course material" (121). Shapiro and Leopold's study focuses on two methods. In the first, students role-played a legal trial, with students researching an issue outside of class, then enacting a mock trial in class (124–125). The second method is described as "scholarly dialogues," where students embody the scholarly writers they have been researching (126). Shapiro and Leopold used a two-pronged heuristic of "Cognitively Challenging" and "Linguistically Relevant" (123) to develop their role-plays, and thus, these activities helped students develop critical thinking and language skills simultaneously.

TESOL professor Tatiana Gordon (2012) reinforced these claims, asserting that role-play "is a powerful language development tool that yields instructional gains on multiple levels" and that it provides opportunities for "[students to] hone their strategic competence and [to be] able to cope independently with the challenges inherent in performing complex literacy tasks" (712). In her analysis, Gordon states that "role-plays are effective in teaching abstract target-language items associated with transformational, social action, and reconstructionist curricula" (716–717). Results from both studies dovetail wonderfully with the social and emotional goals set by Lee and rise to the challenge of helping our students navigate an increasingly complex world by giving them a safe space to enact linguistic practices in "real-world" situations. While these methods of role-play instruction may not be as directly applicable to the real world as, for example, service-learning programs, it offers pushback against the idea of "weak transfer," while simultaneously giving students the opportunity to practice these skills before performing them in high-pressure situations.

Much of the research conducted in role-play pedagogy is centered around TESOL classrooms. Given this, we must ask the question: can there be a line drawn from the findings in TESOL classrooms to first-year composition classes? That line can be examined through the work of Alice Horning (1986). In *Teaching Writing As a Second Language*, she connects first-year writing to learning a new language: "basic writers develop writing skills and achieve proficiency in the same way that other adults develop second language skills...for basic writers, academic, formal, written English is a new and distinct linguistic system" (2). Here we see Horning lay common ground between the skills developed in TESOL and first-year composition classes. While the technical, cognitive abilities of students in these two areas of education are certainly distinct from each other (TESOL students are focused on language acquisition, whereas composition students are focused on developing writing skills), the social and emotional development of these students can be viewed in a shared light. Both sets of students need to develop a sense of context, creativity, and critical thinking to apply their burgeoning skills and to *create* knowledge, rather than simply acquire it.

Given these connections, educators can confidently associate the positive benefits of role-play pedagogy in the TESOL classroom (and its decades of precedent) with the first-year composition classroom.

FROM ROLE-PLAYING (PEDAGOGY) TO ROLE-PLAYING (GAMES)

The overlap between traditional role-play pedagogy and the use of tabletop RPGs may seem intuitive, but does that mean the learning outcomes between the two are similar? Role-play pedagogy gives students the opportunity to practice real-world situations in various roles; in contrast, tabletop role-playing has players assume the roles of purely fictional characters in a game setting. There are a wide variety of tabletop games: some utilize the rolling of dice to help determine outcomes; some do not; some include one player who assumes the role of GM; others do not; some are set in fantasy or science fiction universes; others in modern or realistic settings. Does the fictional component and/or the "play" nature of these games reduce the possibility of educational opportunities for students? Fortunately, the development of the field of game studies over the last half-century, in tandem with the rise in popularity of tabletop RPGs in culture writ large, has provided research to help answer this question.

To address the question of games as effective learning tools, I'd like to take a broad look at the field of games studies using James Paul Gee's (2007) *What Video Games Have to Teach Us About Learning and Literacy*. Granted, this book is specifically geared toward video games (as opposed to tabletop or "analog" games), but the principles Gee introduces are applicable to games in a general sense. It's clear from the beginning of Gee's book that he takes a wide view of literacy: "When people learn to play video games, they are learning a new *literacy*. Of course, this is not how the word 'literacy' is normally used...so why should we think of literacy more broadly?" (17). Gee goes on to answer his own question by discussing how semiotic components are just as worthy to be considered a valid method of communication as textual components are, and how even amongst various textual components (e.g., different genres) there are multiple levels of interpretation which require social context (17–18). Again, we see an emphasis on the social aspect of literacy that relates directly to Lee's framework. Gee's insistence that symbolic systems should be treated with respect (in terms of taking them seriously as a form of literacy) calls to mind Elizabeth Hill Boone and Walter Mignolo's (2020) call for an inclusive definition of writing, where they argue the merit of symbolic systems of language as writing: "If we are to consider thought and communication broadly, we must recognize the supralinguistic ways of presenting knowledge" (71). Maintaining a comprehensive understanding of literacy is a necessity for building an inclusive classroom environment, as shown by a statement released by the Conference on College Composition and Communication. In the statement, the authors show how the continuation of teaching standard, academic English as a benchmark perpetuates institutional white supremacy (Baker-Bell et al. 2020). If we are serious about following Freire's liberatory pedagogy, we must continue to reframe our ideas about what literacy is and can be.

Gee further reinforces the idea of gameplay as a social force of knowledge construction through what he calls "affinity groups" (205), a term he uses to describe what educational scientists Ann Brown and Joseph Campione have called "communities of learners" (203). Gee makes this change from the original term as a rhetorical maneuver because he "[wishes] to avoid the romantic notions that seem to accompany the word 'community'; affinity groups can be good, evil, or anything in between" (206). While Gee discusses several implications about these social systems, what is most relevant here is his discussion of types of knowledge within affinity groups, "Knowledge is not first and foremost in heads, discrete individuals, or books but in *networks of relationships*" (207, emphasis added). Furthermore, he says one role of leaders in affinity groups is to "help members turn their tacit knowledge into *explicit knowledge*, while realizing that much knowledge will always remain tacit...Leaders are not 'bosses,' and only knowledge that is made explicit can be spread and used outside the original affinity group" (207). Here we see Gee firmly within a social constructivism framework, and his implications about tacit and explicit knowledge once again call to mind the constructivist critique of weak transfer. Can the idea of affinity groups help us facilitate "networked" learning, where students synthesize knowledge from both inside and outside the classroom? But Gee continues, saying, "young people who play video games often experience a more intense affinity group, leverage more knowledge from other people and from various tools and technologies, and are more powerfully networked with each other than they are in school" (208). This work is paramount to how we view games. If playing games typically creates affinity groups with stronger bonds than being in school does, we can leverage the use of games inside our classrooms to encourage a sense of collaboration amongst our students.

Perhaps surprisingly (given his book's title), Gee did not mean for his book to be used in a purely educational context. He instead wanted to establish principles that could be used in broad contexts, including but not limited to schools:

> good video games build into their very designs good learning principles…we should use these principles, with or without games, in schools, workplaces, and other learning sites. Second, I wanted to argue that when young people are interacting with video games—and other popular cultural practices—they are learning, and learning in deep ways. Through good game design we can leverage deeper and deeper learning as a form of pleasure in people's everyday lives, without a hint of school or schooling…one way (not the only way) to deliver good learning in schools and workplaces would, indeed, be via games or game-like technologies, though we have to be careful not to co-opt young people's cultures for our own purposes.
>
> *(215)*

Gee's ending sentiment here drives home an integral yet overlooked pillar of socially and culturally situated education: teachers must examine *why* they are teaching what they are teaching. In my experience, students have a good intuition for the intention of a teacher's curriculum. From Gee's work, we can see that games have pedagogical value, but as teachers, we must be transparent and communicative about our goals.

To bring these ideas directly into conversation with tabletop RPGs, I will address their fictional and role-play elements through the work of sociologist Gary Alan Fine (1983). Many studies about the efficacy of tabletop RPGs reference Fine's seminal work, *Shared Fantasy*. Using participant-observer methods, Fine shows that the world of role-playing games is one that includes legitimate sociological elements worthy of study. In conversation with Erving Goffman's ideas on identity construction, Fine shows how players at the tabletop RPG table must navigate multiple personae at once. Participants must not only be "role-players" but also "role-takers," who "must accurately predict and react to the actions of the other participants" (205). This develops sophisticated social communication and collaboration skills among the players, who must also work within the framework of the game's rules. Through the collaboration facilitated by the game, players "seek to develop new and unique cultural systems" (229). In order to effectively create these cultural systems, players must think through symbolic abstractions on multiple levels and from multiple perspectives – a goal that aligns with UNESCO's definition of literacy, Lee's dimensions of learning, and Freire's emphasis on collaborative learning. This alignment shows how tabletop RPGs aren't simply "goofing off" but are helping players develop complex social and emotional skills in a gaming environment.

So, what does this mean for constructivist teachers, beyond the recognition of a happy overlap between two fields of study? First, it gives us confidence to explore games as educational tools in our classrooms. I consider myself lucky because my institution trusts me, even as a teaching assistant, to liberally alter the day-to-day activities within the curriculum. This may not be the case for all writing instructors, so I recognize that the ability to cite the educative value of games is paramount for those interested in using tabletop RPGs in the classroom. All academic fields have had to fight for their legitimacy, and games studies is no exception. Even technical communication (often seen now as the "pragmatic" choice in many English departments) was once seen as the little brother of humanities (Connors [1982] 2004, 3). Second, it orients us to the *types* of value these games have. Intentionality is vital to instruction. The more we can understand about how games operate as collaborative tools, the more effectively we can implement them. Third, it gives us a mirror to reflect our own constructivist practices in other spaces, which can illuminate us to new approaches to our theoretical frameworks. This is simultaneously reinforcing and inventive; the familiarity allows us to more easily draw parallels, but the recontextualization can help shake us free of our entrenched philosophies.

ROLE-PLAY IN THE CLASSROOM

While this chapter's focus is on philosophical overlaps between composition and games, as opposed to the direct application of tabletop RPG mechanics in the classroom, I would like to offer a brief look into how teachers might approach a direct application. Theories of education can influence the way we prepare for teaching, but what does the implementation of tabletop RPGs in the classroom look like, and how do we, as educators, guide our students toward desired learning outcomes using them? Maryanne Cullinan and Jennifer Genova (2023) see the need for a "shared vocabulary" amongst educators who want to use tabletop RPGs in the classroom (7). This is especially important given the vast range of different tabletop

RPGs available. They constructed a learning matrix where educators can align specific learning goals with various aspects of play, which is in line with effective assessment practices (McKeachie and Svinicki 2013, 72–73). Building from the work of Fine and other notable games studies scholars, Cullinan and Genova first built a framework to categorize elements of play: context, materials, structural, and functional (10). From this framework, the authors built a matrix of potential learning outcomes and matched them to questions about the game being used for instruction. Answering these questions helps a teacher determine which types of games to introduce to the class, depending on which learning outcomes are being sought. This is vital work, because certain games are better at honing particular skills such as collaboration or team-building (11). Their learning matrix includes the subcategories academic skills (e.g., reading comprehension, problem solving, written expression), social-emotional skills (communication, flexibility, frustration tolerance), and executive functioning skills (organization, time management, sequencing) (12–14). Once again, we see in these subcategories an alignment with Lee's educational goals. As colleges continue to prioritize preparing students for an increasingly diverse post-academia life, these goals must remain in the forefront. As Cullinan and Genova put it,

> RPGs offer a unique opportunity to support student development in multiple skill areas as well as apply knowledge learned in the classroom to novel situations and changing circumstances… [they] allow teachers to create more dynamic and responsive classroom experiences tailored to the specific needs of the classes, thus producing the integrated skill sets that modern life demands.

> *(14)*

While this is only one example of practical application, Cullinan and Genova's matrix can help teachers organize their use of tabletop RPGs in the classroom to directly impact the interpretative skills of their students – a key element of modern literacy.

OVERCOMING CHALLENGES IN COMPOSITION AND GAMING SPACES

While Freire put forth his critique of the banking model of education over 50 years ago, the implementation of social constructivist methods remains a struggle in many classrooms. Perhaps this comes as no surprise when

we consider that Freire's predecessors were combating top-down educative practices for over a century before the publication of *Pedagogy of
the Oppressed*. Pushing back against an academic structure entrenched
in hundreds of years of oppressive precedent is no easy task, especially
when many of us who attempt to enact this change have educational origins rooted in that same system. The view of students as *tabula rasa* wait-
ing for information to be inscribed into them is not a malicious act by
teachers, but rather a repetition of institutional learning. Many students,
particularly those who have faced systemic marginalization, enter the
composition classroom with a diminished sense of agency, believing that
their perspectives and experiences hold little value in academic spaces. It
is difficult to get students to buy into the potential of their own abilities,
which can lead to further disconnect between teacher and student. This
is often compounded by factors outside the teacher's control, such as curriculum requirements and class size. And even if we follow Freire's lead
and attempt to subvert our own position of authority, we cannot be blind
to the inherent power dynamics present in the classroom – as instructors, we can push our students toward a collaborative learning space, but
ultimately, we still determine their grades. The uphill battle teachers face
in their attempt to create truly inclusive spaces, where students feel comfortable taking risks and expanding their conceptions of critical thinking,
underscores the need for dynamic and creative pedagogical philosophies.

The world of tabletop RPGs faces parallel challenges related to exclusion
and agency. Many traditional or "old-school" tabletop RPGs often perpet-
uate hierarchical dynamics through the presence of the GM, who wields
disproportionate control over the game's narrative and mechanics. While
this structure can enhance storytelling, it also creates an inherent power
imbalance between the GM and players. It's right there in the name: Game
"Master." When the GM asserts excessive control, players may feel dis-
empowered, reduced to passive participants in a story they had hoped to
co-create. Moreover, gatekeeping behaviors within some tabletop RPG
communities exacerbate feelings of exclusion, particularly for newcom-
ers or individuals from historically marginalized groups. These behaviors
often manifest as rigid adherence to traditional gaming norms, such as an
antagonistic GM style or an overemphasis on mastering complex rules systems. These dynamics can discourage creativity and collaboration, leaving
players reluctant to take narrative risks or contribute fully to the game.
We can see how these challenges mirror those of first-year composition

students. Due to historical and cultural precedent, the authority figures at tabletop RPG tables and in composition classrooms alike must take *active* steps to ensure an inclusive, creative environment.

At the heart of addressing exclusion and agency in both composition classrooms and tabletop RPGs is the need to rethink and redistribute power. Freire's dialogic pedagogy offers a framework for fostering inclusive, collaborative environments by dismantling hierarchical structures that traditionally position teachers or GMs as sole authorities – but for the aforementioned reasons, truly internalizing and then implementing a philosophy of constructivism is harder than it seems. When I first started teaching, I believed I was enacting collaborative practices in my composition classrooms. It wasn't until I analogized the constructivist practices I was already participating in at the gaming table that I understood I was falling short, and that I would continue to fall short, of those goals. This type of comparative thinking can help us see our teaching practices in a new light.

I have already referred to the ability of students to intuit their teacher's intentions. The same goes for players and their GM's intentions. Some players, like some students, have no trouble at all jumping into the verbal fray, bringing their own knowledge and experience into the conversation, but many feel uncomfortable doing so. I often find these players lack the confidence to do so because they don't feel connected to the material – just like I find with students who show similar feelings in the composition classroom. If we want to establish an environment where students and players are comfortable incorporating their own ideas, they can't simply be told they have agency; they must *believe it*. In the classroom, this means embracing methods that empower students as co-creators of knowledge rather than passive recipients. For instance, peer-led discussions, collaborative writing, allowing students to pick their own topics, and projects with multiple options (e.g., giving the option to write an analysis or a creative work for the same project), and *genuinely* asking the students for input on the curriculum and lesson planning of the class provide students with opportunities to share their perspectives, negotiate meaning, and take ownership of their learning process. Similarly, GMs can foster player agency by stepping back from an authoritarian role and encouraging shared narrative control. This can be done by physical cues, such as the removal of the GM screen, or by verbal ones, like encouraging players to draw from their own strengths, experience, and hobbies – adding aspects and interests of their own lives to that of their characters – and actively turning over world-building control to player so they can integrate these ideas. These practices allow teachers and GMs to go beyond lip service when it comes to collaboration – the important elements of students' and players' lives *become* the curriculum, they *become* the story.

Confidence and creativity thrive when people feel comfortable and safe, which happens through intentional community-building activities. Of course, you can read this in any number of constructivist-influenced books on teaching, but reading theory only got me so far. I wouldn't say I was initially *unsuccessful* in my efforts to promote collaboration as a teacher, but perhaps my site of learning and my site of instruction were too close. After all, I was a teacher and student in the exact same building. At the heart of collaboration is the idea, "your ideas are as worthy of being heard as mine." It's one thing to write this in a philosophy of teaching statement; it's another to live and believe it. Reflecting on the collaborative practices I've seen instilling players with confidence forced me to reexamine my approach in the classroom, especially when it came to genuine adaptability. As a teacher and a GM, I must be willing to alter (or sometimes, completely abandon) a lesson plan or narrative thread to foster genuine, spontaneous learning and storytelling. It seems a risky move – no one wants to lose the precious time we've spent preparing material – but in my experience, this leads to more creativity and buy-in from both students and players. If we don't take a risk and show vulnerability by explicitly ceding power, how can we expect our students and players to take risks in return?

TOWARD A MORE COLLABORATIVE FUTURE

The reflection of tabletop RPG-inspired practices into composition pedagogy, and vice versa, presents an opportunity to rethink how collaboration and agency are fostered in both educational and recreational spaces. By considering the strengths (and challenges) of both fields, educators and gamers alike can build environments that empower participants to take meaningful risks, embrace their agency, and engage deeply with the process of learning and storytelling. This collaborative approach also invites further exploration and experimentation. As applied studies become more frequent, educators can gather additional evidence about how tabletop RPGs work in the classroom, leading to a greater understanding of how tabletop RPG mechanics influence group dynamics and creativity while yielding insights applicable to classroom management and curriculum design. Future research might examine the long-term impacts of these methods on student outcomes, including their ability to apply critical thinking and collaboration skills in diverse contexts. Ultimately, the dialogue between composition pedagogy and tabletop RPGs is a promising partnership for the enrichment of both fields, offering innovative frameworks for addressing exclusion, fostering agency, and redefining literacy in a rapidly changing world.

Teachers should look to tabletop RPG spaces not only for in-class activities but also for useful parallels that can defamiliarize themselves with their own philosophical groundings. In addition, we should continue broadening our definition of literacy while researching the impact games can have on our students' literacies – on their ability to think about themselves in someone else's shoes, to occupy and interact with multiple personae at once, to read and interpret visual, oral, and textual information, to practice speaking and listening and seeing reactions in a safe space, and to do all this in a way that sparks a lifelong interest in developing these skills beyond the classroom. I will attempt to do the same for myself; to learn from my players and my students and remain adaptable in the face of an ever-changing cultural and academic landscape. Because teaching and gaming are both inseparable from social dynamics, it's become clear to me that striving for active collaboration, shirking power dynamics, and nurturing agency isn't just best practice – it's a necessary part of cultivating comfortable, creative spaces. My motivation for writing this chapter was the opportunity to draw connections between the things I love, to allow myself the time and space to reflect on how the philosophical and theoretical approaches I take in the classroom can be and absolutely are informed by those I take in non-academic activities. I hope, if nothing else, this chapter allowed you to do the same.

REFERENCES

Baker-Bell, April, Bonnie Williams-Farrier, Davena Jackson, Lamar Johnson, Carmen Kynard, and Teaira McMurtry. 2020. "This Ain't Another Statement! This Is a DEMAND for Black Linguistic Justice!" Conference on College Composition and Communication, NCTE. https://cccc.ncte.org/cccc/demand-for-black-linguistic-justice.

Boone, Elizabeth Hill and Walter Mignolo. 2020. "Writing without Words: Alternative Literacies in Mesoamerica and the Andes." In *Literacies: A Critical Sourcebook.* 2nd ed., edited by Ellen Cushman, Christina Haas, and Mike Rose, 60–77: Macmillan Higher Education.

Campbell, Harrison and Andrea Madsen. 2021. "Nothing Like a Good Fiasco! Exploring the Potential of Tabletop Role-Playing Games (TRGs) as Literacy Experiences." *Canadian Journal for New Scholars in Education* 12 (2): 98–105. https://journalhosting.ucalgary.ca/index.php/cjnse/article/view/72728.

Connors, Robert J. 2004. "The Rise of Technical Writing Instruction in America." In *Central Works in Technical Communication*, edited by Johndan Johnson-Eilola and Stuart A. Selber, 3–19: Oxford University Press.

Cullinan, Maryanne and Jennifer Genova. 2023. "Gaming the Systems: A Component Analysis Framework for the Classroom Use of RPGs." *International Journal of Role-Playing* 13 (May): 7–17. https://doi.org/10.33063/ijrp.vi13.305.

Cushman, Ellen, Christina Haas, and Mike Rose, editors. 2020. *Literacies: A Critical Sourcebook*. 2nd ed. Macmillan Higher Education.

Fine, Gary Alan. 1983. *Shared Fantasy: Role-Playing Games as Social Worlds*. University of Chicago Press.

Fox, Richard. 2001. "Constructivism Examined." *Oxford Review of Education* 27 (1): 23–35. https://www.jstor.org/stable/1050991.

Freire, Paulo. 1972. *Pedagogy of the Oppressed*. Translated by Myra Bergman Ramos. Penguin Education.

Freire, Paulo. 2005. *Education for Critical Consciousness*. Continuum.

Gee, James Paul. 2007. *What Video Games Have to Teach Us about Learning and Literacy*. Palgrave Macmillan.

Gordon, Tatiana. 2012. "Using Role-Play to Foster Transformational and Social Action Multiculturalism in the ESL Classroom." *TESOL Journal* 3 (4): 698–721. https://doi.org/10.1002/tesj.32.

Horning, Alice. 1986. *Teaching Writing as a Second Language*. Southern Illinois University Press.

Lee, Carol. 2020. "The Mult-Dimensional Demands of Reading in the Disciplines." In *Literacies: A Critical Sourcebook*. 2nd ed., edited by Ellen Cushman, Christina Haas, and Mike Rose, 619–627: Macmillan Higher Education.

McKeachie, Wilbert and Marilla Svinicki. 2013. "Assessing, Testing, and Evaluating: Grading Is Not the Most Important Function." In *McKeachie's Teaching Tips*. 14th ed., 73–84: Cengage Learning.

Nystrand, Martin. 1993. "Where Did Composition Studies Come From? An Intellectual History." *Written Communication* 10 (3): 267–333.

Shapiro, Shawna and Lisa Leopold. 2012. "A Critical Role for Role-Playing Pedagogy." *TESL Canada Journal* 29 (2): 120–130. https://eric.ed.gov/?id=EJ981501.

UNESCO. 2024. "What You Need to Know about Literacy." *UNESCO*. Updated 11 February 2025. www.unesco.org/en/literacy/need-know.

III

Proficiency Bonus

Disciplinary Challenges and Opportunities

CHAPTER 8

Historiography and History Role-Playing Games

The Past is What We Play It

Stephen Mallory

INTRODUCTION

In *Reality Is Broken,* Jane McGonigal defiantly proclaims that "[g]amers have had enough with reality" (2011), illustrating that shift from the real to the simulated, educators and scholars have encouraged and aided in the deployment of games into classrooms over the last 40 years (Chin, Dukes and Gamson 2009). Games like *Oregon Trail* (Rawitsch, Heinemann and Dillenberger 1971) and *Discovery* (Wesley 1999) came into classrooms some 50 years ago in an attempt to foster deeper engagement with core historical events in the United States through play. Since then, scholars such as Gee (2007; Gee and Hayes 2012), Steinkuehler and Duncan (2008), Evans (2012), and MacCallum-Stewart (2016), amongst many others, have studied why games – digital and analog – foster stronger learning engagement and their efficacy in achieving learning goals. More specifically, these scholars bring together the idea that games allow students and their teachers the opportunity to build learning communities, engage in informed improvisation and storytelling, the heritage of rules, maps, and

DOI: 10.1201/9781003641353-12

counters inform and constrain play, and that the act of play itself serves to warp student expectations of the classroom experience and make the prospect of playing to learn seem subversive.

Understanding what these games mean interrogating the games themselves. This interrogation helps understand the default affordances and constraints presented to the game participants. To achieve this interrogation, participants deploying these games must take the time to understand the essentials of games and their social nature and how the frameworks can be bent and broken to foster new experiences. Using these games can lead to teaching history, formulating a more dynamic perspective, and heightening the tension between game history and documented history. By fostering a playful state, players can embrace their personally developed identity and identify and explore gaps or silences in the historical record. The game's framework allows students to explore history, but through multiple interpretive lenses, players can write histories of their own. This exploration allows students to learn more deeply about significant, yet potentially uncomfortable, aspects of history framed by play.

Analysis of these works all view these games as *fait accompli*; the constant demands for new games mean a steady stream of new content being developed and deployed in books and digital delivery. Playing with history places learning in tension with the labor of education; players often have to learn more about the past to forge their identity and understand the historical context. What is missing is the study of how play generates a consistent stream of counterfactual histories, useful for interrogating documented history, and how the existing historiographic process elevates certain aspects of the record while erasing others.

This analysis will study a supplement for a popular tabletop role-playing game (RPG) series that strives for generic application, allowing participants and designers to overlay this mechanical superstructure on everything from fantastical worlds filled with dragons and elves to science fiction space operas on the edge of the universe. This supplement, developed for an earlier edition of the game system, was explicitly designed and framed as a game for exploring alternate histories through the lens of science fiction. Designed to provide a second framework of alternative history exploration over the generic mechanical frameworks, it allows participants to develop an exploration in any timeframe they see fit by expanding the mythos of conflict provided by the supplement and imagining, like a rock dropped into a pond, what the ripples of their participants' actions will have across time.

Setting this analysis requires briefly exploring what is a *history tabletop role-playing game* (hTTRPG) and how they stand apart from the broader genre of RPGs. This chapter will then briefly define history and historiography; as these are massive fields in their own right, this highlights the works of two specific historians and sociologists that have particular relevance to the use of history in RPG contexts and what it means to participants in the act of playing history RPGs. Because these games place participants as both player and historian, the player's identity as participant and historian must be addressed. Taken together, the idea of history RPGs as player participants as historians means unpacking what it means to be playing with history and how the act of play brings a host of external understandings, cultural pressures, and situations to the game and play experience. When participants play RPGs, they are given agency over their worlds. Further, when history is added, a subject that participants have had exposure to through primary education, a potential common intellectual ground is placed at the table, giving participants a fuzzy starting point for building their games. These games then become as much of an exploration of the ahistorical as their understanding of the past and how the act of play influences that understanding.

INTELLECTUAL GROUNDING

Defining History RPGs

Defining a game has become increasingly contentious as various academics attempt to establish working definitions that all broadly try to develop intellectual and practice boundaries on what is, essentially, technologies that systemized play from the perspective of practitioners (Costikyan 1994; Crawford 2003), philosophical ruminations (Wittegenstein 1958; Suits 1978), and academic explorations (Salen and Zimmerman 2004; McGonigal 2011; Schell 2015). This analysis will bring together two definitions of games. The first defines playing games as "the voluntary attempt to overcome unnecessary obstacles" (Suits 1978, 54–55), but requires expanding further (Torner 2021) and clarifying (Bellomy 2017), leading to the following working definition that is inclusive of analog and RPGs of all stripes. History games must "begin at a clear point in real-world history and that history has to have a manifest effect on the nature of the game experience" (MacCallum-Stewart and Parsler 2007, 204). RPGs often include players responsible for serving as gamemasters, serving multiple roles simultaneously as producers, writers, referees, and general gaffers who fill in the gaps of play in a cooperative role. Therefore, this analysis requires a specific definition for an hTTRPG as an artifact in which participants attempt to overcome unnecessary obstacles, where humans perform the necessary calculations to determine the outcomes of those attempts, physical materials serve as randomizers and seed information for determining outcomes while optionally serving as both representational items and game-state tracking devices, adjudicated by a referee, while the game content beginning at a clear point in real-world history with that history having a manifest effect on the nature of the game experience.

If hTTRPG are artifacts that live in and between play and history, and that games are systematized play, this analysis has only touched upon half of the artifact of study. Understanding what history is and the process of writing history, historiography, is required. By understanding how history is written and its impacts once deployed, the thematic framing of hTTRPGs becomes contentious sites of debate and uneven knowledge and understanding not just by the historian but reflected through the player who has been taught the past through specific lenses.

History and Historiography

Understanding two essential and potentially assumed elements must be unpacked before moving forward. The first is that hTTRPGs are structured around written history, and the second is that these games implicitly engage participants in historiography. Historiography is the practice, techniques, and theoretical approaches to writing history. History is the creation of a narrative, reliant upon dramatic structures to generate meaning for both historian and audience, with the historian serving the role of chronicler and creator, weaving events together into a coherent structure (White 1973a, 1973b). The historian is a filter, making value determinations of information gathered from the archives and regarding interpretation and accuracy, creating an engaging narrative that entices the audience to engage with and consume the historical text. History, by the very nature of historiography, is never exclusively an objective creation; it is subject to the conventions of narrative, interpretation, and historians' biases.

These biases appear throughout historical texts, reflecting the editorial choices made by the historian through the historiographic processes as silences or gaps in the narrative. Trouillot (1995) describes three elements that determine these silences. The first is understanding the sociohistorical processes implicitly used by the historian to determine the facts of the historical matter being translated into a narrative. The second is understanding how this narrative is ultimately created. The third and final element is realizing that the process of determining fact and crafting narrative exists on a spectrum, where the creation of the historical text exists in a fluid space where the boundaries between objective fact and narrative embellishment are constantly shifting. This makes the creation of history an exclusionary act determined by the historical context and situation of the author (Trouillot 1995, 23). These exclusions are ultimately silences, or intentional gaps in the historical narratives, that occur when the historian determines the facts, assembled into and stored in an archive, retrieved and arranged into the final narrative when the historian determines what should or should not have retrospective significance (Trouillot 1995, 25). Silences reflect the sociocultural and historical contexts of the historian, who grapples with events that "deal with the impossible only after the impossible had become fact; and even then, the facts were not always accepted as such" (Trouillot 1995, 89). Silences occur when historians must reconcile events with their existing sociocultural context, which is in tension between "what happened and that which is said to have happened" (Trouillot 1995, 106). With these tension-derived narratives, game designers for hTTRPGs use their understanding of history to frame their work and thus provide a second layer of historiographic labor in modifying existing history to work within the rule-based structures of the game. hTTRPGs become integral to generating dynamic archives and establishing and perpetuating specific historical narratives.

What does this mean? Designers who make hTTRPGs bring their own interpretation of history to the game and frame that interpretation in the service of the game's rules. Participants, players, and game masters bring their understanding of history to their game sessions, and these various interpretations may, in turn, synch or conflict, leading to continued negotiation through play. Because of the localized, personal nature of historical understanding, participants playing hTTRPGs can lead to various outcomes, from encouraging more profound engagement with the history used in the game to participants improvising their interpretations of history over those provided in the game materials. In both cases, the question of identity and the participants becomes a key analysis point.

Tabletop RPGs and Identity

One of the things that makes tabletop RPGs broadly, and the use of hTTRPGs, so seductive is that the games explore, question, and answer essential frameworks of player identity. These are interactive assemblages that do more than foster engagement toward implicit or explicit goals; they provide a locus for exploring questions of personal identity and creating game-focused affinity spaces, as well as larger communities that serve as micro-sites of learning that extend beyond normative learning locations.

Tabletop RPGs allow players to grapple with essential questions of identity through a cascade of representations. Discussions of this cascade are not particularly novel in Game Studies, as RPGs allow players to simultaneously engage with multiple player identity representations. Players have their virtual representation, their physical representation, and their projective representation (Gee 2007, 54–56). The virtual representation is the player's assumed identity while playing the game, the physical representation is the player's real-world identity, and the projective representation is the identity that the player fosters through gameplay, embodying the goals and desires that the player's physical and virtual representations come together during the act of play.

While tabletop RPGs draw inspiration from numerous source materials, playing these games specifically affords participants "another way to make sense of our real-world experiences" (Evans 2012, 191). There are generalized discussions on players in relationship with the rules that help understand why players play games (Bartle 2003) this sort of analysis only extends to the boundaries of the game itself. In Bartle's terms, an achiever exists only when in conjunction with mechanical structures that encourage achieving behaviors as a mechanical extension of identity. When players engage with tabletop RPGs, these are players who are ultimately creating imaginary echoes of themselves (Evans 2012, 192), creating opportunities "informed by [our] social experiences in that shared, social fantasy, and perhaps reflected on with a little more knowledge" (Evans 2012, 192) than before playing the game. Playing a tabletop RPG means "participating in a complex form of identity play that involves the creation of a shared fiction that centers on the relationship between multiple players and character identities" (Evans 2012, 192).

Playing with History

Games structure play allows participants to experience and explore multiple avenues within the provided framework. Interactivity allows players to explore the histories they know, the histories in the documentation, and their response to those histories. Players playing hTTRPGs bring their embodied knowledge to the table, allowing them to engage, reinforce, or challenge the information they know in an interactive space, becoming a site where participants learn together. Even if the referee and players have sufficient mastery and understanding of the game and content presented in that game, the act of play provides a means of exploring and finding alternative histories that the collected participants may not have learned previously. These games are filled with interconnected rules and narrative affordances that typically encourage participants to explore what is and is not possible. The presented game thus provides a framework inviting discussion, debate, and even potential research as players establish and reinforce a social contract outlining the social rules of the table working in conjunction with the rules of the game.

Playing with history means using these hTTRPGs and engaging in collective challenges within a social nexus that engages with the past to create an alternative historical narrative that is structured around the events determined by the players. The game critiqued in this analysis embrace the idea of endogenous play. As Lloyd Reiber (1996) describes, endogenous play is the tight overlap between gameplay, content, and practices surrounding that content. The game materials presented in this analysis were designed and developed by professional game designers and developers as historical supplements for larger game systems. These supplements were all released commercially, conforming to the conventions of play established within various market genres at the time of their release, developed outside of the constraints of edutainment or specific, state-mandated curricular goals. Playing games occurs at a social nexus; play is an act of exploration, a struggle alongside and against the game's rules. The game systematizes these rules. These rules can also foster and encourage socially agreed-upon modifications and conventions of behavior that modify the systematized rules (Sicart 2014). Play, and the games that frame it, is about engaging with the game's challenges.

CASE STUDY: GURPS – ALTERNATE HISTORY

This case study analyzes a specific sourcebook developed for a commercial game system, exploring the above concept of playing with history using hTTRPGs and the ahistorical narratives that players will derive from that activity. This study intends to utilize the existing gameplay framework designed implicitly or explicitly as a content-neutral game framework. These frameworks, or game systems, provide structures for determining how to develop and overcome challenges during play and the flexibility to encourage referees and players to bend or break the rules during play as they see fit.

Using the above framework and analysis as a starting point, this case study will be structured around the following questions:

1. What is the implicit historical narrative provided by the supplement?

2. What sort of agency do players have within that narrative structure?

3. How well does the framework of the game engine mesh with the historical framework?

These questions are ultimately explored through a close reading of the provided text. It must be noted that the text referenced here is within a game framework that is currently supported, with additional content under development and release as of the time of this writing.

Steve Jackson developed the *Generic Universal Role Playing System* (GURPS) in 1986. The *GURPS* system, on release, was still aimed at the fantasy market and leaned heavily on swords and sorcery as a theme, but as the system matured, with the fourth edition of rules being published in 2006, so has the content being offered. Currently available, *GURPS* allows players to use the core ruleset to create their own game worlds, or players can pick up sourcebooks based on genres like Fantasy, Horror, Martial Arts, Superheroes, Space Opera, and alternate history in their Infinite Worlds supplement. Previous editions of *GURPS* also allowed players to engage with licensed properties like *Conan the Barbarian*, *Discworld*, evolutions of other game systems like *Traveller*, or explicitly grounded historical books such as Imperial Rome, Ancient Greece, Age of Napoleon, Ancient Egypt, or a five-book series that covers World War II from the standard to the science fiction-esque dubbed Weird War II. It is worth noting that, as of 2024, the current edition of GURPS does not have *any* explicitly framed historical sourcebooks as previous editions. Rather, they, like other engines, have generalized much of this sort of content into broader sourcebooks like the one studied here.

This analysis is going to study the supplement *Alternate Worlds* (Hite, Jackson and Ford 2006), produced for the fourth edition of GURPS, and explicitly intended to give players an opportunity to explore divergent historical narratives, in turn, creating a divergent narrative inspired by those provided in the text. Framed within the standard GURPS universe, *Alternate History* serves two purposes. The first is that, when deployed as written, it provides players and referees plenty of science fiction tropes, such as time travel, to insert themselves into divergent histories for adventuring. The second is that the book, given the generic nature of the system, also provides rules and frameworks where "[y]ou could can even build a game world – an infinity of them – from scratch, using this books alternate Earth design systems and advice" (Hite, Jackson and Ford 2006, 4), letting participants pick an important moment in history, choosing an alternative outcome, and then create a world based how the players believe that outcome cascades.

With this in mind, the sort of historical narrative the supplement provides is bifurcated. The source material, grounded in the *standard setting*, is roughly based on reality and the world around us in the moment of play. By utilizing science fiction tropes, players can explore existing alternative historical narratives provided by the text, adventuring across the past as members of the Infinity Patrol, protecting both the core timeline and homeline, and that trans-dimensional/time travel is possible, known as the secret. This means players could chase threats back in time to prevent the Nazis from developing a Nuclear Weapon, or go back and kill George Washington, or radically diverge the homeline from what we currently experience (Hite, Jackson and Ford 2006, 8–25), with explanations for this movement framed as everything from paranormal to technological in method to account for the generic nature of the system. Provided threats to the homeline range from Centrum (Hite, Jackson and Ford 2006, 46–56), based on the proposed Anglo-French alliance of 1939, Nazis (Hite, Jackson and Ford 2006, 56–67), and the supernatural horror of the Cabal (Hite, Jackson and Ford 2006, 68–69). With appropriate time, players should be able to find a narrative hook to intertwine this text with other GURPS games regardless of their foundational genre and provide them a basis for time-traveling, inter-spatial adventures.

The narrative structure developed by the *Alternate Worlds* supplement provides a fairly tight structure to work within. After all, like other tabletop RPG structures, the emphasis here is on the social contract between players and referees as much as it is on the rules as written. While the GURPS system is highly generalized toward different play-styles, as tabletop RPGs have matured, understanding the social dynamics and their relationship with play and games have also matured. While the origins of these games are deeply rooted in wargaming, which is rife with rules to recreate the complexities and verisimilitude of armed conflict, tabletop RPGs can swing between RPGs and RPGs. Some groups lean heavily into following the rules as written and cleaving their play closer to the wargaming structures provided in the rules, while others lean more into the social, theater-of-the-mind, improvisation acting aspects that tabletop RPGs also afford. While each game has particular affordances and constraints, lending certain game styles to be easier to implement, the emphasis in tabletop RPGs has been that style is ultimately afforded by the player, falling somewhere on a spectrum between *hack and slash* with a heavy emphasis on maximizing characters to face and overcome mechanics-focused challenges and *immersive storytelling* where the wargame-based combat mechanics can – and often encouraged in more recent game systems (Wizards of the Coast 2014, 34) – to take a backseat to narrative constraints and affordances. Like *Dungeons and Dragons*, *GURPS* allows players to find a game somewhere in between those two extremes. As a result, the players significantly impact the narrative structure, particularly the historical narrative being recreated. The *GURPS* system, by design, provides a generic framework of tools for players and referees/gamemasters to overlay their particular goals, demands, and frameworks. Whether they realize it or not, this does place both players and gamemasters into the position of historians and brings with them all of the pitfalls and promises of historiography.

When players and gamemasters cocreate the narrative of their game worlds through playing their hTTRPG, they create historical events for their shared game world that are worthy of historiographical analysis and history production. When looking at published works in tabletop RPG spaces, in games not necessarily history-based, players often rise from locally known heroes to heroes of such power and ability that their reknown is known to the very gods of the universe. In published module series for games like *Dungeons and Dragons: 3rd Edition* and the *Dragonlance Chronicles* (Hickman et al. 2006), players rise from local heroes adventuring around their hometown of Solace, and by the end of the first series of modules, they have fought and defeated the leader of one of the vaunted Dragon Armies, rebuilding ancient alliances, and bringing proof of the existence of the Gods back to the people of Ansalon. These sorts of modules effectively constrain how and what sort of history is written; the designers have a laid-out agenda, highlighting specific events, locations, people, and places, and the module itself is arranged to provide players the opportunity to write their histories based on the outcomes of their path through the module itself.

Using *GURPS: Alternate History* as a guide, gamemasters and players cleave much closer to historians and historiographers as they develop their own unique game world and alternate histories therein than they imagine. As a field and practice, history is inherently creative and subjective, and when brought together into an interactive affinity space like an hTTRPG, players and gamemasters become historians of their own world. This means, they bring with them their own biases, perspectives, and narrative constraints to the works they research and create. The practice of writing history, historiography, emphasizes the need for deep research, engagement with primary and secondary sources, and ultimately crafting a narrative using those curated sources to explain and explore events, people, and places in the past. When gamemasters and players do the same for their game worlds, nominally called worldbuilding, they do the same, constraining their history and historiographical processes to be applied to their game world specifically, even if that work can be "bent, twisted, spindled, and mutilated to suit a homebrew, a corporate campaign setting, or some combination of the two" (Baur 2012, 87–99). Historians, and the gamemasters who develop their homebrew game worlds, write with the idea that "there are ultimately an infinite number of stories contained therein, all different in their details, each unlike every other" (White 1973a, 1973b, 294). These infinite stories can find their interactive expression in the games played using hTTRPGs in ways that past historians may not have considered but still cannot shake a concerning but with it an educationally relevant perspective. As gamemasters develop their own game worlds, particularly when framed within historical contexts like hTTRPG play, then they implicitly bring their own biases to the game. The same can be said of the players within the game world; the characters they create and how the embody those characters include all of the biases and understandings of history that the player carries with them as embodied representations of the player into their character-based representation. The GURPS system, by design, provides incredible potential for agency in the narrative structure, limited only by the negotiations and understandings established between participants at the table and the available resources to understand the (a) historical narrative they are working within.

Because *Alternate Worlds* allows a nearly infinite number of alternative histories to be created and provides the framework to do just that, and the same can be said for the nearly infinite number of popular historical moments around which these histories can be explored, the potential is there for gamemasters and players to bring with them their own biases to the histories of the past. Good historiography is ultimately grounded in historical thinking (Wineburg 2010, 2–4). Being a historian is less about embracing and reinforcing popular myths, such as the Confederacy winning the Civil War. Creating history-based worlds for hTTRPGs means thinking historically, and not trusting interpretations of these mythic times, places, and events, but engaging in the following when reviewing historical works:

1. Sourcing: identifying who wrote the historical work and what biases they brought to it

2. Contextualizing: identifying when the work was written and what events were occurring during its distribution

3. Close Reading: what does the document say and the language used to say it

4. Using Background Knowledge: use a broad base of existing historical knowledge and information to read and understand the document in question

5. Reading the Silences: begin tracking and identifying what was left out of the analysis

6. Corroboration: ask the same questions of multiple sources to determine common areas of agreement and disagreement

With these six points in mind, even relying on popular tropes and lead to deeply flawed histories, even those popularly reflected and amplified. Creating an Alternative History seems like an easy task, one that relies on existing popular knowledge of the past, but is in order to maintain internal consistency for the history-based game world, designers and gamemasters need to do significant research to give their world sufficient verisimilitude and depth to afford game players proper agency to write their characters place in that historical record. That said, if designers and gamemasters do embody these six elements, not only will their worldbuilding be stronger and reflect a care and understanding of history that will work closely with player capabilities and agency, but it will also prevent that hTTRPG from falling into the pitfalls of popular history that often rely on weakly sourced, silenced histories that elevate myth over contentious fact. This is a difficult task to complete, particularly when most individuals history education in the United States stops in High School and engaged with content that was hyper-focused on state curricular goals that are, themselves, warped by cultural myth and market focuses (Loewen 2007).

This ultimately allows a perfect overlay of the game engine with the historical frameworks defined by the participants at the table. That is not to say there are no issues with using the supplement; *Alternate Worlds* perfectly embodies the science fiction trope of traveling back in time to fix the future with amazing foreknowledge (Carnes 2014, 9). hTTRPGs can be considered popular deployments of the role-immersion games imagined by Mark Carnes, where games can encourage participants to engage more deeply with history through play (Carnes 2014, 8–10). While Carnes describes this role immersion as a blend of research and improvisational acting, games like *Alternate Worlds* potentially offer far more structure and conflict-resolution capabilities than the free-form style he imagines. Rather than dealing strictly with negotiation and soft structures for compliance and negotiation, games like GURPS allow players to potentially more deeply inhabit historical characters because of the emphasis on abstracting oratory, performance, or intimidation skills that a reluctant or poor performer may have trouble embodying. Players whose natural identity may be shy, meek, or speak poorly can role-play and embody a new identity, and relying on dice rolls and statistics allows them to embody a very different persona.

Playing these sorts of games, particularly ones that explore alternative histories, means that players need an understanding of both the rules, the history as written, and the history as presented. This alone provides excellent opportunities for use in a classroom context, where students would need to research and rewrite counterfactual histories to understand the world in which they are playing. Regardless of educational demands, participants would need to establish a specific cultural competency with the past as known and the alternate history presented to role-play the game and solidify their identity in the game event. Much of this is largely ignored if the chosen game relies more on roll-playing, where historical/ahistorical background becomes less critical and merely window-dressing to the mechanical engagement loops whose outcomes are determined by dice rolling and numeric calculations.

DISCUSSION

The text featured here falls within a reasonably discrete hTTRPG development philosophy. This reflects not only when they were developed but also the affordances and constraints of the game systems in which they were developed and released. The *Alternate Worlds* text can be seen as a looser example of the hegemony of play (Fron et al. 2007). It emphasizes creative labor on both the gamemaster and the players to bring their perspectives into the games they will be playing, with all the biases and tastes therein. These biases and tastes assumed who was playing, why, and what they wanted to play. Even when framed in historical contexts and the identities players assume within those contexts, the developers' biases and tastes are evident, as is the potential for ahistorical outcomes.

Alternate Worlds reflects a greater level of creative trust and freedom by the designers toward the players and the game masters. This freedom allows players to have greater agency within the alternate worlds they create and the alternate histories contained therein. As noted above, this does place a greater level of labor on the gamemaster and the players to provide sufficient historical foreknowledge to establish the game narrative context and help players build a sufficiently grounded identity in the game world. Players and gamemasters much work together to build a greater understanding of the state of the alternate worlds and their alternate histories that are a part of the game, even if they follow the default campaign guidelines.

The *GURPS* system, by being generic, creates additional player and gamemaster labor, allowing players to have greater agency in modifying or creating new historical narratives. Players can play a central part in the histories they engage with, as determined by fellow players and the gamemasters. Rather than being anonymous bystanders to the flow of history, *Alternate Worlds* places players central to the engagement, modification, and erasure of histories across alternate worlds. Even taking into account the biases and tastes of the players, the social negotiation on how these historical/ahistorical narratives play out becomes far more dynamic in the

GURPS framework. This dynamism increases when considering the character identities that players inhabit while playing the game, visiting worlds where the player and their characters historical foreknowledge may be useful and necessary to succeed as they adventure and potentially change history. This is all mediated, of course, but the player and gamemasters' biases and tastes, by the potential for exploration and even critical engagement (Mallory 2023) with the past through exploring ahistorical worlds, exist within the GURPS framework. Even when framed in historical contexts and the identities players assume within those contexts, the developers' biases and tastes are evident, as is the potential for ahistorical outcomes.

Further, this entire analysis dances between three terms, two of which are familiar in the realm of analog games. These terms are role-playing, roll-playing, and the odd one out, role-immersion play. Role-play and roll-play have two distinct meanings. Role-play allows participants "to unpack different relationships of varying amounts of power and knowledge" (Miller 2021), thus "blurring the lines between explicit game rules and implicit social contracts" (Miller 2021). This form of improvisational acting relies as much on the dice roll as it does on the participants embodying their characters through play based on the particular situation. This can often lead to participants "are briefly dispatched to the past in order to fix [a problem], carrying a tool kit of contemporary problem-solving skills" (Carnes 2014, 9). By contrast, rollplay relies exclusively on the dice's random roll and the game's mechanical outcomes to determine outcomes. When put into a historical context, though, where participants may need to know more than what they have encountered in history books in order to fully inhabit their role within the past, a third type of play can be utilized in these contexts. Role-immersion games potentially "provide access to…often untapped wellsprings of motivation and imagination" (13) by requiring participants to deeply engage with the past through research through this unique form of role-play that requires research, dedication, and intentionally resisting the above "Connecticut Yankee in King Arthur's Court" problem. An hTTRPG will likely require all three in some form, requiring participants to do significant research, inhabit their roles, and rely on mechanical determinants to fill in the gaps.

This places hTTRPGs in a unique position. On the one hand, they are constrained by expectations of research and content accuracy based on the constraints of the game system. On the other hand, few game designers and players have sufficient background in historiography and thinking like historians to fully engage with and expand the research and accuracy provided by the core rulebooks. Game systems like GURPS intentionally market themselves as being flexible, only limited by the player's and game-masters' imagination, allowing whatever games they conceive to become a reality. This means that players and gamemasters have agency over the sort of game they design and consume, resisting specific standards and practices to prevent the deployment of unethical, immoral histories that embrace or take existing historical events to their most extreme. Creating or defining an ethical or worthwhile practice to prevent the exploitation or enumeration of far more dark alternative histories in an hTTRPG space falls beyond the game's scope. After all, once the players have the books in their hands, there is nothing that the designers can do about participants completely ignoring designer recommendations.

Creating a more ethical hTTRPG ultimately becomes a question that is too complex for this analysis, demanding a variety of designers with deep backgrounds in history and historiography, ethics, morality, and game design to bring their various skills to bear in and around these playful artifacts. These unicorn designers can be found in the field of history, where they are still working in a field in deep crisis. Historians have all but abdicated their work of informing people about the past and its impact on the present to popular histories of dubious quality and inter-active media whose own interpretations of history are constrained by the rules, mechanics, and data used within the game that are, in turn, warped and modified by the designers. Top-selling games like *Hearts of Iron IV* (Paradox Development Studio 2016), which purports to be a history game, erase all atrocities, including the holocaust, to tell a sanitized version of World War II that "teaches people to learn that there are no isolated answers, that everything is connected" (Hall 2016) yet ignores the approximately 1,000 civilians who died per hour from 1939 to 1945. The responsibility for creating these designers falls on higher education, which has begun to develop more robust game design and development programs and sufficiently robust programs that embrace both developing sufficient design agendas for students and their abilities to create cohesive interactive structures and ground their works sufficiently deep research.

Ultimately, it means that the game designers themselves position them-selves in a place where they implicitly ignore much of their role in terms of ethical implications once the game is distributed to the public. After all, many games, including *Dungeons and Dragons*, emphasize the role that players and game masters alike have in modifying the game rules as they see fit, creating their fantasy worlds with rules that "help you [Dungeon Master] and the other players have a good time, but the rules are not in charge" (Wizards of the Coast 2014, 4). This positioning means that, despite the designer's or publisher's intentions, game content created for private consumption and distributed locally that is disturbing or unethical may be deployed. Content from previous iterations of these sorts of games range from the vaguely insulting to the offensive, including *AD&D* 1st Edition *Dungeon Masters Guide* (Gygax 1979) and its infamous harlot table (191) that describes a variety of colorful prostitutes, placing home creators and modifiers in a position where to create more ethical and approachable game world, they must have a deep understanding of the rules and the content as is before stripping out or heavily modifying the content to meet modern, existing standards of equity and inclusion.

While these game systems encourage players and game masters alike to have this level of knowledge, creating an ethical game world demands the social interaction around which play demands. Creating a historical world means bringing all participants together to mold the game world, their experiences, and what sort of history will be created from these playful interactions that will still be rife with the participants' biases and narrative demands. If these fantasy worlds are based on real human history, how these players deal with concepts of slavery, racism, and misogyny is critical. The resulting games can follow the explicit rules of *Advanced Dungeons and Dragons* and place hard limitations on character abilities and capabilities based on race and gender (Gygax 1978, 13–18), as intended by the designer (Riggs 2024), or they can create their own game worlds where these limitations do not exist. They can create new engagements with history freed from past realities to explore these worlds through role-play and adventure, using their interactivity as a fulcrum around which interrogating the past can and should occur.

CONCLUSION

It should be little wonder that, since 2000, Steve Jackson Games has quietly walked away from explicitly historical games or game sourcebooks with their properties. The latest revision of GURPS, of which *Alternate Worlds* is a part, has quietly moved away from explicitly historical texts and, instead, relies on a larger volume of themed texts to provide players and gamemasters the agency to develop their own historically themed games. While this does help erase the potential of the designers to explicitly overlay their own biases and preferences from history on the game, it does elevate the player and gamemasters' biases and preferences. While this will undoubtedly help players forge stronger identity connections with their characters, they will implicitly bring in their perceptions and understandings of history to the game.

Ultimately, shifting toward the player and gamemaster-centered history games in hTTRPGs creates positive and negative opportunities. hTTRPGs allow players to create their interpretation of historical worlds, events, and people, giving participants greater agency to engage/reengage with historical texts. Simultaneously, it also places participants where a greater criticality in the texts they are using becomes necessary. Pulling popular history texts and bringing their agendas, biases, and frameworks makes the games dangerously unique by repeating and amplifying historical narratives of dubious research or assertion. These ahistorical games walk a fine line between historical recreation, science fiction alternate histories, and historiography, where the games create new historical narratives. It is up to the next generation of game design teachers, instructors, and critical media scholars to instill greater ethical standards reflected through stronger design agendas reflected in deeper research grounding and game structures that guide designers and the hTTRPGs they make toward more ethical and worthwhile games.

REFERENCES

Bartle, Richard. 2003. *Designing Virtual Worlds*. Indianapolis: New Riders.

Baur, Wolfgang. 2012. *Complete Kobold Guide to Game Design*. Kirkland: Kobold Press.

Bellomy, Ian. 2017. "What Counts: Configuring the Human in Platform Studies." *Analog Game Studies* (4). https://analoggamestudies.org/2017/03/what-counts/.

Carnes, Mark C. 2014. *Minds on Fire: How Role-Immersion Games Transform College*. Cambridge: Harvard University Press.

Chin, Jeffrey, Richard Dukes, and William Gamson. 2009. "Assessment in Simulation and Gaming: A Review of the Last 40 Years." *Simulation & Gaming* (SAGE Publications) 40 (4): 553–568.

Costikyan, Greg. 1994. "I Have No Words & I Must Design: Toward a Critical Vocabulary for Games." *Interactive Fantasy: The Journal of Role-Playing and Story-Making Systems* (2): 22–38.

Crawford, Chris. 2003. *On Game Design*. Indianapolis: New Riders Publishing.

Evans, Monica. 2012. "The Secret Lives of Elven Paladins." In *Dungeons and Dragons and Philosophy: Raiding the Temple of Wisdom*, edited by Jon Cogburn and Mark Silcox, 179–192. Chicago: Carus Publishing Company.

Fron, Janine, Tracy Fullerton, Jacquelyn Ford Morie, and Celia Pearce. 2007. "The Hegemony of Play." In *Situated Play: Proceedings of DIGRA 2007 Conference*https://dl.digra.org/index.php/dl/article/view/283/283

Gee, James Paul. 2007. *What Video Games Have to Teach Us about Learning and Literacy.* New York: Palgrave MacMillan.

Gee, James Paul, and E. Hayes. 2012. "Nurturing Affinity Spaces and Game-Based Learning." In *Games, Learning, and Society*, edited by Constance Steinkuhler, Kurt Squire and Sasha Barab, 129–153. New York: Cambridge University Press.

Gygax, Gary. 1978. *Advanced Dungeons and Dragons: Players Handbook.* Lake Geneva: TSR Games.

Gygax, Gary. 1979. *Advanced Dungeons and Dragons: Dungeon Master Guide.* Lake Geneva: TSR Games.

Hall, Charlie. 2016. "Hearts of Iron 4 and the Hard Work of History." *Polygon.* January 25. Accessed July 27, 2020. https://www.polygon.com/features/2016/1/25/10806780/hearts-of-iron-4-and-the-hard-work-of-history.

Hickman, Travy, Harold Johnson, Douglas Niles, Michael Dobson, Clark Valentine, and Sean MacDonald. 2006. *Dragonlance: Dragons of Autumn.* Lake Geneva: Sovereign Press.

Hite, Kenneth, Steve Jackson, and John M. Ford. 2006. *GURPS: Infinite Worlds*, edited by Andrew Hackard. Austin: Steve Jackson Games.

Loewen, James W. 2007. *Lies My Teacher Told Me: Everything Your High School History Textbook Got Wrong.* New York: The New Press.

MacCallum-Stewart, Esther. 2016. "Wargaming (as) Literature." In *Zones of Control: Perspectives on Wargaming*, edited by Pat Harrigan and Matthew G. Kirschenbaum, 555–572. Cambridge: The MIT Press.

MacCallum-Stewart, Esther, and Justin Parsler. 2007. "Controversies: Historicising the Computer Game." *Situated Play, Proceedings of DIGRA 2007 Conference.* https://www.digra.org/wp-content/uploads/digital-library/07312.51468.pdf.

Mallory, Stephen. 2023. "Playing as People: Critical Pedagogy and Historical Role Immersion Games." *Visual Arts Research* (49), No. 2, 102–114.

McGonigal, Jane. 2011. *Reality Is Broken: Why Games Make Us Better and How They Can Change the World.* New York: Penguin.

Miller, Josh Aaron. 2021. "Roleplaying as a Solution to the Quarterbacking Problem of Cooperative and Educational Games." Analog Game Studies. Accessed February 14, 2025. https://analoggamestudies.org/2021/06/roleplaying-as-a-solution-to-the-quarterbacking-problem-of-cooperative-and-educational-games/.

Paradox Development Studio. 2016. *Hearts of Iron IV.* Digital Game. Stockholm, June 6.

Rawitsch, Don, Bill Heinemann, and Paul Dillenberger. 1971. *The Oregon Trail.* Digital Game. MECC, December 3.

Reiber, Lloyd P. 1996. "Seriously Considering Play: Designing Interactive Learning Environments Based on the Blending of Microworlds, Simulations and Games." *Educational Technology Research and Development* (44), 43–58.

Riggs, Ben. 2024. *Ben Riggs.* July 7. Accessed January 1, 2025. https://www.writerbenriggs. com/blog.

Salen, Katie, and Eric Zimmerman. 2004. *Rules of Play.* Cambridge: The MIT Press.

Schell, Jesse. 2015. *The Art of Game Design: A Book of Lenses.* New York: CRC Press.

Sicart, Miguel. 2014. *Play Matters.* Cambridge: The MIT Press.

Steinkuehler, Constance, and Sean Duncan. 2008. "Scientific Habits of Mind in Virtual Worlds." *Journal of Science Education and Technology* (17), No.6, 530–543.

Suits, Bernard. 1978. *The Grasshopper: Games, Life and Utopia.* Toronto: University of Toronto Press.

Torner, Evan. 2021. *Boardgame Historian – Geschichte und Gesellschaft in analogen Spielen.* October 18. Accessed October 16, 2024. https://bghistorian. hypotheses.org/2030.

Trouillot, Michel-Rolph. 1995. *Silencing the Past: Power and the Production of History.* Boston: Beacon Press.

Wesley, John. 1999. *Discovery – Teachers Guide.* Culver City: Interact.

White, Hayden V. 1973a. "Interpretation in History." *New Literary History* (4), No. 2. 281–314.

White, Hayden V. 1973b. *Metahistory: The Historical Imagination in Nineteenth-Century Europe.* Baltimore: Johns Hopkins University Press.

Wineburg, Sam. 2010. "Thinking Like a Historian." *Teaching with Primary Sources Quarterly* 2–4.

Wittegenstein, Ludwig. 1958. *Philosophical Investigations.* 2nd ed. Translated by G.E.M. Anscombe. Oxford: Basil Blackwell.

Wizards of the Coast. 2014. *Dungeons and Dragons Dungeons Masters Guide.* Renton: Hasbro.

CHAPTER 9

Edu-larp and Positive Psychology

Theory, Practice, and Case Study

Leland Masek

INTRODUCTION

Educational live action role-playing (edu-larp) has several traditions in communities focused on pedagogy, games, play, and design. Edu-larp is often compared to drama education (Mochocki 2013), emotional skills education (Maragliano 2019), and is being progressively brought into a variety of pedagogical contexts (Robinson et al. 2023). It has been applied in several ways, such as computer-human interaction (Robinson et al. 2023), math (Maragliano et al. 2021), challenges asylum seekers face (Maragliano 2019), and national history (Mochocki 2014). There are also entire schools that are dedicated to utilizing edu-larp as a primary tool for all topics in education, notably Østerskov Efterskole (Hyltoft 2008) and Efterskolen Epos (Westborg 2019) both in Denmark. There are also numerous companies and programs that seek to integrate edu-larp more closely into public school systems. While the practitioners of modern edu-larp are often framed as radical or disconnected from other pedagogical theory and practice,[1] they can also be seen as embodying numerous components of the psychology of learning. This text aims to integrate some of the useful theories of psychology that are critically relevant to

DOI: 10.1201/9781003641353-13

design choices by edu-larp practitioners. The text will go over three different paradigms of the psychology of learning: behaviorism, cognitivism, and constructivism and address specific ways edu-larp can embody these educational techniques. Furthermore, this text will illustrate these points with concrete examples from an edu-larp program from 2018 to present by the city of Tampere that educated ages 7–12 on positive psychological (see Seligman 2010) principles.

In the first section, behaviorist positive psychological education will be described through the lens of normative gamification methods. In essence, a game environment that has a fictional world designed to embody literature-driven content with game rewards and progression attached to the student learning that content. Secondly, cognitivist models amplify this approach through a variety of framing techniques applicable for children's developmental characteristics such as featuring concrete fictional examples, verbal talkbacks, and framed discussion of game and play moments. Finally, Constructivism will address how edu-larp is a unique context of educational experience in helpful and potentially unhelpful ways. Specifically play scholarship will address the experience of playfulness and how it intersects with educational experience. Specific techniques will be discussed from De Koven's The Well-Played Game (for a reprint, see De Koven 2013) and Stenros's work on one-sided and unplayful play styles (Stenros 2015). Through these lenses, there will be a deeper theoretical understanding of how education in a playful experience is affected. By integrating these theoretical paradigms into how they are applied in practice in a specific edu-larp program, this work hopes to extend the discourse on academic theories of education, psychology, and edu-larp.

BACKGROUND

One of the core challenges of connecting edu-larp into a larger historical framework is that connected practices can use different names such as education simulations and game-based education. In order to better integrate understandings of the pedagogical potential of edu-larp it is helpful to give a brief overview on the plurality of education techniques and theories with major overlaps in their structure. For this piece, I will follow Robinson et al. who defined edu-larp as "a semi-structured role-playing activity, in which participants engage a subject matter by taking on particular roles and/or personas and enacting situations and scenarios to create immersive learning" (Robinson et al. 2023, 1).[2] Semi-structured role-playing with an immersive learning potential has several potential historical starting points.

In a very broad sense, components underpinning edu-larp have been used as pedagogical tools in our earliest records of education. In a certain way, *Socratic Dialogues* feature key components: they present a fictionalized representation of Socrates engaging in debates with various philosophical figures (Kahn 1997) and are often used as experiential pedagogical tools to spark real debates with students on the questions the textual characters ask and discuss (Altorf 2019). Some authors see these texts as intentionally open to spark this kind of imagined argument by being "something that is still alive - with things still unsaid in it. What is unfinished is also an opening, an invitation - here from Plato and Socrates" (Molander 1990, 230). Taken together, students are presented a compelling fictionalized frame where they have active and specific roles to play and their experience in these roles is intended to educate them – sounds like edu-larp!

Now, while the above interpretation is meant to highlight how an immersive act of imagination on a specific pedagogical concept is a broad and ancient education tool, specific techniques and components of edu-larp are explicitly starting in the modern era. Edu-larp is an international pedagogical phenomenon which dates back to the 1916 long-term educative imagination games promoted by Inokentiy Nikolaevich Zhukov. In 1918, 700 participants aged 12–14 in the school system of CHITA in the USSR played a two and a half year long-term larp designed by him to learn core school subject matter. These ideas were implemented in Russian and Soviet schools in a variety of ways throughout the 20th century. This pedagogical movement saw the intentional leveraging of imaginary role-playing applied in public school settings based on Soviet and Russian psychological theory. While this tradition eventually became a propaganda tool, the concept of explicit imaginary, playful activity to teach children content has a broad impact (Kot 2012; Harviainen et al. 2018).

The Nordic larp community has promoted edu-larp in the European education system, especially in the 2000s. There is an entire full-time edu-larp school called Østerskov Efterskole in Denmark founded in 2006 by Nordic larpers associated with the annual larp convention Knutepunkt (Hyltoft 2008). This convention also promotes practitioners and researchers on the topic with an annual edu-larp Conference held since 2014 (Westborg 2019). There are also a number of historical and pedagogical overviews of Nordic-style edu-larp[3] (Temte et al. 2013; Mochocki 2020).

In the United States, edu-larp has also seen an explosion of interest, especially since the 1990s which was heavily influenced by the history of adventure education programs and outdoor summer camps in the United States (Miles and Priest 1990). This partly explains why these programs are called things like the *Adventure Game Theater* (founded in 1986), now called the Wayfinder Experience (see pbs.org; Wayfinderexperience. com), *Renaissance Adventures* (founded in 1995) (see website Renaissance Adventures Nov. 2024), or *Guardian Adventures* (founded in 1999) (see website Guardian Adventures 2024). This history is critical to understand the resulting programmatic pedagogical intent, as their goals are frequently socio-emotional, like programs such as Outward Bound. Outward Bound focuses on the motivational self-learning of success in risky, challenging, novel environments (Walsh and Golins 1976). It is common for this form of edu-larp to feature "an Adventure Quest where young adventurers enter a land of mystery and wonder" (Renaissance Adventures Nov. 2024) or "educational adventures" (Guardian Adventures Nov. 2024), where the primary goal includes enabling children to "achieve their personal goals and experience self-fulfillment and empowerment" (Renaissance Adventures web Nov. 2024). American edu-larp then later also integrates more traditional school topics such as STEM education (see website Guardian Adventures 2024).[4]

Taken together, edu-larp is an educational technique used for possibly thousands of years, often by dissociated groups working in moderate isolation. This chapter hopes to build on an integration between different approaches to edu-larp based on the psychology of learning. At this point, it's probably important to understand the position of the author of this text. Leland Masek is an edu-larp designer from the United States who first professionally designed edu-larps starting with Guardian Adventures in 2014. Since then, he has worked at a number of edu-larp programs, was on the founding team for two original programs in the United States, and is currently based in Tampere Finland since 2018. He is involved in the Nordic larp scene and runs games multiple times a year through the *Games As Art Center* (Gamesasartcenter.com, 2024) which also hosts a weekly afterschool edu-larp program through the Tampere Public City afterschool funding body Lupa Harrastaa (began in 2018) called *Live Action Gaming Club*.[5] This 60- to 120-minute weekly program uses a variety of games and fictional scenarios in its design and will provide concrete examples referred to throughout the text. Children most often play heroic characters in adventurous storylines. Costuming has varied through-out the years due to feasibility. Notably, physical immersion/high fidelity aesthetic is not a primary target. It utilizes designed toys of various types including foam swords, interactive puppets, digital character sheets, and printed puzzles. The author also does not use a very strong division between "games" and "larp" for example, so while the author's designed games may be outside a reader's view of larp, the core principles, should for the most part, be malleable enough to still be relevant to other design principles.

BEHAVIORISM

Behaviorist educational paradigms are a 20th-century psychological framework that aimed to provide an empirical study of how learning can be proven to happen. Initiated by works like John B. Watson's "Psychology as the behaviorist views it" (Watson 1913), this movement exclusively cared about trackable external actions, rather than any non-observable concepts of experience. They frequently cited two key mechanisms by which behavior is modified in a way that can be seen as a type of learning. Classical conditioning is where a stimulus is co-occurring with another stimulus, thus teaching the receptor to associate the two. Secondly, operant conditioning is where a specific result is occurring in succession with a specific behavior, thus teaching the individual that the action should lead to the result. In addition, they had two categories of behavioral reactions, "reinforcers" which were stimuli found to increase the likelihood of a response behavior and "punishers" which were stimuli found to decrease the likelihood of a behavior. By pairing these two sets of concepts, behaviorist psychologists created a paradigm of education whereby external controllers were often able to teach, usually animals, a variety of tasks. In this paradigm, thinking and emotions are generally viewed as a "black box" (Tomic 1993) that could not be rigorously understood and thus was ignored. This framework has been robustly criticized[6] both factually and ideologically which will be discussed in the section on Cognitivism.

In terms of edu-larp, American adventure education does have a history of being seen as a black box of learning, a phrase common to behaviorism (McKenzie 2000). In contemporary edu-larp, there is a robust ability to leverage these techniques to gain benefits in education. Firstly, play itself has been studied as a reinforcer (Humphreys and Einon 1981). In this way, assuming an edu-larp includes enjoyable actions of play, then these could all be seen as classical conditioning techniques whereby pedagogical content becomes associated with the enjoyable actions of play. Past edu-larp theorists have drawn these connections, stating that role-playing is an intrinsically rewarding activity (Bowman & Standiford 2015). Similarly, the presence of engaging games with a figure presenting positive psychological techniques can create a potentially strong associative effect for students. Modeling is a technique often supported in general education theory as well (Haston 2007) in essence having a teacher, or a character, doing a technique and having students mimic them. In another way, game rewards can be paired with children's learning content, creating an environment of operant conditioning. This framework is similar to how gamification of education uses techniques such as a "leaderboard and distribution of achievement badges and rewards" (Caponetto et al. 2014, 55).

In the edu-larp program run in Tampere from 2018 to 2024, specific elements were modeled for students based upon positive psychological literature. Firstly, positive framing is a fundamental of how the instructor runs the program to model educated principles. The teacher aims to speak in positive, supportive statements first and in most of the communications within the program. Whenever a behavior is seen as potentially problematic, the instructor first compliments several students who are pursuing the desired behavior before intervening in any problematic act. This embodies one of the core premises of positive psychology: focusing on things that are going well first and foremost even if there is something not going well that you wish to fix (Seligman 2010). In addition, the instructor aims to compliment each student for things that they are doing well regularly and explicitly states gratitude for students doing anything requested of them (Emmons and Shelton 2002). The above elements could occur in any pedagogical context, in terms of edu-larp specifically characters in many interactions similarly embody the above traits, preferences for positivity, and strengths orientation. This operates as a form of classical conditioning whereby the students grow acclimated to seeing the instructor, the space, and the stories within in as one paired with positive psychological behavior.

The program also uses a reward system, where students gain in-game benefits for embodying positive psychological traits themselves, as a form of operant conditioning. See Figure 9.1 for an anonymized character sheet used in the program. Students received experience points for taking risks in active games (passion, fight, brave) for playing new games (game) and demonstrating positive psychological choices in a game context (gratitude, optimism, goal setting).

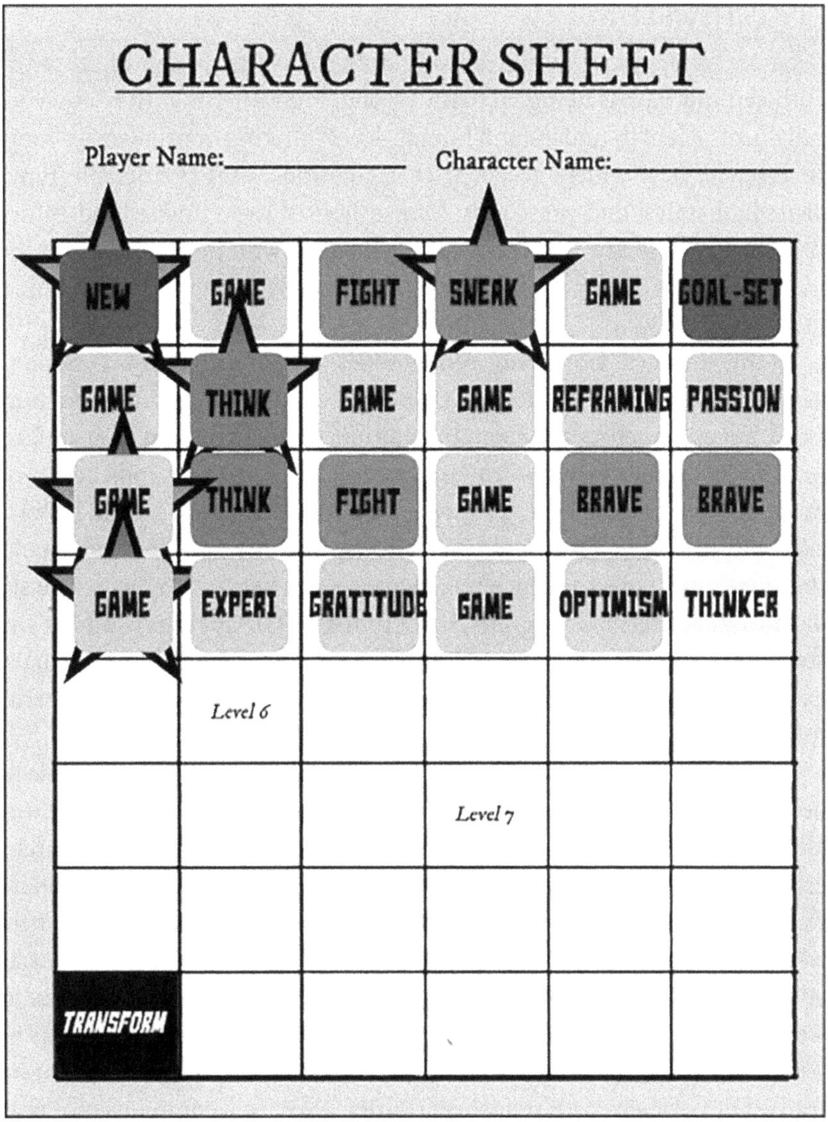

CHARACTER SHEET

Player Name:_____ Character Name:_____

NEW	GAME	FIGHT	SNEAK	GAME	GOAL-SET
GAME	THINK	GAME	GAME	REFRAMING	PASSION
GAME	THINK	FIGHT	GAME	BRAVE	BRAVE
GAME	EXPERI	GRATITUDE	GAME	OPTIMISM	THINKER
	Level 6				
			Level 7		
TRANSFORM					

FIGURE 9.1 Example character sheet.

In this way, we can see a clear way that edu-larp can apply behaviorist techniques:

Classical conditioning: While engaged in enjoyable edu-larping, instructors and characters can present content regularly.

Operant conditioning: When students demonstrate content, in-game benefits can be given to them.

COGNITIVISM

Behaviorist techniques were robustly criticized in the second half of the 20th century, not as being factually wrong, but rather that they are woefully insufficient to understand human-level thinking or problem-solving. In essence, it is widely accepted that cognition uses predictable types of mental states, and previously known heuristics to understand future situations. There are also ideological problems with behaviorism, as the movement was deeply invested in and intimately connected to eugenics[7] (Yakushko 2019).

In this way, behavioral education models, focusing on reinforcers, punishers, classical conditioning, and operant conditioning, can be seen as valid, but extremely insufficient. In addition, they can be seen as, if applied in isolation, offensively minimizing the role of the person and their own internal thoughts and feelings during education. There are several historical trends that have confronted behaviorism and attempted to understand the "black box" of experience in a rigorous and helpful way with one set of movements termed "cognitivism" (Tomic 1993). Cognitivism took the stance that certain internal, predictable, consistent aspects of individuals' experience must be studied to understand their behavior, including learning behaviors.

A key step for cognitivism came from the observation that animals in behavioral training paradigms had certain behaviors that were contextually systematic, thus not purely genetic, and not taught by the researchers attempting to control them. Even more importantly, the behaviors were not even controllable by the scientist, where reinforcers or punishers were unable to stop the behavior. For example, Rhesus monkeys in science labs would actively seek to look out of the window in their cages to watch the "normal comings and goings" (White 1959, 298) of scientists in a laboratory. The monkey's watching behavior furthermore could not be trained out of them with punishers (Butler 1953). In a commonsense way, it is obvious that the monkeys enjoyed watching the scientists doing their busy science business. This among other observations became known as "intrinsic motivation" theory.[8]

Since then, several scientific models of intrinsic motivation have been widely established and empirically tested. Important intrinsic motivation theorists include Deci and Ryan's Self-Determination Theory (SDT Deci and Ryan 2012). SDT began from a controversial observation that external rewards can undermine motivation when they conflict with what would otherwise be intrinsically motivated tasks (Ryan and Deci 2024). Their theory argues for three psychological intrinsic needs that support motivation: autonomy, relatedness, and competence. Autonomy is generally described as the perception that one's own behavior as coming from the self instead of an external controller referred to as perceived locus of causality (PLOC; Deci and Ryan 2000, 234). Competence refers to a belief that one can affect the environment, which is measured by positive feedback for actions instead of negative feedback (PLOC; Deci and Ryan 2000, 235). Taken together, it refers to positive feedback that someone thinks they deserve. Finally, SDT promotes relatedness as a distal factor where a present external authority figure having secure, engaged attachment with the individual enables intrinsic motivation, especially if that authority figure is providing the feedback. In conclusion, they "summarize, intrinsic motivation involves people freely engaging in activities that they find interesting, that provide novelty and optimal challenge" (235). Luckily, an activity freely engaged with, providing novelty, and optimal challenge is also a classic view for a well-designed game!

Edu-larp has been studied a few times as supporting intrinsic motivation in learning (Brom et al. 2019; Hixson and Eike 2025). Several aspects of SDT can be designed for in larping activities. Firstly, it is important for the design of any game for it not to end up feeling "controlling" for student players. Autonomy can be promoted by enabling the enactment of student ideas in imaginary scenarios. For example, teachers can learn the improvisational theater tenet of seeking to support others imaginary ideas (Spolin 1999) popularized as performers saying "yes and" to other players' imaginary offers. Competence can be designed by ensuring players are set up to receive positive feedback they feel they deserve. This is like designing for challenges that students have just enough skill to succeed at which is a long-standing design principle aiming at *flow state* in game-based education (Perttula et al. 2017).

For the edu-larp program in Tampere, several aspects of SDT are designed for. Firstly, as seen in Figure 9.1, each "choice" that players make in the fictional world provides a free-choice option. This technique is used to invite students to share their own views, if the pre-designed options do not align with their desires. This design aims to help students feel a PLOC over the choice and the results.[9] Secondly, the program validates very creative, even unpredictable, ideas from its students. For example, recently, a student "leveled up" and asked if they could transform their character

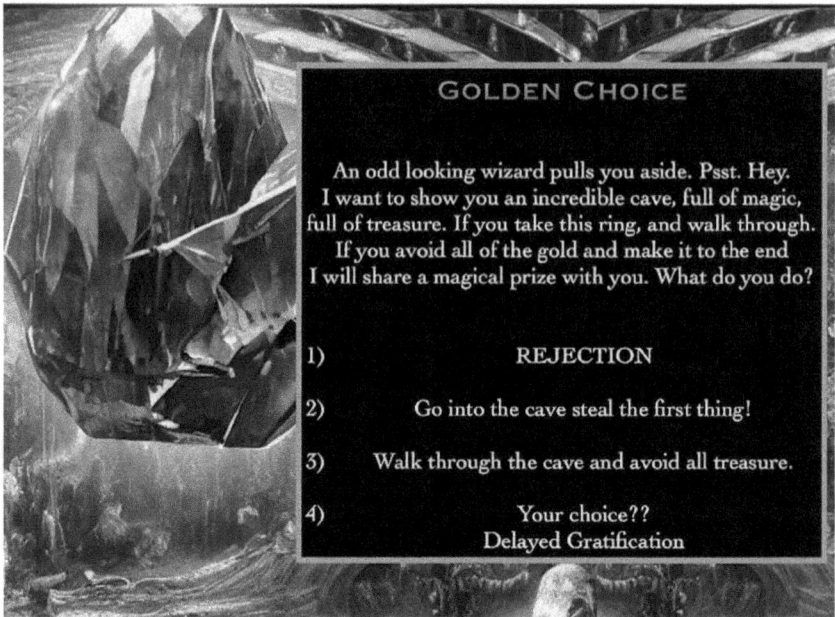

FIGURE 9.2   A choice structure from Live Action Gaming Club.

to "being made of rubber." While it is still unclear what the implications of this transformation are, it is widely accepted that they are "now made of rubber." Hopefully, this has left the student to feel they are in an environment of high PLOC. In addition, feedback in the program designs for competence by focusing on winning rather than having a "losing" state. In essence, if a student is embodying a positive psychological trait, such as delayed gratification, they receive positive feedback without punishment toward non-presentation of the desired content. Finally, the instructor aims to be actively engaged with students and reinforcing an emotionally related position (Figure 9.1).

Autonomy: Free choice is uniquely possible in a high imagination larp environment.

Competence: Games and role-play interactions can focus on positive feedback, rather than negative feedback.

Relatedness: Instructor relationship is highly important.

CONSTRUCTIVISM

Constructivism is an expansion of cognitivism that emphasizes how individuals may fundamentally experience different things in the same conditions. Rather than exclusively looking at learning through a lens of objective agreement, where all students experience the same thing, constructivism argues that education should come "from our own interpretations of our experiences" (Ertmer and Newby 1993 online). This is further broken down into environmental and learner factors.

In the constructivist model, edu-larp becomes a very specific form of pedagogical context: one that is playful. While some edu-larps may not intend playfulness from its participants, many do. Playfulness is already a complicated term, so in this text, I use a contemporary definition of playfulness as engagement prioritizing (Masek 2024). In essence, a playful edu-larp places the learner in an environment of active engagement, with emotional desire for the activities involved and a socially shared atmosphere amplifying the experience, while simultaneously intentionally removing barriers that might disrupt their engagement. This view of playfulness is highly relevant to learning as engagement is generally seen as a key factor for students to successfully learning (Boekaerts 2016).

Through a constructivist lens, a playful environment has several psychologically relevant factors. Historically, play has been considered a critical activity for learning usually through the theoretical works of Piaget and Vygotsky:

> Whereas Vygotsky's cultural-historical approach deems play to be a driving force of development, during which multiple processes of new knowledge and skills acquisition are realized, Piaget considered play to be more of a measure of development, as the complexity of play marked the cognitive development of the child.
>
> *(Veraksa et al. 2022)*

In practice with edu-larp, we can apply Piaget's model to enable a variety of forms of play available to engage learners. Piaget separates play into several stages, all relevant to the design of edu-larp (see Table 9.1).

For example, Piaget's theories have clear recommendations to run edu-larps for children ages 4–7 as mostly self-guided discovery actions through play. Very young edu-larpers, according to Piaget, would not have the cognitive capacity to understand a verbal explanation of a fictional scenario. Rather than telling them "rules" or what they are "role-playing," he would encourage letting children explore things physically like letting them put on pre-selected costumes and the teacher can just "act" as a character facilitating the imagination of the students.[10]

TABLE 9.1   Example of Piaget model of play and short relevance to edu-larp

Type of play	Short definition	Edu-larp design practice	Examples
Sensorimotor play	Playful physical actions. Usually, repetitions with enjoyably predictable results.	Engaging physical environments, props, and toys. Creating interactions with teachers that are very predictable.	1. Costuming – Give students physical props to play and imagine with. 2. Have characters/ instructors give predictable, extremely emotional reactions to students.
Symbolic play	Imagination play	Create character traits that children recognize and enjoy recreating	Character designs can set up certain with tropic behaviors such as "hero," but also "protector of animals" or "speech in front of a Senate."
Play with rules	Games of competition/ cooperation	Use games	Puzzles, competitions, and cooperative games designed with content in mind

Vygotsky's model views play as more central in a social-education mechanism. For Vygotsky, play is a form where younger players interact with a "More Knowledgeable Other" who teaches them socialized ideology to better enable their goals at their appropriate "Zone of Proximal Development" (Veraksa et al. 2022). This theoretical paradigm can be applied by, for example, setting up games with a gradient of playstyles from the students' current approach to content with a fictional character whose responsibility is guiding them toward some desired content knowledge.

In addition to the psychology of play for children, the academic play literature has some critical components for edu-larp designers. In the edu-larp program in Tampere, there are two play-theories that are utilized and highly recommended for future edu-larp programming. Firstly, De Koven's The Well-Played Game (for a reprint, see De Koven 2013) is a trove of information on the practicalities of running game-based programming for children. One influential tool he argues for is the "out of play" area where students can go to stop playing if needing rest or if they are upset. This tool is invaluable for several reasons. Firstly, students often need help not attempting to continue engaging in play even when they are no longer in a positive emotional state. For example, if a student is greatly upset by something in a game or play scenario, they can sometimes "lash out" with game objects/toys, etc., attempting to be in the game, while not playing. These events are essentially never productive. If a student is stressed, if their ego is on the line with an interaction, it is better for them to take a moment to stop playing, maybe talking with other players or instructors out of character, before they return to the play-space capable of being in a play-mindset. The out-of-play area (see Figure 9.3) also allows the act of non-play to be a non-judged choice, and rather a component of the space that everyone occupies at the beginning of the program and often at different times during it. It is helpful if the out-of-play is in a visually supported area in the program, where students can watch the other games in case they wish to re-initiate in their own volition.

FIGURE 9.3 Behind the cones, you see the "out-of-play" area demarcated by cones.

The second important play principle that affects edu-larp programs is one-sided play (Stenros 2015). One-sided play is a situation where one student is highly engaged by a playstyle, while an external student is not engaged or often upset by an act of play, yet is still directly involved in some component of it. In practice, this is quite a difficult situation as the second student not playing does not necessarily undermine the engagement from the first student. In addition, the second student can often get quite upset as their protests to end the play are ignored. A short example is if one student has a joke they enjoy, another student finds it annoying, the first student keeps telling the joke. This is a component of many inter-student conflicts we face in the Live Action Gaming Club. This language of "one-sided" play being forbidden is much more helpful than fairly ambiguous cues as "being nice" or "don't bully." This kind of problematic playstyle is a unique problem in playful environments as students prioritize their engagement so high they are sometimes pursuing impulsive (Proyer 2017) and non-conscientious (Proyer and Jehle 2013) choices, both of which are psychological concomitants with playfulness.

These educational considerations structurally enable students to healthily reduce their engagement when needed. This is a unique level of problem in a playful environment. Engagement prioritization also implies an engagement bias by the student. Some students may in the state of play engage in activities they normally know are unacceptable. In this way, we see the strength and issues with creating a playful education space. If student's engagement is desired, as is common, then playful design is effective; however, inconsiderate engagement at all times is not universally helpful to an education space. So, in this way, playful education spaces including edu-larp should not only consider engagement techniques but also more advanced disengagement techniques.

Psychology of Play: Design for playstyles aligned with cognitive development. Utilize characters who act as *more knowledgeable others* enabling students to be in their *zone of proximal development*.

Play Theory: Utilize *out-of-play areas* and *one-sided play* awareness to also facilitate healthy disengagement.

DISCUSSION AND CONCLUSION

This text has aimed to bring forward a diverse approach to how the psychology of learning is relevant to edu-larp designers. Three different discourses of psychology of learning were briefly presented: behaviorism, cognitivism, and constructivism. Each of these discourses was connected to the design of edu-larp, sometimes by referencing large pools of research and design recommendations such as in the field of gamification, game-based learning, and playfulness literature. Finally, each category was illustrated through specific techniques applied in an edu-larp program run in Tampere, Finland.

Taken together, edu-larp has a host of ways it can be connected to the psychology of learning. In addition, specific components often used in edu-larp have unique ways of enacting educating principles. Firstly, the role of imagination offers more flexibility for setting up an environment for education. While numerous environments are impossible to enact in an education setting, asking students to imagine and fill the gaps of certain components of a larped environment is much more doable. In addition, playful environments can be extremely useful to enable student engagement with topics and material. Playful environments however also have unique problems, especially at curtailing engagement that is unhelpful for learning. In summation, the following concepts, readings, and examples are listed below for readers:

Behaviorism: Classical and operant conditioning, reinforcers and punishers, connected to gamification in education (Caponetto et al. 2014). *Examples: Fictional worlds where target content is present and repeated. In-game rewards for learning.*

Cognitivism: Self-determination theory in education (Reeve 2002), flow theory in education games (Kiili et al. 2014), connected to game-based learning (Plass et al. 2015). *Examples: Free choice, "Yes And" improvised moments, Positive Feedback.*

Constructivism: Psychology of play (Nicolopoulou 1993) and play theory (De Koven 2013; Stenros 2015). *Examples: Costuming/physical assets, Predictable and reactive characters, more knowledgeable other characters, out-of-play area, one-sided play awareness.*

There are several fertile terrains for future study of psychology and edu-larp design both in general and specifically when targeting positive psychological content. As discussed at the beginning, a primary barrier is that most practitioners and theoreticians operate in relative isolation from each other without a shared vocabulary. To bring diverse practices together in edu-larp, I argue that a critical topic for further study is *Playfulness*.

Playfulness is a critical contemporary term in both positive psychology (Shen and Masek 2024) and game studies (Masek and Stenros 2021). Playfulness research holds practical design implications both specifically in designing games targeting mental health improvement (Masek 2023a) and designing diverse playful rules in game-like situations (Masek 2023b). Edu-larp holds the exciting possibility to practically integrate these kinds of findings. In conclusion, even with its potentially thousand-year-old beginnings, edu-larp research and practice is in an exciting position to advance contemporary education!

NOTES

1 See Mochocki's (2014) discussion of the challenges of utilizing edu-larp in the public school system of Poland.

2 For a literature review on the topic, see Bowman (2014) who does not specifically define Edu-larp but describes the essential components very similarly as "Edu-larp can offer greater and lesser degrees of drama, simulation, and game, but should always feature the live action element of physical enactment, some degree of role-playing, and the basic framework of a game structure" (Bowman 2014, 120).

3 While Mochoki terms this "Nordic-American" edu-larp, he is clearly discussing the group I term "Nordic." His view that this community is influenced by American scholars is compelling. It is clear though that he is not engaged with the longer history of American edu-larp which will be discussed in the next section. He is clearly referencing Nordic edu-larp, and he seems unaware of American edu-larp as he places the beginning of the history as KP's founding in 1997 (193) which notably is 11 years after the founding of the originating American edu-larp adventure camp.

4 While some readers may not agree these are educational larps, that would seem quite silly as they match the criteria of presented by Robinson et al. (2023) and Bowman (2014), and call themselves educational live action role-playing games.

5 This is the program that will be referred to throughout the text.

6 Though not disproven or made irrelevant.

7 Removing the ideological effects of eugenics is an important activity for any psychologist or educator. Behaviorism essentially viewed individuals who learned slowly as "worse" genetically, as they were uninterested in any other explanation besides the context of learning and the genetic makeup of the individual. Edu-larp educators should certainly take a more human-approach to their students and understand those who are not presenting an expected or desired behavior are having different experiences and have a different history of experience and should not be seen as "worse."

8 Presumably termed "intrinsic" because it came from the animal, rather than the "extrinsic" source of a behavioral scientist attempting to control them.

9 When a student does this, it does require a creative skillset by the game runner to meaningfully create a result that makes sense.

10 There are of course critiques and disagreements to Piaget's model (for one connected to Edu-larp see Kapitany, Hampejs and Goldstein 2022).

REFERENCES

Altorf, Hannah Marije. "Dialogue and discussion: Reflections on a Socratic method." *Arts and Humanities in Higher Education* 18, no. 1 (2019): 60–75.

Boekaerts, Monique. "Engagement as an inherent aspect of the learning process." *Learning and instruction* 43 (2016): 76–83.

Bowman, Sarah Lynne. "Educational live action role-playing games: A secondary literature review." *The Wyrd Con Companion Book* 3 (2014): 112–131.

Bowman, S. L., & Standiford, A. "Educational Larp in the middle school classroom-a mixed method case study." *International Journal of Role-Playing*, 5 (2015): 4–25.

Brom, Cyril, Viktor Dobrovolný, Filip Dechterenko, Tereza Stárková, and Edita Bromová. "It's better to enjoy learning than playing: Motivational effects of an educational live action role-playing game." *Frontline Learning Research* 7, no. 3 (2019): 64–90.

Butler, Robert A. "Discrimination learning by rhesus monkeys to visual-exploration motivation." *Journal of Comparative and Physiological Psychology* 46, no. 2 (1953): 95.

Caponetto, Ilaria, Jeffrey Earp, and Michela Ott. "Gamification and education: A literature review." In *European Conference on Games Based Learning*, vol. 1, p. 50. Cham: Springer Nature Switzerland, Academic Conferences International Limited, 2014.

De Koven, Bernard. *The well-played game: A player's philosophy*. Cambridge, Massachusetts: MIT Press, 2013.

Deci, Edward L., and Richard M. Ryan. "The" what" and" why" of goal pursuits: Human needs and the self-determination of behavior." *Psychological Inquiry* 11, no. 4 (2000): 227–268.

Deci, Edward L., and Richard M. Ryan. "Self-determination theory." *Handbook of Theories of Social Psychology* 1, no. 20 (2012): 416–436.

Emmons, Robert A., and Charles M. Shelton. "Gratitude and the science of positive psychology." *Handbook of Positive Psychology* 18 (2002): 459–471.

Ertmer, Peggy A., and Timothy J. Newby. "Behaviorism, cognitivism, constructivism: Comparing critical features from an instructional design perspective." *Performance Improvement Quarterly* 6, no. 4 (1993): 50–72.

Games as Art Center. *Games as Art Center*, 2024, Nov. 2021. https://gamesasartcenter.com/

Guardian Adventures. *History*, 2024, Nov. 2021. https://guardup.com/about-us/history/

Harviainen, J. Tuomas, Rafael Bienia, Simon Brind, Michael Hitchens, Yaraslau I. Kot, Esther MacCallum-Stewart, David W. Simkins, Jaakko Stenros, and Ian Sturrock. "Live-action role-playing games." In *Role-playing game studies*, pp. 87–106. Routledge, 2018.

Haston, Warren. "Teacher modeling as an effective teaching strategy." *Music Educators Journal* 93, no. 4 (2007): 26–30.

Hixson, Sarah West, and Rachel J. Eike. "Mixed-methods assessment of an apparel edu-larp rooted in self-determination theory." *International Journal of Fashion Design, Technology and Education* 18, no. 1 (2025): 58–70.

Humphreys, Anne P., and Dorothy F. Einon. "Play as a reinforcer for maze-learning in juvenile rats." *Animal Behaviour* 29, no. 1 (1981): 259–270.

Hyltoft, Malik. "The role-players' school: Østerskov Efterskole." *Playground Worlds* (2008): 12–25.

Kahn, Charles H. *Plato and the Socratic dialogue: The philosophical use of a literary form.* Cambridge, UK: Cambridge University Press, 1997.

Kapitany, Rohan, Tomas Hampejs, and Thalia R. Goldstein. "Pretensive shared reality: From childhood pretense to adult imaginative play." *Frontiers in Psychology* 13 (2022): 774085.

Kiili, Kristian, Timo Lainema, Sara de Freitas, and Sylvester Arnab. "Flow framework for analyzing the quality of educational games." *Entertainment Computing* 5, no. 4 (2014): 367–377.

Kot, Yaraslau I. "Educational larp: Topics for consideration." *Wyrd Con Companion Book* (2012): 118–127.

Maragliano, Andrea. "Edu-larp paths in education: A pedagogic research on ethnic prejudice and empathy through games." In *Conference Proceedings. The Future of Education 2019.* 2019.

Maragliano, Andrea, Josef Kundràt, Francesca Morselli, and Elisabetta Robotti. "Starflyer: An Edu-larp project for ethic and math teaching and learning." In *European Conference on Games Based Learning*, pp. 947–XIX. Reading, UK: Academic Conferences International Limited, 2021.

Masek, Leland. "How playfulness can enable greater understanding of game-based adult mental health interventions." In *International Simulation and Gaming Association Conference*, pp. 171–184. Cham: Springer, 2023a.

Masek, Leland. "Criticizing Caillois: Examining how players perceive rules in play and games." In *Conference Proceedings of DiGRA 2023 Conference: Limits and Margins of Games Settings.* Tampere: DiGRA, 2023b.

Masek, Leland, and Jaakko Stenros. "The meaning of playfulness: A review of the contemporary definitions of the concept across disciplines." *Eludamos: Journal for Computer Game Culture* 12, no. 1 (2021): 13–37.

McKenzie, Marcia D. "How are adventure education program outcomes achieved?: A review of the literature." *Journal of Outdoor and Environmental Education* 5, no. 1 (2000): 19–27.

Miles, John C., and Simon Priest. *Adventure education.* State College, PA: Venture Publishing, Inc., 1990.

Mochocki, Michał. "Edu-larp as revision of subject-matter knowledge." *International Journal of Role-Playing* 4 (2013): 55–75.

Mochocki, Michał. "Larping the past: Research report on high-school edu-larp." In *Wyrd Con Companion Book 2014*, pp. 132–149. Costa Mesa, CA: Wyrd Con, 2014.

Mochocki, Michał. "Rhetorics and mechanics of player safety in the Nordic-American larp discourse." *Homo Ludens* 1, no. 13 (2020): 179–202.

Molander, Bengt. "Socratic dialogue: On dialogue and discussion in the formation of knowledge." In *Artificial intelligence, culture and language: On education and work*, pp. 229–243. London: Springer, 1990.

Nicolopoulou, Ageliki. "Play, cognitive development, and the social world: Piaget, Vygotsky, and beyond." *Human Development* 36, no. 1 (1993): 1–23.

Perttula, Arttu, Kristian Kiili, Antero Lindstedt, and Pauliina Tuomi. "Flow experience in game-based learning—A systematic literature review." *International Journal of Serious Games* 4, no. 1 (2017): 57–72.

Plass, Jan L., Bruce D. Homer, and Charles K. Kinzer. "Foundations of game-based learning." *Educational Psychologist* 50, no. 4 (2015): 258–283.

Proyer, René T. "A new structural model for the study of adult playfulness: Assessment and exploration of an understudied individual differences variable." *Personality and Individual Differences* 108 (2017): 113–122.

Proyer, René T., and Nicole Jehle. "The basic components of adult playfulness and their relation with personality: The hierarchical factor structure of seventeen instruments." *Personality and Individual Differences* 55, no. 7 (2013): 811–816.

Public Broadcasting Service. *Mindful Parenting: Raising Happy, Healthy Kids: The Play is the Thing*, Nov. 2024, published 1998. https://www.pbs.org/bodyandsoul/217/game.htm

Reeve, Johnmarshall. "Self-determination theory applied to educational settings." In E. L. Deci & R. M. Ryan (Eds.), *Handbook of self-determination research* (pp. 183–203). Rochester, NY: University of Rochester Press, 2002.

Renaissance Adventures. *Award-Winning Programs for Creative Kids*, 2024, Nov. 21. https://www.renaissanceadventures.com/kids-camps-boulder-denver/program-types/

Roberts, Brent W., Carl Lejuez, Robert F. Krueger, Jessica M. Richards, and Patrick L. Hill. "What is conscientiousness and how can it be assessed?" *Developmental Psychology* 50, no. 5 (2014): 1315.

Robinson, Raquel B., Karin Johansson, James Collin Fey, Elena Márquez Segura, Jon Back, Annika Waern, Sarah Lynne Bowman, and Katherine Isbister. "Edu-larp@ CHI." In *Extended Abstracts of the 2023 CHI Conference on Human Factors in Computing Systems*, Association for Computing Machinery, New York, NY, USA, Article 346, 1–5, 2023. https://doi.org/10.1145/3544549.3573819

Ryan, Richard M., and Edward L. Deci. "Self-determination theory." In *Encyclopedia of quality of life and well-being research*, pp. 6229–6235. Cham: Springer International Publishing, 2024.

Seligman, Martin. "Flourish: Positive psychology and positive interventions." *The Tanner Lectures on Human Values* 31, no. 4 (2010): 1–56.

Shen, Xiangyou, and Leland Masek. "The playful mediator, moderator, or outcome? An integrative review of the roles of play and playfulness in adult-centered psychological interventions for mental health." *The Journal of Positive Psychology* 19, no. 6 (2024): 1037–1050.

Spolin, Viola. *Improvisation for the theater: A handbook of teaching and directing techniques*. Evanston, Illinois: Northwestern University Press, 1999.

Stenros, Jaakko. Playfulness, play, and games: A constructionist ludology approach. Tampere: Tampere University Press, 2015.

Temte, Bjoern F., Morgan Jarl, and Henrik Schoenau-Fog. "Edu-larp: Teaching, learning and engaging through roleplay and interactive narratives." In *Interactive Storytelling: 6th International Conference, ICIDS 2013*, Istanbul, Turkey, November 6–9, 2013, Proceedings, vol. 8230, p. 272. Springer, 2013.

Tomic, Welco. "Behaviorism and cognitivism in education." *Psychology-Savannah* 30 (1993): 38–38.

Veraksa, Nikolay, Yeshe Colliver, and Vera Sukhikh. "Piaget and Vygotsky's play theories: The profile of twenty-first-century evidence." In *Piaget and Vygotsky in XXI century: Discourse in early childhood education*, pp. 165–190. Cham: Springer International Publishing, 2022.

Walsh, Victor, and Gerald Golins. The exploration of the Outward Bound process. Denver: Colorado Outward Bound School, 1976.

Watson, John B. "Psychology as the behaviorist views it." *Psychological Review* 20, no. 2 (1913): 158.

Wayfinder Experience. *Wayfinder's History! A Company for the Community*, 2024, Nov. 21. https://wayfinderexperience.com/about/history/

Westborg, Josefin. "Overview of Edu-Larp Conference 2019." (2019).

White, Robert W. "Motivation reconsidered: The concept of competence." *Psychological Review* 66, no. 5 (1959): 297.

Yakushko, Oksana. "Eugenics and its evolution in the history of western psychology: A critical archival review." *Psychotherapy and Politics International* 17, no. 2 (2019): e1495.

CHAPTER 10

Playing a Role in Democracy

Political Live Action Role-Playing Games, Activism, and Deliberation

Karin Johansson, Johanna Koljonen,
Jaakko Stenros, PerOla Öberg
and Sarah Lynne Bowman

INTRODUCTION

This chapter explores political live action role-playing (larp) through the lens of *Nordic larp*, a design discourse and artistic movement grounded in leisure role-play that nonetheless has engaged seriously with real-world themes for decades. It discusses how cultural and societal specificities shaped larp in the Nordics, enabling it to become culturally positioned as just another form of expression, suited not just for escapist but also educational and artistic uses. To explore the potential of Nordic larp specifically as an educational tool for civic skills, this chapter contextualizes larp within a century of democratic skill training through role-playing activities, and further through comparisons with *deliberative events*, in which participants from different social and ideological backgrounds discuss political topics.

Activities recognizable as role-playing reach back through human history; the word itself pre-dates leisure role-playing games by over half a

DOI: 10.1201/9781003641353-14

century, and spread through use specifically in educational and therapeutic contexts (e.g., Moreno 2014). Since at least the 1920s, these methodologies have been used in connection with political or civic education (e.g., Wisemee n.d.; Moreno 2014). In a 1966 psychology study of the *role-play effect*, Alan Elms showed that discussing political issues while portraying characters with views different from one's own would lead to greater attitude change than being exposed to similar information without the role-taking. By the 1970s, simulation and role-playing pedagogy were firmly established in education, forecasting, and professional training (see Bowman 1949 for an early example; Garvey and Garvey 1967).

One place the term "role-play" could not be found at all is in the first edition of *Dungeons & Dragons* (Gygax and Arneson 1974), a publication considered the birth of recreational *role-playing games* (RPGs) as they are known today (Peterson 2012). The term only attached itself to this novel pastime because early players recognized the game's combination of role-taking, storytelling, and tactical decision-making as something they were already familiar with from non-leisure contexts (see Peterson 2022).

Academic game studies understands role-playing games both as activities where participants engage in co-creative rule-bound pretend play, for a bounded period of time, acting as if they are characters in a shared, fictional reality – and as the rule systems that enable this activity (see Zagal and Deterding 2024). In the late 1970s, *larp* emerged as an embodied form of role-playing, where the players physically enact and perform their fictional characters.

Larp is commonly a subcultural leisure practice, either organized as non-profit events or run by small businesses. It also intersects with other professions. As examples, larp is produced in contemporary arts contexts with arts funding; as brand activations for entertainment IP; as a tool for audience development and citizen participation by arts institutions and public organizations such as museums; and as an intervention in educational activities and professional training. The play cultures making and participating in larps are sometimes surrounded by small, but vibrant discourse communities systematically documenting, developing, and researching the design and development of larp as a medium (Torner 2024). One such movement is Nordic larp, whose context and practices are of particular relevance to political education and the focus of this chapter (Stenros and Montola 2010a).

Role-playing games can train participant skills at cognitive, affective, and behavioral levels simultaneously, providing experiential, multimodal learning opportunities often absent in traditional educational methods (for example, see Cullinan and Genova 2023; Bowman et al. 2024). As an often highly embodied and social form of role-playing, larp is touted as a space in which players can experience increased motivation, agency, and empowerment, increasing perceived competence or self-efficacy in political discussions, negotiations, debates, and other spaces of persuasion (Bowman 2014). The high degree of player engagement and experiential nature of larp has led to increased interest in its application (Johansson et al. 2024) in formal, non-formal, and informal learning environments (Westborg 2023). Larps created with learning outcomes in mind are often called *edu-larps.*

Larp is an interesting testbed for social and political problem-solving (Bowman 2010), enabling players to experience, influence, and reconstruct political systems. Beyond such structures, players can also explore socio-economic and cultural aspects of political decision-making, such as the impacts of economic systems on a community (McDiarmid 2015), and explore important social issues through play (Brown 2016). Political play is embedded even in larps considered to be designed for entertainment purposes, e.g., in many fantasy (Budai and Hammock 2014) and World of Darkness games such as *Vampire: the Masquerade* (By Night Studios 2014), sometimes leading to the transfer of relevant skills in daily life (Bowman 2010).

Larps with political content are not necessarily designed, organized, or played with the purpose of exploring an explicit political goal, conveying an explicit message about democracy, or replicating political processes (Harviainen 2016). However, as this chapter will explore, some larps are. More could productively be designed for such impacts – including specifically around evidence-based democracy-supporting processes grounded in political science research (Rantanen 2016), e.g. *deliberation.* The century-long history of what we today would recognize as educational role-playing supports our hypothesis that larp may be well-suited not just for teaching democratic values, but also for further developing tools and methods for deliberative events through a fictional lens.

While the established practices of educational games have not always been well-known in subcultural gaming communities, there are also examples of influence between that field and the discourse communities creating larps for transformative leisure, including the Nordic larp movement. This chapter specifically addresses *political larps*, i.e., larps specifically focused on political themes, whether societal (e.g., systems of governance) or individual (e.g., identity), and explicitly designed with political aims, e.g., activism, awareness-raising, and building democratic skills. Examples from Nordic larps include subject matter such as immigration (*Europa* 2001; Gräslund 2010), environmental issues (*Baltic Warriors* 2015; Arjoranta 2015; Pettersson 2021a, 2021b); life under occupation (*Halat Hisar* 2013, 2016, Eng. State of Siege; Pettersson 2014; Pöllänen and Arjoranta 2021); and the outbreak of HIV/AIDS in the 1980s (*Just a Little Lovin'* 2011; Groth, Grasmo, and Edland 2021; Levin 2023).

Our analysis is informed by role-playing game studies and theories of political larp (Harviainen 2016; Lehto 2016; Rantanten 2016; Turkington 2016), transformative game design (Bowman, Diakolambrianou, and Brind 2024), and political science, in particular deliberation research (see e.g., Jennstål, Uba, and Öberg 2021). We take a special interest in larps that feature deliberation as an activity.[1]

Despite this potential, in some cultural contexts engaging with serious themes in any kind of role-playing game can be perceived as controversial, because of underlying cultural notions around play, role-playing, and fun; e.g. that a "game" would necessarily involve playful competition or might trivialize the subject matter (see Sutton-Smith 1997; Masek and Stenros 2021). Many larps and other role-playing games are not really games in the sense that they can be won or lost (see Stenros 2017), but even where that is understood, the embodiment of characters outside formal arts contexts can still be viewed with suspicion. To some among the general public, the term "larp" in itself can connote fantasy escapism in a negative way and is used derogatorily when discussing adult pretend play (Klenell 2019). We are hoping this chapter can help challenge any such lingering prejudice against role-playing pedagogy and against role-playing as an artistic or transformative leisure practice.

Effectively employed, edu-larp and political larp can contribute to strengthening the skills needed for civic engagement in support of functioning democracies. This chapter features a discussion of role-play as a method for developing political and civic skills, and an overview of types of political larps. It includes a brief discussion of how specific societal circumstances shaped larp in the Nordics in general, as well as the distinct international movement still commonly referred to as Nordic larp. This discussion is followed by detailed examples of Nordic larps with political themes and larps in which deliberation is specifically present. The potential for intentionally applying larp design to deliberative skills training or deliberative events is discussed. Furthermore, challenges of using larp as a tool for political or educational aims are addressed, especially weighing concerns about portrayals of historical events, diverse backgrounds, and marginalized identities. Further research directions are outlined.

LARP AS A METHOD FOR POLITICAL SKILL DEVELOPMENT

Larp as Serious Pretend Play

Play is a foundational quality of all mammals. Role-play, role-playing games, and larps are built on the typically human behavior of acting "as if," what play scholars call *pretend play* or, when done collaboratively with others, *sociodramatic play* (Burghardt 2005). Role-playing games geared for more mature players tend to be more complex and systemic than children's pretend play, resulting in what psychologists have termed a *pretensive shared reality* (Kapitany, Hampejs, and Goldstein 2022). In larps, participants are *pretending to believe* (Pohjola 2004) in the reality of their fictional character within the fictional situation.

Different cultures have varying tolerance for adults engaging in pretend play at all, which historically contributed to a dismissal or even stigmatization of role-playing and larp as outsider "geek" culture. However, today such cultural expressions dominate the mainstream, and tabletop role-playing is more popular than ever (see e.g., Pesce 2022). In some educational contexts, role-playing is completely normalized, while in others remains suspect because of its association with "fun."

Playing and playfulness are generally associated with frivolity, yet play often feels very serious (Sutton-Smith 1997; Masek and Stenros 2021). When playing a game, it can be the only thing that matters to the players in the moment, even as they also know it does not matter at all. Across genres of play, playing with serious topics is very common; experiences that are serious or sad can be just as meaningful or satisfying as those that are light-hearted or escapist.

A meaningful player experience does not require one's character to succeed in their goals (i.e., "win"), especially if the larp explores the human condition or societal power structures. The player may "win" a deep insight or satisfyingly tragic narrative even when their character loses everything.

Embodying a character who fails or suffers can become a *positive negative experience* for the participant (Hopeametsä 2008; Montola 2010), resulting in moments of *positive discomfort* that can become educational, especially when paired with debriefing and other forms of post-game processing (Bjørkelo and Jørgensen 2018).

The presence of serious themes, challenging content, and educational applications would allow placing these larps within the larger frame of serious games, i.e., the use of a game for an educational or political purpose (see e.g. Abt 1970; Deterding 2014; Klabbers 1999). But because of the relative irrelevance to Nordic larps of winning and losing, they are by some definitions not games at all (Stenros 2017). Serious larps are therefore more commonly framed as leisure, hobbies, or art.

INTERACTIONS BETWEEN EDUCATIONAL AND LEISURE ROLE-PLAY

Role-Play before Role-Playing Games

Long before the publication of *Dungeons & Dragons*, role-playing and simulation tools had been used in fields as diverse as psychology, military simulation, civic education, and activist interventions. For example, wargaming, originally *Kriegsspiel*, was developed in the 18th century from variants of *chess* (Peterson 2012) and included as part of military training in early 19th-century Prussia. Character role-play was not part of these games.

Role-playing with a purpose emerged in the field of psychology with Jacob Moreno's improvisation method *Theatre of Spontaneity* in 1910s Vienna. He (and later Zerka Moreno) developed it, based e.g., on experiences of group work in marginalized communities, into *psychodrama* and *sociodrama* (Blatner 2004). Moreno's methods, contextualizing individual psychology socially and societally, would influence most later educational and therapeutic role-playing practices directly or indirectly; a 1943 paper of Moreno is said to have introduced the term to the English language (see McCallum-Stewart 2016). The US RAND Corporation adopted the word in the 1950s for their political-military simulation games studying nuclear deterrence, (see Peterson 2012). These games would in turn inspire a wide range of training simulations with role-play, often with both diplomatic and tactical elements, used by decision-makers as well as within formal education and business environments. They also had a direct effect on recreational tactical board games at least since the 1960s (Trammell 2023).

Moreno's role-play methodologies remain in therapeutic use and have an offshoot in experiential pedagogy (see e.g. Giacomucci, Junqueira Fleury, and Altınay, 2025), but were particularly popular in the 1970s (see Blatner 2004). By that time, role-playing methods in training and education were common enough to merit an international association, ISAGA, organizing practitioners of simulation games (ISAGA 2024). This coincides with great interest in the political artistic practices of Augusto Boal, *Theatre of the Oppressed* (also *Forum Theatre*; and including *Invisible theatre*. Boal 2002). Forum Theatre involves actors improvising their performance based on concerns of community members, who can shift between spectating and actively influencing the performance.

From this contemporary context, *Dungeons & Dragons* (1974) eventually sourced the term "role-play," which soon became primarily associated with trivial leisure pastimes. It appears that the vital traditions of educational role-play shifted away from framing their activities as such in response. While tracing subsequent influences in detail is out of scope for this study, the development and reception of any post-*Dungeons & Dragons* role-playing-adjacent activity or intervention would likely have been influenced in some way by cultural ideas about leisure role-play, just as leisure role-players and game designers might have been exposed to e.g. Model UN (see below).

ROLE-PLAY IN CIVICS AND DEMOCRACY EDUCATION

Role-playing has been used since the early 20th century in civic education. An early example of role-play-based democracy training is Fogelstad Women's Citizenship School, which in Sweden in the 1920s used role-playing scenarios to foster women's democratic skills and emancipation (Kulturföreningen Fogelstad 2024). The League of Nations simulations began in 1921 at the University of Oxford (Wisemee n.d.), and would develop into *Model United Nations* (The New York Times 1947; United Nations n.d.), which still engages over 400,000 children per year globally (UNA-UK 2023).

Among the plethora of contemporary examples of educational interventions that employ embodied role-play, but are not conceptualized as larps or positioned within a role-playing game tradition, many engage with political themes and center deliberative activities. This type of work is commissioned among others by:

- non-profits, e.g., Plan International's role-play on political climate change negotiations (Plan International and FN förbundet n.d.);

- museums, e.g., The National Museum of American Democracy's US State Department diplomacy simulations for classroom use (National Museum of American Diplomacy n.d.), or the Nobel Prize Museum's (2017) role-play about regulating genetic engineering implementations;

- higher education, e.g., to practice deliberation skills within the pedagogy faculty and the Deliberative Citizenship Initiative at Davidson College in the United States (Worl 2022); or teaching history, as in the dozens of semester-long scenarios developed, published, and taught by the Reacting to the Past Consortium, e.g., role-playing the development of early American democracy (Weidenfeld and Fernandez 2017);

- political institutions, e.g., the role-playing scenarios provided by EU institutions for classroom use (European Parliament n.d.; European Union Learning Corner n.d.);

- networks organized around specific methods or pedagogies, e.g., the international organization Bridging Ages, which teaches local human rights issues through time travel narratives featuring costuming, props, and character embodiment. Example scenarios include deliberation about female circumcision in rural Tanzania, and engaging thousands of Estonian students in understanding the negotiations surrounding the country's liberation (Bridging Ages n.d.); and

- and organizations providing immersive simulation training for policymakers, e.g. the Crossroads Foundation, which brought its *A Day in The Life of a Refugee* to the World Economic Forum in Davos (Beale 2016).

Even our limited study of Nordic larp discourse found specific instances of cross-pollination. Design features of *Model United Nations* were analyzed as early as the 1990s (Granhagen 1997). Boals's Theatre of the Oppressed and Invisible Theatre have been discussed in larp contexts at least as long (e.g., Belarbi 2010), with a resurgence of interest in the last decade. Boal is also influential in other larp design communities; in a recent keynote, Brazilian scholar Tadau Rodrigues Iuama (2022) boldly asserted, "I am pretty sure if Boal was alive today, he would not talk about theatre; he would talk about larps."

Contemporary examples of educational role-playing whose developers have engaged both with this long tradition, and with leisure role-playing design and Nordic larp specifically, support our hypotheses that systematic evaluation and exchange of similar design theories and implementation practices could strengthen both practices. For example, the Swedish *Electionville* (Sharing Sweden 2025), designed by larp practitioners, is a democratic governance simulation consisting of a floor-sized board game with role-playing phases. It has been used in over 20 countries, including Uganda, Albania, Romania, Moldavia, and Peru (Sharing Sweden 2025; Svenska institutet 2025), as well as in Ukraine specifically for citizen reflection on the war's effects on democracy (Fabel 2023).

HOW CAN ROLE-PLAY AFFECT POLITICAL SKILLS AND ATTITUDES?

Since the mid-1960s, psychologists have observed *the role-playing effect*, in which participants playing characters who discuss political views different from their own show a greater attitude change afterward than members of a control group exposed to similar information, but who did not role-play (Elms 1966). As a tool for political education, role-play can increase students' democratic attitudes (Rombot, Sunaryati, and Ariani 2018), foster critical thinking (Berry and Kowal 2022), increase student engagement in discussions (Stevens 2015), increase collaborative capacities in negotiating political issues (Rumore, Schenk, and Susskind 2016), and enhance students' political knowledge. Thus, role-play has the potential to increase motivation to engage in politics and participate in decision-making (Lo 2015).

Such effects are often observable in leisure role-playing games as well. Recent studies of the popular tabletop RPG *Dungeons & Dragons* (1974) suggest that the co-creative nature of the playing process itself makes the medium inherently democratic (Garcia 2016; Haarman 2022, 2023), and therefore an important space for the development of democratic skills, as well as moral development (Hollander 2021; Wright 2020). As examples, players often explore perspectives different than their own, discuss topics in-character, reach consensus on joint action, and engage in team work to enact these decisions, experiencing and exercising agency in the fictional world: all skills relevant to democratic participation.

Shared reimagining of oneself and society in a larp often requires changing perspectives and elaborating different worldviews through empathy and negotiation (see Kangas, Loponen, and Särkijärvi 2016). Such skills can transfer beyond the game to player attitudes and behavior in daily life (Westborg and Bowman In press). In sum, intentionally designing such games for democratic education purposes has the potential to significantly increase their impacts.

The Nordic leisure larp community has designed for political and attitude impacts outside and after the larp since the 1990s (see, e.g., larps for escaping, exploring, exposing, and imposing in Stenros and Montola 2010b). One such discussion relates to the spillover of aspects of the character performance to the player – and vice versa – which the community identifies as *bleed* (Montola 2010). larps that are intentionally designed to have a political effect beyond the larp aim for an experience of *memetic bleed,* a phenomenon "in which ideas, thoughts, opinions, convictions, ideologies and similar cognitive constructs bleed between player and character" (Hugaas 2019; 2024). In the case of intentionally designed larps, the goal is a specific form of spillover called *political bleed-out* in which players "can't help but take some of the viewpoints with them into the outside world" (Harviainen 2016). Furthermore, the political standpoints of larp designers can affect the content of the larp, e.g., *design bleed* (Toft and Harrer 2020).

Such impacts can arise from the worldview of the character embodied by the player, witnessing the views expressed by other characters, or the philosophy expressed by the larp as a whole. This latter philosophy may run counter to the represented actions, e.g., a larp with deeply humanistic intentions featuring play on dehumanization for political aims. Through intention-setting, bleed, processing, taking action, and/or other impactful factors, larps can become transformational, expanding beyond the containment of the game experiences itself (Bowman, Diakolambrianou, and Brind 2024). In some cases, the players transform the design itself through these framing activities (Back, Segura, and Waern 2017), exerting agency not only as characters but also as players. Designing and organizing such larp can also be transformative for their creators.

POLITICAL LARPS AND NORDIC LARP

Types of Political Larp

J. Tuomas Harviainen (2016) proposes a typology based on organization theory (Whittington 2006) to distinguish between different kinds of political larps. Larps in the *Practices: Politics at Play* category include political dynamics such as in-character negotiations, while those in *Praxis: Illustrating Oppressive Structures* may also have explicitly critical or political dimensions, although neither are designed for political impact beyond the experience itself. The third category, *Practitioners: Influencing Players,* aims to affect participants with the intention of also changing their behavior later.

Tanja Lehto (2016) categorizes larps explicitly aiming to affect participants in terms of *skill development, awareness-raising,* or *direct action.* Awareness-raising, understood as a first step toward politicizing an issue, maps onto Harvianen's *Illustrating Oppressive Structures,* while skill development and direct action involve *Influencing Players.* Examples of direct action in our data include e.g., performative activism, for instance larps played in public spaces and visible to a non-participating audience (see e.g., Pettersson 2021a, 2021b), and could extend to civil disobedience, as when a larp produced in an authoritarian country intentionally challenges regime-sanctioned historical narratives (see Andersen and Aarebrot 2009).

These typologies help us conceptualize political larps in terms of designer intent as well as player experience. The formal qualities of larp as a form of role-play typically involving larger numbers of participants in specific settings with specified social rules, roles, and expectations, make it unusually suited for the exploration of individual agency and human interactions within a political framework. Arguably, such elements are almost inevitably present in larp (see e.g. Bowman 2010; Koljonen 2011), as characters within a setting have different goals, resources, and access to processes through which to negotiate conflicts of interest.

As a result, larps have commonly included elements of politics at play since at least the 1980s, e.g., fantasy larps often feature kingdoms with hierarchical societies. Even when these are entirely romanticized, political practices such as "petitioning the king" can still occur. In the popular larps of the *Vampire: the Masquerade* franchise, Machiavellian politicking is a central feature and navigating limited political agency through activities like lobbying, scheming, or serving on advisory councils becomes central to gameplay (see e.g., *Mind's Eye Theatre*, By Night Studios 2014). When hierarchical fictional societies are portrayed with even a smidgen of realism, players may find their character's experiences "illustrating oppressive structures," whether or not that was intended. Not everyone larping for escapism and fun is interested in such themes, although a larp reproducing hegemonic political values is inevitably political too (Kangas 2015; Rantanen 2016).

Lest all larps fall into the "political" category, Teemu Rantanen (2016) practically limits his analysis to "larp that acts as a means or medium for political actions." In these, he identifies two styles: *simulation/allegory* and *utopian/dystopian*. Simulation/allegory-type political larps present an interpretation of a real-world political issue or situation, which is dynamically modeled and explored, whether as realistically as the medium permits, or transposed into an analogous, allegorical setting. Utopian or (more commonly) dystopian political larp instead project political choices through time to a desirable or undesirable outcome, their settings essentially telling a story about consequences to convince an audience about the validity of the political interpretation. This story too can be told directly or metaphorically. These "styles" do not straightforwardly map onto settings or genres; a dystopian sci-fi story can be allegorical of some current situation, a realistic or indeed metaphorical projection of where we might be headed, or just a cluster of aesthetics and tropes without political intent.

Rantanen (2016) also describes the two audiences of political larp: those participating in the event and those exposed to its messages or perspectives in other ways. Larp can affect this secondary audience e.g., through interventions in public spaces (see *Dublin2* below), inviting media coverage of the larp and/or its themes (see *Halat Hisar* below), or inviting policymakers or other stakeholders to play (see *Baltic Warriors* below). Secondary audience effects can also happen in smaller ways, as when the impact of a specific larp makes its wider leisure community more engaged in an issue (see *Just a Little Lovin'* below). The kinds of political larp we will discuss more deeply have an explicitly activist or transformative agenda, whether to raise awareness among the participants, to affect their behaviors after the larp, or to act directly in society.

Edu-larp with political themes are a special category in that all education has transformative goals, even when that is limited to awareness-raising, e.g. the Norwegian *Prisoner for a Day* (2012) in which students experienced elements of historical carceral conditions. Edu-larp with explicit political elements can also serve entirely unrelated learning goals. For example, in *Franska revolutionen* (2010, Eng. The French Revolution; LajvVerkstaden 2025a), participants play members of different revolutionary factions interacting at an inn during the revolution of 1789, culminating in a tribunal on the fate of the nobles. In addition to teaching historical dynamics and outcomes in a manner suitable for seventh to ninth graders, the larp's learning goals are also integrated into arts subjects in the Swedish national curriculum (for more on learning objectives in educational RPGs, see Geneuss 2021; Cullinan and Genova 2023).

NORDIC LARP

Larp in the Nordics as a Nordic Phenomenon

Political larp of the types described above are particularly common within the Nordic larp movement and its related international discourse communities. Understanding how this kind of larp became normalized very early in the Nordics requires us to consider the specific cultural and political context in which they developed. In most places around the world where tabletop role-playing games were played, larp organically emerged between late 1970s and early 1990s. Pre-internet, without detailed information about the production, game design, play, or organizational practices of other groups, the term soon described a wide variety of only superficially similar activities. This history has not been closely studied, but some factors contributing to local specificities have been hypothesized.

In the Nordics, most people have easy access to the outdoors. Short distances to wild-looking spaces and the *freedom to roam* – a universal right to freely access wilderness, government owned and even private undeveloped land for non-commercial leisure and recreation – made fantasy larp easy and cheap for young people to stage in suitable environments, encouraging bodily interactions with the setting (see Harviainen et al. 2018). Free education and healthcare, the generous national student support of the time, and long paid vacations made leisure time abundant and co-creating and regularly participating in multi-day larp events feasible.

In the Nordic social democracies, not just sports and scouting but a wide range of youth leisure activities were encouraged to self-organize into clubs and non-profit associations (Stenros and Montola 2010b). States viewed support for teens and young adults participating in civil society organizations as a public investment in civic skills and democracy, while for the young people themselves, it provided important resources. Registered associations enabled even minors to access services, open bank accounts, rent venues, or receive public funding for activities and events created by young people for each other. Financial amounts were trivial, but significant to young people in non-profit environments, and somewhat widened access to the hobbies in question.

Sverok, the Swedish association for role and conflict play, including larp, was formed in 1988 (Brodén 2008) and grew rapidly into one of Sweden's largest cultural civic organizations with 195,000 members (Harding 2012). Starting or joining a local gaming club was easy and affordable, but required simple but formal statutes, annual meetings, board members, deliberating, voting, and other functions of a democratic association, training members for leadership and civic participation (Brodén 2008). In other Nordic countries, national gaming federations were less prominent, but local clubs were similarly organized.

The "Satanic panic" around role-playing games that originated in the United States (Laycock 2015) hit Sweden in the 1990s (Seter 2024, 125-129), with accusation of the hobby fostering satanism, murderers (Müller 2011), and in a bizarre local twist also anarchist revolutionaries (see Örnstedt and Sjöstedt 1997). This provided an opportunity for gaming societies and the related structures such as fanzines to organize in response. Sverok systematically demanded corrections for erroneous media reporting, rallied responses, and lobbied public officials, while fanzines offered practical advice recommendations for how to engage with the media or concerned neighbors and relatives (Nelson 1996a, 1996b, 1997). Some Swedish larp designers later cited these attacks "as the impetus that first started them thinking about using role-playing games to change society" (Stenros and Montola 2010b).

Such factors rooted leisure larp in the Nordics strongly in democratic process and norms, and inspired in many participants a sense of personal responsibility for making things happen in the world. Engaging with public funding, first in the youth culture category and later as an art practice or for educational purposes, trained larp-makers in conceptualizing and communicating their own work in terms of both utility and cultural value.

From Larp in the Nordics to Nordic Larp

Playing together at pan-Scandinavian larp events and nascent online contacts between larp associations across the Nordics led in 1997 to the founding of an annual larp conference rotating between Norway, Sweden, Denmark, and Finland, referred to each year by its name in the host language: Knutepunkt, Knutpunkt, Knudepunkt, or Solmukohta, respectively (Harviainen et al. 2018). Curiosity about the unfamiliar design practices of other larp cultures incentivized participants to start documenting and reflecting on their own work (e.g., Gade, Thorup, and Sander 2003; Saitta, Holm-Andersen, and Back 2014). As making and playing larp is very time-consuming, learning from each other was also a practical necessity. "Nordic larp" gradually grew distinct from "larp in the Nordic countries" into a highly mediated practice and discourse community, with documenting, theorizing, and systematizing larp design as central activities (Stenros 2014). With the publication of *Nordic larp* (Stenros and Montola 2010a), both the term and movement gained brand recognition, value, and cultural cachet.

Larpers had already shared ideas in writing in their local languages, for example through larp and role-playing fanzines like the Danish *Semper Bonus* (late 1990s); the Finnish *Larppaaja* (1995–2003); and the Swedish *Strapats* (1992–1997) and *Fëa Livia* (1993–2006). As Finnish is unrelated to the Scandinavian languages but most Nordics are fluent in English, this became the shared language of the Nordic larp discourse first in web forums and underground fanzines like *panclou* (1998–2004), and later in formal publications like *Playground Magazine* (2011–2012, 2024–ongoing). Starting in 2001, para-academic anthologies would be published most years in conjunction with the Knutepunkt conferences, with 31 books to date, most openly available online. Nordiclarp.org has published over 500 online magazine articles, and the annual Nordic Larp Talks currently totals over 140 short YouTube lectures.

This wealth of publicly accessible design documentation and aesthetic discussion in English made Nordic larp a particularly influential discourse community, in a way that risks obscuring similar work in independent larp traditions and performance practices elsewhere. With time, practitioners from dozens of countries found their way into Nordic larp communities, fruitfully challenging and further developing the discourse. Since the community includes such cultural diversity among designers, the word "Nordic" in Nordic larp is justly contested (Stenros 2014).

Nordic Larp as Bespoke Design

The tradition that would later be identified as Nordic larp got its start by challenging the then contemporary understanding of the form, rebelling against a perceived mainstream dominated by fantasy, cyberpunk, and vampire larp, and set out to explore serious topics, everyday environments, and social realism (see Stenros and Montola 2010a). The pattern of challenging emerging design norms continued within the Nordic larp movement itself. A commitment to indexical fidelity, the ideal of a *360° illusion* in the larp environment (Koljonen 2007; Waern, Montola, and Stenros 2009) was followed and challenged by abstract minimalist larp designed to be played in theater blackboxes (Stenros, Andresen, and Nielsen 2016). Larps requiring up to 50 hours of preparations (reading, meetings, costume creation, etc.), were challenged by non-verbal larp inspired by dance and somatic practice whose four-hour duration included all onboarding (see e.g., Essendrop 2018). Even the questioning of mainstream larp's fascination with popular entertainment settings and tropes produced its inevitable counter-reaction. Although serious and realist larp continue, genre larp has also been re-embraced, including hommages to commercial IP, e.g., the Harry Potter-inspired *College of Wizardry* (2014; Stenros and Montola 2017).

This dynamic rapidly made Nordic larp impossible to define through its themes or formal qualities. A term sometimes used instead is *bespoke design* (Koljonen 2019). While present in other design discourses, in larp, the term refers to the understanding that the optimal qualities and creation process for any larp must be determined for each individual work based on the experience it is intended to enable for each participant, and how that is intended to affect them.[2] Conceptualizing larp design as a skill set and toolbox, in combination with Nordic larp's easy familiarity with serious topics, organically expanded it from a leisure activity toward fields like art and education.

Contemporary Position of Nordic Larp and Larp in the Nordics

In the Nordic countries today, larp is commonly recognized as a form of expression. Artistically or politically interesting Nordic larp are occasionally covered in the mainstream media (see e.g., Pettersson 2014) or presented in museum contexts. Larps and larp designers can receive arts funding and grants, and larp is gaining recognition as a pedagogic tool. Thousands of Swedish schoolchildren have experienced curriculum-specific edu-larp from organizations such as LajvVerkstaden (2025b) and Lajvbyrån (2025); Denmark even has two boarding schools taught in part or in whole through larp pedagogy, Østerskov Efterskole (n.d.) and Efterskolen Epos (n.d.).

Current and former larpers in positions of influence (e.g., policymakers, headmasters, journalists, cultural funders) contribute to openness toward institutional engagement with the medium. When a former Sverok larper, Amanda Lind, became Swedish Minister of Culture, she said larp had opened doors for her and contributed to collaborative skills (Josefsson 2019). Heikki Holmås, a former Minister of International Development of Norway who has attended several Nordic larps, has explicitly stated that they in his view have a great deal of political potential in helping people understand each other's perspectives (Giæver 2012).

POLITICAL NORDIC LARP

Examples of Large-Scale Political Nordic Larp

In addition to viewing larp in terms of aesthetics and craftsmanship, Nordic larp discourse is about engaging with ideas. In line with a longer history of role-players debating challenges within their hobby (see Peterson 2022), early Nordic fanzines include articles reflecting critically on the making or content of larp, e.g., the balancing of authenticity and racism in historical settings (Rislund 1997), or gender roles and male monopolization (Jonnmyren and Lindberg 1997). Political analysis and cultural criticism are present in most Nordic larp-related publications, and one of the para-academic Knutepunkt books, *Larp Politics: Systems, Theory, and Gender in Action* (Kangas et al. 2016), focuses specifically on political aspects of larp.

In the 1990s, larp like many forms of entertainment often unthinkingly reproduced generic dystopian cyberpunk tropes of oppression and violence for fun. Seminal works of proto-Nordic larp were explicitly created in response, e.g. the multi-day *Kybergenesis* (1997; Hassel 1997; Halvorsen 1997; Grasmo 1998). The political analysis of its backstory was perhaps not nuanced but aspects of it – AIs running the world and humans exerting what power they can over each other – seem prescient today. Within the metaphorical setting, the larp attempted physical and psychological realism for heightened impact. Although its attempts at awareness-raising were aimed primarily at the players, the larp's impressive production in fact placed its anti-authoritarian critique in front of a much larger secondary audience through media reports including a segment on the Norwegian national TV news (NRK 1997).

Within the nascent Nordic larp discourse, as larps like *Kybergenesis* became shared reference points, political uses of dystopian sci-fi settings soon became established practice and their use became more precise. For example, in *Last Will* (2014), citizens give up their rights and freedoms in exchange for food and shelter. The larp was designed to spark reflections on modern enslavement (Strand, Gamero, and Stenler 2015), raising awareness (Lehto 2016) through a political allegory (Rantanen 2016).

An early example of larp with elements of direct action was the dystopian art larp *AmerikA* (2000; Fatland 2009), taking over a central Oslo square with the blessing of the municipality. Fifty tonnes of garbage were turned into a stylized trash heap on which hundreds of participants embodied fictional characters for three days in a critique of consumerism, US cultural imperialism, and the sensationalism of dawning reality entertainment. Larp rarely engages with audiences, but in *pervasive* larp (Montola, Stenros, and Waern 2009), situated as a seamless or permeable fictional layer on top of real-world environments, the fiction can interact with non-players. Passers-by could follow *AmerikA* from an elevated street by the square, through web cameras, or by taking on fictional roles as visiting tourists, whose gawking and "slumming" made sense within the larp fiction (Fatland 2009).

Similarly, *System Danmarc* (2005) was played in a public square in Copenhagen. It was a three-day larp about a future Denmark with a democratic deficit, for which a city block was built out of shipping containers to house "Class C" citizens, an encampment "reserved for the citizens deemed useless for the society" (Munthe-Kaas 2010). The visibility of the larp's set in the cityscape also made it a public intervention requiring significant municipal cooperation.

A simulation-style political larp played in a public square was *Dublin2* (2011), a combination of larp, public artwork, and activism. Played in a central Helsinki square, the larp was set in a "self-formed camp of irregular migrants" in an unnamed Southern European city, with a container detention cell, and a barbed-wire fence with guard towers representing a national border toward the better-resourced but dysfunctional refugee processing of Northern Europe. Created to debate the EU's Dublin II framework, its participants played asylum seekers and Frontex officials with a real-world lawyer, NGO representatives, and a journalist participating as themselves. The backstories were based on real people, in consultation with refugees and stakeholders including Finnish Border Guards. Passers-by were invited to engage with the fiction; notable interactions included a non-player improvising the role of a lawyer to negotiate a character out of lockup, real refugees who happened upon the event advising the participants, and casual racist verbal attacks from people apparently not noticing the camp was fictive (Kaljonen and Raekallio 2012; Arjoranta 2015).

Equally fact-based, but at the opposite end of the simulation/allegory scale, was *Baltic Warriors* (2014–2015), a Nordic larp integrated into a transmedia awareness-raising campaign about seabed eutrophication that toured seven cities around the Baltic Sea with support from the Goethe Institut. In addition to its environmental awareness-raising, the larp also had the educational goal of illuminating how political decisions are made, and participants portrayed politicians, lobbyists, experts, activists, and concerned citizens at a public debate about the issue. As discussions were interrupted by zombie Vikings representing the dead seabed (Pohjola 2016), stakeholders joined forces to defeat the threat using clean water. After the larp, a panel of real politicians and lobbyists discussed the issues portrayed in the larp some of them had just played– sometimes even in characer as each other, arguing positions different from their own (Pettersson 2021a, 2021b; Lehto 2016).

Halat hisar (2013, 2016) was a political allegory about daily life in occupied Finland, in an alternate-reality contemporary setting. Created by Palestinian and Finnish larp designers with Finnish arts funding and significant media interest, *Halat hisar* modeled complex political and personal dynamics based on the situation in the West Bank, and between Palestinians and the global north (Pettersson 2014; Pöllänen and Arjoranta 2021). As a side effect of this awareness-raising setting, participants found themselves practicing real-world skills like media criticism or peacefully protesting and resisting arrest. A workshop had to be added at the last minute for the latter when it became obvious that most Northern European participants had no experience in a skillset the Palestinian designers took for granted.

Inadvertent skills training also happened at *1942: Noen å Stole På?* (2000, 2017; Eng. 1942: Someone to trust?; Fatland 2010), which simulated daily life in a Norwegian village under German occupation for several days. The characters were based on first-hand accounts of historical people and their day-to-day routines; players took on the roles of ordinary Norwegians, German soldiers, refugees, and resistance fighters. The design specifically guided toward realistic, mundane, and ethically complicated actions, centering resilience and resistance while challenging romanticized historical narratives. In addition to demonstrating the power dynamics and information flows of daily life under occupation, the simulation approach revealed to participants how differently prepared they were for e.g., cutting firewood, cooking for large numbers of people on limited resources, or fishing for sustenance.

As we have seen, political larp with large sets, pervasive elements, or interesting concepts can reach a wider audience beyond the players themselves and powerfully impact participants. They are however difficult to scale. Most political Nordic larp are smaller in participant number and duration, and playable in a few hours in a theater blackbox, e.g. *Beyond the Barricades* (2015; Wei and Göthberg 2015), a rollicking and ultimately heartbreaking larp about "ten friends on a barricade in revolutionary Paris" in 1832, encouraging self-reflection about friendship, idealism, and activism. Others do not require any special space or equipment at all, such as *My Sister, Malala* (2016, Helin 2016), which focuses on Pakistani girls and "empowerment, online harassment and human rights". Political larp can also lean toward pure abstraction, such as *Restrictions* (2016; Bushyager, Stark, and Westerling 2016), a dance-based larp about how gender affects how we move our bodies.

Edu-larps with political themes are also typically at this smaller scale. Although Nordic classroom larp with humanist or democratic values may appear progressive in other contexts, edu-larp intended for public schools typically refrain from taking stances on specific political issues, focusing e.g., on political skill building instead. In *Ulkoavaruuden muukalaiset ja enemmistön tyrannia* (2015, Eng. Strangers from Outer Space and the Tyranny of the Majority; Korhonen 2015; Lehto 2016), players write the final speech of an election campaign in a titillating alien invasion setting.

Political larp that make vivid unjust situations and dynamics often involve challenging emotional content. This discomfort has been seen to enhance learning, e.g., after a larp about asylum seeking (Bjørkelo and Jørgensen 2018). Such findings echo studies on political educational role-playing games developed outside the larp community; researchers studying a *Reacting to the Past* historical simulation teaching political theory found increased student engagement when experiencing negative emotions (Weidenfeld and Fernandez 2017).

However, political larp can also be light-hearted, using satire and dark humor to engage players. *Ockulta medborgarbyrån* (2016, Eng. Occult Citizens' Bureau; Lajvhistoria n.d.), a humoristic larp where the Swedish bureaucracy has been taken over by the Inferno, is an example of this. *The Future Is Straight* (2022; Grasmo, Sihvonen, and Stenros In press), a pitch-black comedy about a conversion camp for gay and trans people, played by a majority of LGBTQ participants, is another.

Empowerment, Allyship – And Misery Tourism?

Tensions around who can tell or portray which stories are common across the arts, especially those involving role-taking, but are complicated in larp by its position straddling escapist leisure, embodied performance, political activism, educational goals, and contemporary art.

In Nordic larp, gender parity in larp communities is common and there is a sizable base of queer, trans, and neurodivergent players, but people of color often still experience challenges in feeling included in the community (see Kemper 2018; Kemper, Saitta, and Koljonen 2020). Even where more diverse events and communities exist, the long-standing stereotype that role-playing games are a primarily White cis-male middle-class activity (see Amherst 2016) can dissuade people with more marginalized identities from engaging with them unless the communications and culture of events center inclusion.

Leonard, Janjetovic, and Usman (2021) have warned that larp engaging with themes of marginalization risk becoming a form of dark tourism (Roberts and Stone 2014), "in which privileged individuals voluntarily enter disaster zones due to a mix of motives that include voyeurism and vicarious danger exposure." In larp, such practices can also be interpreted as *identity tourism* (Nakamura 1995) and misery tourism. Furthermore, playing marginalizations the player does not experience in their lives may have unintended consequences, e.g., cultural appropriation and unintentionally portraying harmful stereotypes (Kessock 2014; Kangas 2017).

Within Nordic larp and many other play cultures today, awareness of these dynamics is relatively high. Players engaging with real-world themes are often explicitly instructed never to assume they will understand the lived experience of the groups the larp portrays, and reminded that any recreation is by necessity simplified and temporary. The ability of players to opt out of fictional experiences that prove too much can also be framed in contrast to the limited agency of the actual people in the real situation to increase empathy.

Best practice for moving from stereotypes to nuanced representations includes e.g., using cultural consultants and including designers with relevant backgrounds throughout the design and implementation process (Leonard, Janjetovic, and Usman 2021). Even so, designers should not assume a consultant from a marginalized background speaks for everyone with that life experience (Kemper et al. 2018). To further complicate matters, not engaging with diverse representations for fear of misrepresentation can lead to a narrow portrayal of the world and a feeling of erasure for members of that community (Holkar 2016).

Handling sensitive content with insufficient care or lack of nuance is especially likely to negatively impact marginalized players. If stakeholders are likely to participate in a larp on a real-world theme, this is of particular concern; an unrealistic or simplified portrayal may be experienced as offensive, but a too realistic portrayal be inaccessible for participants experiencing similar dynamics in their lives. The social vigilance required to guard against such impacts may in itself hinder access to the same degree of empowerment and agency that larp affords to players from privilege (Kemper, Saitta, and Koljonen 2020).

Leonard, Janjetovic, and Usman (2021) suggest these risks should be weighed against benefits of larp, such as perspective taking and empathy. With sufficient awareness of the limitations any representation entails, opting into a serious larp can become the starting point for an openness to shift one's perspective and to learning more about the complex difficulties faced by others (see e.g., Bjørkelo and Jørgensen 2018).

Furthermore, the same qualities that allow for e.g., stereotypical representations in larp create space in the artform for counternarratives and explorations of cultural heritage, for example for marginalized queer communities (Baird 2022; Levin 2023). Jonaya Kemper (2017, 2020), informed by perspectives of players with minority backgrounds, discusses the empowering experience of *emancipatory bleed*; whether in an escapist or serious larp, challenging oppressive in-game structures or playing a character with more agency than a marginalized player experiences in daily life can be profoundly liberating.

The Example of Just a Little Lovin'

A highly acclaimed larp that faced allegations of "misery tourism" is the four-day *Just a Little Lovin'* (2011–2019; Groth, Grasmo, and Edland 2021), which follows interconnected groups of friends through the three first years of the AIDS epidemic in New York City. In advance of its first Norwegian production, a debate erupted in the culture pages of Swedish newspapers, after a professional critic with no connection to the larp milieu suggested its topic and presentation cheapened a still-painful tragedy. In the following debate, another critic wrongly assumed the designers and players would be predominantly straight (see Gerge 2012). For the larp's predominantly LGBTQ+ designers and players, the work was an exploration of community history and a chance to center queer perspectives on friendship, joy, and chosen family, against the historical background of prejudice, grief, and fear. A more precise criticism would have been the limited way in which Norwegian designers and Nordic players could reflect or portray the complex specificities of ethnic diversity within New York subcultural milieus of the 1980s; later productions of the larp have attempted to address this challenge and worked on its framing. Across its eight runs so far, the larp has also attracted LGBTQIA+ players from New York, including some from the directly affected generations later expressing that the larp was well-handled and accurate to their experience.

It is likely that some players chose to participate in *Just a Little Lovin'* because of its artistic acclaim rather than a personal connection to its themes, and stereotypes may unthinkingly have been recreated in play. This is however not significantly different from the staging and reception of e.g., a stage play or film on the same topics and milieus. Contrary to assumptions underlying public criticisms of the project, *Just a Little Lovin'* was a participatory artwork by LGTBQ creators about issues of personal relevance to themselves and their LGBTQIA+ and ally players.

While primarily intended as liberating and awareness-raising, the larp also had behavior-changing impacts on its participants. Learning about LGTBQ stigmatization and the politicization of healthcare drove many players to platform or work with HIV/AIDS or related causes, generating secondary audience reach e.g., through a player joining their local Pride organizing committees after never taking part in Pride before the larp (Levin 2023); organizers and players producing an exhibition of paintings produced for the larp as well as a public performance inspired by it as part of a wide commemoration of World AIDS Day at the Oslo railway station (Standberg 2011); or players instigating and producing a documentary series (Sveriges Radio2012) about AIDS history for Swedish radio.

Even though not all criticism has been factually grounded, studying and critiquing individual larps from representational perspectives remains vitally important. Concerns about role-taking and respect should be appropriately integrated in any larp's design, communication and framing, especially when designing for audiences with varying levels of awareness or cultural knowledge outside of their own backgrounds.

LARP AND DELIBERATION

What Is Deliberation?

As we have shown, role-playing and specifically bespoke larp, such as that of Nordic larp and related communities, have demonstrated usefulness in democratic education. Examples include increasing awareness of and personally engaging people in specific issues and structural dynamics; adding nuance, complexity, and first-person perspectives to simplified media narratives; and training skills such as non-violent protest, public speaking, and persuasive argumentation. Of particular interest to us is using larp specifically in relation to *democratic deliberation*, a set of skills and practices creating environments of depolarization in which civil political discussions can be given and reasons exchanged. Deliberation can have many goals relevant to democratic engagement, such as creating consensus on a specific issue, fostering greater mutual understanding, or establishing shared group identity (Felicetti et al. 2012; Hartz-Karp et al. 2010). As traditional democratic institutions fail to engage especially younger generations, there is a need to experiment with innovative formats for democracy, including deliberation (Freedom House 2024).

Deliberative democracy is a normative ideal in which people discuss political issues that impact their lives based on equal status and mutual respect. It contrasts with other forms of political exchange, such as debate. Debates tend to be limited to efforts to prevail in supporting certain predetermined outcomes, while the *Oxford Handbook of Deliberative Democracy* (Bächtiger et al. 2018, 2) defines deliberation as "mutual communication that involves weighing and reflecting on preferences, values, and interests regarding matters of common concern." A deliberative process involves concerted efforts of those impacted by a decision to engage with all the relevant arguments in good faith, and integrate valid arguments into this reasoning, whether or not they initially agree with the conclusions these inform.

Democratic deliberation as both a skill and a praxis is a vital part of a functioning democracy. Research has shown that deliberative events with favorable conditions for mutual and respectful exchange of opinions, such as citizen's assemblies, can decrease polarization and foster mutual understanding even between people with very diverse opinions on sensitive matters (Grönlund, Herne, and Setälä 2015), and increase civic engagement (Knobloch and Gastil 2015).

In deliberation, participants should be ready to explain and justify any claims and opinions, but also to carefully weigh and seriously consider information provided by others. In order for deliberation to also be considered democratic, the process should include citizen stakeholders in equal participation, and the deliberation should be consequential to actual decision-making. Core skills for deliberation include the ability to explain positions to a relevant audience; build up arguments based on authenticity, rather than through propagandistic lies, manipulation, or the use of rhetoric; listen and take on different perspectives; be prepared to change position; and foster empathy toward those with different opinions (Bächtiger et al. 2018). Deliberation does not necessarily aim for full consensus; clarifying differences in opinion can be enough, potentially producing a "meta-consensus" on which kind of arguments are relevant in a specific discussion (Dryzek and Niemeyer 2006).

Deliberative theory scholars have largely moved away from considering only interactions that fulfill high normative ideals as deliberative, now also embracing less-than-perfect forms of deliberation (Bächtiger et al. 2018). Current democratic deliberation research explores how deliberative fora should foster not only fact-based argumentation but also alternative and less formal modes of communication such as storytelling, narratives, testimony, and humor. This practice might help address questions of who feels welcome in formal deliberation environments, is emboldened to assert one's views, or has been socially primed to provide "reasons" in a manner that others find persuasive (Sanders 1997; Young 2022). There is growing agreement that the neutrality-only language of rational reason-giving might disadvantage already marginalized groups in civil society, and that deliberation takes as many forms as there are diverse cultures.

An exchange of reasons remains at the core of deliberative theory, but reasons are now understood as legitimately expressed in many ways, including the use of storytelling, bodily expressions, as well as certain kinds of rhetoric (Jennstål and Öberg 2019). This understanding also suggests the need to adopt a permissive view of what should be deemed acceptable claims; as long as speakers do not make threats or tell lies, other participants should listen.

Deliberation and Larp

Rantanen (2016) observes that political larp, like other kinds of political communication, have typically been designed to transmit a specific political message. Even when different viewpoints and perspectives on an issue are enacted, the framing selected by the designers guides and privileges certain outcomes and interpretations. The players' freedom to shape their character, its choices, and the larp itself, could however be argued to be fundamentally deliberative. These qualities could be intentionally enhanced to create larp for political deliberation instead of political messaging (Rantanen 2016).

The process of role-play itself can impact political views (Elms 1966); strengthen engagement in deliberation skill training (Levine 2018); and be utilized for actual deliberation, with potentially powerful results (Gordon, Haas, and Michelson 2017). The social *alibi* (Deterding 2018) provided by the role-taking creates a permission structure for engaging with opposing perspectives without losing face, especially when combined with the overall playful framing afforded by larp, e.g., the fictional setting, pretending, and improvisation.

Empathy, active listening, and taking initiative are central skills in both democratic deliberation (Bächtiger et al. 2018) and playing larp (Pothong et al. 2021). Even conflict-centered larp, like all competitive games, have a non-competitive core; engaging playfully around their characters' varying, individual perspectives requires participants to listen to and trust each other at least on some level (Piven and Cloward 2005; Huizinga 1955). Characters have conflicts, but their players should remain in a collaborative mode, lest out-of-character social conflicts erupt (Bowman 2013).

That said, larps are often optimized for generating high-intensity situations. As in drama and comedy generally, escalated conflicts are common, and character opinions may be exaggeratedly hard-set. This is also true for most Nordic political larp discussed above, even when enacted in a way that centers co-creation, listening, civility, and trust among the players out of character. There are however examples of larp in a more deliberative style, often recreating historical or contemporary deliberative events or processes.

In *Suffragette!* (2014; Suffragette n.d.), a larp about women's rights activists produced in partnership with the Hallwyl Museum in Stockholm (Hallwylska Museet 2014), characters discussed how best to protest for women' s right to vote: peacefully or militantly. Different opinions of diverse groups advocating for votes for women were represented, and the characters worked toward constructing a common agenda between the subgroups, as well as preparing slogans and other messaging. Another example is *Vår skyldighet* (2015, Eng. Our Duty), which was arranged as part of the Calling for Peace event in Varberg, Sweden, and commemorated the 1915 Peace Congress. Participants played delegates from each of the organizations that had been present in deliberations at the original congress, and the larp was partially staged in public spaces (Vår skyldighet n.d.). Unlike in historical reenactment, the participants of these larp had agency to genuinely deliberate, and outcomes could differ from the historical situation.

Larps with deliberative elements have also been based on entirely fictional or even allegorical premises, e.g., *The Circle of Life* (Klanac and Ståh 2016), based on the animated film *The Lion King* (1994), in which participants played animals deliberating whether to be ruled by the lion or find another form of governance. In *Magica Moriens* (2021; Föreningen Ursula 2024), dwindling magic allegorically represented climate change, and the magician characters deliberated to decide how to handle the future.

Although the above larps were not designed with democratic deliberation specifically in mind, the examples show that larps could be purposely created for training deliberation or skills that support it, e.g., listening, reason-giving, and civility in communicating disagreements. Such larps may also illustrate how different social positions can affect one's agency and perspectives. In Rantanen's (2016) strict definition, for a larp to be truly deliberative, participants should have real agency over their characters' viewpoints and the larp as a whole. These qualities would be most important were a larp to be integrated into the overall facilitated framework of a real-world deliberative process.

Larps designed by stakeholders with different positions on an issue, separately or together, could hypothetically also be a medium for reason-giving, allowing them to reflect on and model their understandings of complex aspects of an issue including needs, resources, loyalties, and power relationships. These may be difficult to dynamically represent in other forms of communication such as speeches.

A possible further direction to explore would be using larp as a medium for theory-driven experiments in political science or to teach practices such as strategic peacebuilding (Schirch 2005), for example through a larp in which characters used both democratic skills escalating political conflict (e.g., non-violent protest) and de-escalating it (e.g., deliberation among lawmakers, negotiating terms with the authorities). Such practices could demonstrate to participants the necessity of multi-pronged approaches to addressing political issues, employing multiple skill sets and tactics in collaboration, rather than focusing on one specific practice. The systems-building capabilities of larp design make such a model playable at a small scale, with different factions enacting unique peacebuilding activities throughout the larp.

DESIGN CONCERNS IN LARP FOR POLITICAL EDUCATION

Within Nordic larp design discourse, "everything is a designable surface" (Koljonen et al. 2019); suggesting that not just traditional elements of game design but *all* aspects of the physical and social environment in a bespoke larp from room temperature to out-of-character interactions will affect player outcomes. In practice, many design choices are predetermined, e.g., the duration of an edu-larp by the structure of a school day, or participant number by room size at the venue. Others will be ruled out by feasibility constraints relating to the resources of the design team (e.g., budget, skills), or those of the prospective participants, e.g., their available preparation time or ability to memorize facts.

Participants experience a larp through the actions and choices afforded within the larp's physical and social environments, restricted and focused by elements such as the setting, genre, characters, and mechanics, but also e.g., the cultural expectations of each participant (Lampo 2015). A central design question in any larp therefore becomes to identify the *verbs* or activities the participants will actually engage in as their characters (Torner 2019; Townser and Li 2019; Brind 2022), and to ensure these activities are thematically coherent with the larp's impact goals, as well as meaningful and possible to perform during play (Diakolambrianou et al. 2024).

Importance of Framing Activities

The participants' understanding of the larp's fiction as well as its rules and game mechanics is established in advance of playing (Harviainen 2007). In the last decade, the careful design of this frame-setting stage has become understood as completely central to predictably ensuring the participants' ability to play any specific larp; to their shared understanding of play culture, norms, processes, and objectives; and to their trust in the designers, facilitators, each other, and themselves as players. Pre-game frame-setting begins with how a larp's existence and relevance to specific audiences is communicated, and continues all the way through to the on-site on-boarding into the play experience, through e.g., workshops (see Koljonen et al. 2019).

Framing activities continue after the run-time, e.g., *de-roling* or stepping out of character, reflection, or debriefing questions, as well as post-larp integration practices. All of this framing is of particular importance in transformative larp design, e.g., when aiming for educational or therapeutic impacts (Bowman et al. 2024), including any larp designed for awareness-raising or to change real-world behaviors of the participants. Many of the political larps discussed above use real-world contextualization to scaffold the participants' post-larp integration of their play experience through e.g., presenting real-world information in writing, documentaries, or lectures before, during, and/or after the event, and offering discussion opportunities with real-world stakeholders.

In educational settings, engaging critically with themes such as political polarization carries with it risks of some students being unable or unwilling to internalize their play experiences, or even of their engaging in antisocial out-of-character behaviors. Such risks can be mitigated through framing activities such as structured debriefing and pre- and post-game learning materials on the central themes (see e.g. Aarebrot and Nielsen 2012).

In political discourse analysis, "framing" refers to the selection of which aspects of a perceived reality to emphasize in order to make certain conclusions or solutions more salient (Rantanen 2016). In political larp, this rhetorical framing is made present through the framing activities participants engage in as part of the experience. This is illustrated by *System Danmarc* (2005), which culminated in the screening of a documentary about social inequality in contemporary Denmark just as the game ended. As participants had not been explicitly told about the larp's political intentions in advance, this element of the work partly backfired, with angry reactions to the film's perspective retroactively redefining the meaning of their experience (Kangas 2015). Players felt the larp had first encouraged in-character oppression and carnivalistic portrayals of "C-class citizens" but was now judging this play as immoral instead of using the experience to encourage participants to reflect on real-world inequities. Such non-transparent design choices can decrease trust in the process and its organizers and affect players' perceptions of safety (Torner 2013), which in turn can interfere with learning goals especially when dealing with politically charged content.

Perhaps because shock tactics have historically been an accepted part of activist art, *System Denmark's* reframing gambit may not ultimately have undermined the larp's impact. In a rare post-larp survey, answered by half of the players, "82% had an experience of democratic deficiency, 97% had an experience of social injustice during the larp; 97% viewed the game experience as positive" (Munthe-Kaas 2010) (Unfortunately, these statistics do not illuminate whether or not players' post-game values, awareness, attitudes, or skills changed after the larp, leaving its educational impacts less clear). We assert that making the intent and processes of a political larp legible before, during, and after the experience, i.e., designing for transparency (Torner 2013), is more likely to produce more predictable outcomes and encourage an open rather than a confrontational stance to the message.

In a one-time leisure larp, it might be enough for the expectation-setting, play experience, and post-play integration activities to be internally coherent, and if possible deliver a satisfying sense of closure. In a larp with transformative goals, the question of which kinds of actions a designer would like their participants to take also extends beyond the event itself. If the larp is part of a longer transformative process, the event should allow players to contextualize their experience but also invite later engagement by, e.g., exploring relevant questions in the curriculum later in a school term, engaging with relevant stakeholders after the larp, or offering assistance or volunteering around the larp's themes.

Considerations around safety are also important to integrate into framing activities. In the past decades, safety structures within larp design are increasingly systematic and normalized within Nordic larp, although practices vary. Awareness of and design for participant well-being, including physical and emotional safety and the ability of all participants to opt out of unwelcome situations and calibrate the intensity of their interactions, should be integrated in all phases and levels of a larp's design. Clearly communicating the nature and themes ahead of time is key, as is establishing common limits before playing begins (see Koljonen 2020). That these processes will take place cannot be assumed of all larp, as play cultures and designer skills vary, and even risk is handled well, it can seldom be entirely eliminated (Losilla 2024). Even when participants are well-informed adults consenting to the interactions and feeling freely able to leave, the use of real-world manipulative techniques and high-intensity physical situations should be very limited; with minors, e.g., in many edu-larp, such elements are risky to include (Järvelä 2012). Also, informed consent is not always possible due to the emergent nature of co-creative play, which increases risk compared to more static forms of media.

Finally, larp can be used for good or ill, progressive or reactionary, democratic or totalitarian purposes. Like any other technology, it is not good or bad, nor is it neutral (Kranzberg 1986); it has tendencies, better suited for some purposes than others. As a social technology that requires buy-in from participants, from a political perspective, larp will affect and be affected by players (Flanagan, Howe, and Nissenbaum 2008). Values are built into technologies and can also be actively built into design, including values surrounding justice and morality. Although beyond the scope of this study and counter to our normative goals, it is just as possible to design participatory work for exclusionary ideals such as nationalism, xenophobia, fascism, or authoritarianism. When designing or evaluating any educational larp, it is therefore important to critically consider the ideologies informing them, the experience of engaging with them, and the types of participation invited. This analysis should be extended beyond the larp's setting, events, and mechanics, to its framing activities, facilitation, and wider context, as impacts can extend beyond the play group itself, particularly if a larp is widely promoted, documented, or otherwise disseminated.

CONCLUSION

This chapter establishes that the use of role-playing and larp-adjacent activities in democratic skills training pre-dates leisure role-playing by over half a century, and that educational role-playing games are now an established field in themselves. Design movements such as Nordic larp have 30 years of documented experimentation in using larp to promote awareness-raising and activism on societal issues, as well as to teach political and democratic skills. All this suggests larp has immediate potential as a social technology for political education, democratic skills training, and policy development.

In this age of stressed democracies and democratic deficits, combining larp with democratic deliberation is of particular interest. Larp is built on co-creation, dialogue, and understanding different perspectives, qualities equally central to deliberative methodologies. Democratic deliberation has been demonstrated within the field of political science to, for instance, foster mutual understanding, create consensus on specific issues, and decrease polarization. Finding successful ways to combine the artistic, role-taking, and somatic aspects of larp with deliberation events, whether as a training method or as part of deliberative processes, has strong transformative potential.

The decades worth of documented collaboration between players and designers developed within bespoke larp communities, including educational larp design, could add new dimensions to deliberative events. Similarly, existing deliberation research might be adapted to and tested in edu-larp contexts, potentially offering new directions for unanswered questions about when and how larp works best for engaging with societal topics and democratic skill training. For example, does a fictional or historical setting make it easier to engage with a sensitive contemporary issue? Is it helpful to ask participants to play roles far from their everyday lives, or to act in positions of authority they seldom can access?

From our perspective, while gathering data is helpful in understanding larp's impacts, larp's value does not need the validation of instrumental uses. Playing together is enough in itself: creating community, building trust, finding respite, feeling joy, and sharing the human condition. While these things will have inherent value in any future, preferring some futures over others should make us very eager to contribute to democratic resilience and the revitalization or recreation of our political systems. This contribution requires not just systems literacy and the skills of governance, citizenship, and political change, but the ability to collectively imagine and actually model where other paths might take us. A well-honed toolkit for imagining, creating, and testing alternative worlds and social realities together is a valuable thing indeed.

AUTHOR DISCLOSURE

Karin Johansson has contributed extensive composition on early drafts; primary and secondary source research; and citation work.

Johanna Koljonen has contributed extensive composition in the revision and post-review stages of this chapter, including significant restructuring, rewriting, and refinement of the argument, and citation work.

Jaakko Stenros has contributed in the revision and post-review stages of this chapter, including rewriting, commenting, restructuring, refinement of the argument, and citation work.

PerOla Öberg has contributed substantial written work and citations to the sections regarding deliberation and its comparison with political larp.

Sarah Lynne Bowman has contributed extensive composition and citation in several drafts.

ACKNOWLEDGMENTS

This research is co-funded by the European Union's Horizon Europe project Larpocracy: Developing Spaces for Deliberation and Democratic Skills through Role-playing. Larpocracy integrates perspectives from researchers on game studies, larp design, transformative play, political science, and human-computer interaction. The project aims to explore larp in relation to democratic processes, including deliberative events, and how the combination can promote civic outcomes related to democratic participation. Special thanks to Annika Waern, the project lead and main architect.

NOTES

1   The analysis presented in this chapter draws from years of practitioner experience in the Nordic larp movement and adjacent role-play spaces. The dataset at the core of the analysis comes from an exploratory scoping review seeking connections between larp and politics, first in two Swedish larp magazines, *Fëa livia* and *StrapatS*, whose issues from the 1990s were reviewed for political or democracy-focused content. This study was then expanded into the wider Nordic larp literature. Further instances of larp and politics were found by following references, and through our own experience as researchers and/or members of these respective communities, e.g., Nordic larp, role-playing game studies, edu-larp, and political science.

  A common challenge in larp studies is the ephemeral nature of the events that are being studied; if larps are not documented, they vanish the moment they end (Koljonen 2008; Stenros and Montola 2011). While the Nordic larp discourse community is better than most at documenting their works, it historically prioritised documenting and sharing what they had learned about larp design rather than the precise details of previous iterations. These gaps in design documentation means historical analysis in this paper is based on partial, sometimes even fragmentary accounts, making impossible systematic reviews and comparisons of, for instance, the design and structure of large numbers of larp with regard to the degree of activities related to democratic skill training in comparison to dramatic social play.

2   To delimit this chapter to the Nordic larp design discourse, our use of "bespoke design" refers to concepts within that community (see, e.g., Koljonen et al. 2019). However, we are aware that many wider design theories exist that also present perspectives on bespoke design, value-driven design, participatory design, human-centered design, critical design, each with their own implications. We reserve a careful consideration of these design philosophies for future work.

REFERENCES

Aarebrot, Erik, and Martin Nielsen. 2012. "Prisoner for a Day: Creating a Game without Winners." In *Playing the Learning Game: A Practical Introduction to Educational Roleplaying*, edited by Martin Eckoff Andresen. Fantasiforbundet.

Abt, C. Clark. 1970. *Serious Games*. Viking Press.

Amherst, Christopher. 2016. "Representation and Social Capital: What the Larp Census reveals about Community." In *Larp Realia: Analysis, Design, and Discussions of Nordic Larp*, edited by Jukka Särkijärvi, Mika Loponen, and Kaisa Kangas. Ropecon ry.

Andersen, Anita Myhre, and Erik Aarebrot. 2009. "Larp in Kamensky forest." In *Larp, the Universe, and Everything*, edited by Matthijs Holter, Eirik Fatland, and Even Tømte. Knutepunkt 2009.

Arjoranta, Jonne. 2015. "Larp as Playful Resistance." Paper presented at Adult Play, University of Tampere, Finland, May 10–12, 2015.

Bächtiger, André, John S. Dryzek, Jane Mansbridge, and Mark D. Warren.eds. 2018. *The Oxford Handbook of Deliberative Democracy*. Oxford Handbooks. Oxford University Press.

Back, Jon, Elena Márquez Segura, and Annika Waern. 2017. "Designing for Transformative Play." *ACM Transactions on Computer-Human Interaction* 24 (3): 18:1–18:28. https://doi.org/10.1145/3057921.

Baird, Josephine. 2022. "Learning About Ourselves: Communicating, Connecting and Contemplating Trans Experience through Play." *Gamevironments* 17: 355–402.

Beale, Charlotte. 2016. "When Davos Delegates Pretended to Be Refugees." *The Independent*, January 23. https://www.independent.co.uk/news/world/europe/davos-delegates-experience-refugee-life-for-75-minutes-a6828886.html.

Belarbi, Samir. 2010. "Föreningen visionära vetenskapsmäns årliga kongress. Sailing the Seas of Mental Disorder." In *Nordic Larp*, edited by Jaakko Stenros and Markus Montola. Fëa Livia.

Berry, Laurie A., and Kristin B. Kowal. 2022. "Effect of Role-Play in Online Discussions on Student Engagement and Critical Thinking | Online Learning." *Online Learning: 2022 OLC Conference Special Issue* 26 (3): 4–21.

Bjørkelo, Kristian A., and Kristine Jørgensen. 2018. "The Asylum Seekers Larp: The Positive Discomfort of Transgressive Realism." In *Proceedings of Nordic DiGRA 2018*.

Blatner, Adam. 2004. *Foundations of Psychodrama: History, Drama, and Practice*. Fourth Edition. Springer Publishing Company.

Boal, Augusto. 2002. *Games for Actors and Non-Actors*. Second Edition. Routledge.

Bowman, Claude C. 1949. "Role-Playing and the Development of Insight." *Social Forces* 28 (2): 195–199.

Bowman, Sarah Lynne. 2010. *The Functions of Role-Playing Games: How Participants Create Community, Solve Problems, and Explore Identity*. McFarland & Company, Inc.

Bowman, Sarah Lynne. 2013. "Social Conflict in Role-Playing Communities: An Exploratory Qualitative Study." *International Journal of Role-Playing* (4): 4–25. https://doi.org/10.33063/ijrp.vi4.183.

Bowman, Sarah Lynne. 2014. "Educational Live Action Role-Playing Games: A Secondary Literature Review." In *Wyrd Con Companion Book 2014*, edited by Sarah Lynne Bowman. Wyrd Con.

Bowman, Sarah Lynne, Josephine Baird, Kjell Hedgard Hugaas, Elektra Diakolambrianou, and Taisto Suominen. 2024. "Chapter 7: Research in Transformative Game Design." In *Transformative Role-Playing Game Design*. Acta Universitatis Upsaliensis, edited by Sarah Lynne Bowman, Elektra Diakolambrianou, and Simon Brind. Transformative Play Research 1. Uppsala University Publications.

Bowman, Sarah Lynne, Elektra Diakolambrianou, and Simon Brind, eds. 2024. *Transformative Role-Playing Game Design*. Acta Universitatis Upsaliensis. Transformative Play Research 1. Uppsala University Publications.

Bowman, Sarah Lynne, Elektra Diakolambrianou, Kjell Hedgard Hugaas, Josefin Westborg, and Josephine Baird. 2024. "Chapter 2: Transformative Role-Playing Games: Types, Purposes, and Features." In *Transformative Role-playing Game Design*. Acta Universitatis Upsaliensis, edited by Sarah Lynne Bowman, Elektra Diakolambrianou, and Simon Brind. Transformative Play Research 1. Uppsala University Publications.

Bridging Ages. n.d. "International Organization in Applied Heritage and Time Travels." Accessed July 6, 2023. https://bridgingages.com/.

Brind, Simon. 2022. "Combat Narratology – Strategies for the Resolution of Narrative Crisis in Participatory Fiction." Ph.D. diss., University of the West of England. https://uwe-repository.worktribe.com/output/9955142.

Brodén, Martin, ed. 2008. *Sverok 20 År*. Bilda Idé.

Brown, Maury. 2016. "Creating a Culture of Trust through Safety and Calibration Larp Mechanics." *Nordiclarp.org*, September 9.

Budai, Sarah, and Kristin Hammock. 2014. "The State of Amtgard." In *The Wyrd Con Companion Book 2014*, edited by Sarah Lynne Bowman, 11–27. Wyrd Con.

Burghardt, Gordon. M. 2005. *The Genesis of Animal Play. Testing the Limits*. The MIT Press.

Bushyager, Misha, Lizzie Stark, and Anna Westerling, eds. 2016. *#Feminism. A Nano-Game Anthology*. Fëa Livia.

By Night Studios. 2014. *Mind's Eye Theatre: Vampire: The Masquerade Quick Start Guide*. By Night.

Cullinan, Maryanne, and Jennifer Genova. 2023. "Gaming the Systems: A Component Analysis Framework for the Classroom Use of RPGs." *International Journal of Role-Playing* 13: 7–17.

Deterding, Sebastian. 2014. "The Ambiguity of Games: Histories and Rhetorics of the Gameful World." In *The Gameful World. Approaches, Issues, Application*, edited by Steffen P. Walz and Sebastian Deterding. The MIT Press.

Deterding, Sebastian. 2018. "Alibis for Adult Play: A Goffmanian Account of Escaping Embarrassment in Adult Play." *Games and Culture* 13 (3): 260–279.

Diakolambrianou, Elektra, Sarah Lynne Bowman, Simon Brind, Josefin Westborg, and Kjell Hedgard Hugaas. 2024. "Theory, Key Concepts, and Inspirational Materials." In *Transformative Role-Playing Game Design*, edited by Sarah Lynne Bowman, Elektra Diakolambrianou, and Simon Brind, 80–139. Acta Universitatis Upsaliensis. Transformative Play Research 1. Uppsala University Publications.

Dryzek, John S., and Simon Niemeyer. 2006. "Reconciling Pluralism and Consensus as Political Ideals." *American Journal of Political Science* 50 (3): 634–649.

Efterskolen Epos. n.d. "Start." Accessed September 5, 2025. https://efterskolen-epos.dk/.

Elms, A. C. 1966. "Influence of Fantasy Ability on Attitude Change through Role Playing." *Journal of Personality and Social Psychology* 4 (1): 36–43. https://doi.org/10.1037/h0023509.

Essendrop, Nina Runa. 2018. "Retrospect: Nina Runa Essendrop." *Fantasiforbundet*, January 10. https://youtu.be/YeqRyvYiibE?si=DxYvPl_jg5lIXEQS.

European Parliament. n.d. "Role Play Game | Visiting." *European Parliament*. Accessed November 19, 2024. https://visiting.europarl.europa.eu/en/education-learning/role-play-game.

European Union Learning Corner. n.d. "Role-Play EU Decision-Making." Accessed January 15, 2025. https://learning-corner.learning.europa.eu/learning-materials/role-play-eu-decision-making-0_en.

Fabel. 2023. "Electionville in Ukraine." November 8. https://fabel.se/2023/11/08/electionville-in-ukraine/.

Fatland, Eirik. 2009. "Excavating AmerikA." In *Larp, the Universe, and Everything*, edited by Matthijs Holter, Eirik Fatland, and Even Tømte. Knutepunkt 2009.

Fatland, Eirik. 2010. "1942 – Noen å stole på." In *Nordic Larp*, edited by Jaakko Stenros and Markus Montola. Fëa Livia.

Felicetti, Andrea, John Gastil, Janette Hartz-Karp, and Lyn Carson. 2012. "Collective Identity and Voice at the Australian Citizens' Parliament." *Journal of Public Deliberation* 8 (1): Article 5: 1–27.

Flanagan, Mary, Daniel C. Howe, and Helen Nissenbaum. 2008. "Embodying Values in Technology: Theory and Practice." In *Information Technology and Moral Philosophy*, edited by Jeroen van den Hoven and John Weckert. Cambridge Studies in Philosophy and Public Policy. Cambridge University Press.

Föreningen Ursula. 2024. "Magica Moriens – Föreningen Ursula." Accessed January 15, 2025. https://www.foreningenursula.se/magica-moriens/.

Freedom House. 2024. "Why Are Youth Dissatisfied with Democracy?" September 14. https://freedomhouse.org/article/why-are-youth-dissatisfied-democracy.

Gade, Morten, Line Thorup, and Mikkel Sander, eds. 2003. *As Larp Grows Up: Theory and Methods in Larp*. Projektgruppen KP03.

Garcia, Antero. 2016. "Teacher as Dungeon Master: Connected Learning, Democratic Classrooms, and Rolling for Initiative." In *The Role-Playing Society: Essays on the Cultural Influence of RPGs*, edited by Andrew Byers and Francesco Crocco. McFarland.

Garvey, Dale M., and Sancha K. Garvey. 1967. "Simulation, Role-Playing, and Sociodrama in the Social Studies: With an Annotated Bibliography." *The Emporia State Research Studies* 16 (2): 5–34

Geneuss, Katrin. 2021. "The Use of the Role-Playing Technique STARS in Formal Didactic Contexts." *International Journal of Role-Playing* 11: 114–131.

Gerge, Tova. 2012. "Larp and Aesthetic Responsibility. When Just a Little Lovin' Became an Art Debate." In *States of Play: Nordic Larp around the World*, edited by Juhana Pettersson. Pohjoismaisen roolipelaamisen seura.

Giacomucci, Scott, Heloisa Junqueira Fleury, and Deniz Altınay. 2025. *Psychodrama in Education. Creativity and Experiential Teaching around the World.* Springer.

Giæver, Ole Peder. 2012. "LARPs Can Change the World." *Imagonem*, March 27. https://imagonem.org/2012/03/27/larps-can-change-the-world/.

Gordon, Eric, Jason Haas, and Becky Michelson. 2017. "Civic Creativity: Role-Playing Games in Deliberative Process." *International Journal of Communication* 11 (0): 19.

Granhagen, Maria. 1997. "FN-rollspel." *StrapatS*. Issue 46, June. https://alexandria.dk/sv/magazines?issue=735

Gräslund, Susanne. 2010. "Europa. Intimate Refugee Role Reversal." In *Nordic Larp*, edited by Jaakko Stenros and Markus Montola. Fëa Livia.

Grasmo, Hanne. 1998. *Levande rollespill LAIV*. Gyldendal.

Grasmo, Hanne, Tanja Sihvonen, and Jaakko Stenros. In press. "(Ir)resistible Bodies. Larp as Sociocultural Technology for Building Queer Heterotopias." Forthcoming in *Playing Politics in Digital Spaces: Life After Social Media,* edited by Sybille Lammes, Frans-Willem Korsten, Bram Ieven, Alex Gekker, Frank Chouraqui, Saniye Ince, Eleni Maragkou, and Sara Polak. Routledge.

Grönlund, Kimmo, Kaisa Herne, and Maija Setälä. 2015. "Does Enclave Deliberation Polarize Opinions?" *Political Behavior* 37 (4): 995–1020. https://doi.org/10.1007/s11109-015-9304-x.

Groth, Anna Emilie, Hanne "Hank" Grasmo, and Tor Kjetil Edland. 2021. *Just a Little Lovin': The Larp Script*. Drøbak. https://researchportal.tuni.fi/en/publications/just-a-little-lovin-the-larp-script.

Gygax, Gary, and Dave Arneson. 1974. *Dungeons & Dragons*. TSR, Inc.

Haarman, Susan. 2022. "Dungeons & Dragons & Dewey: The Potential for Dramatic Rehearsal and Civic Outcomes in Tabletop Role-Playing Games." *Philosophical Studies in Education* 53 (2022): 56–70.

Haarman, Susan. 2023. "Dungeons & Dragons & Dewey: Toward a Ludic Pedagogy of Democratic Civic Life through the Philosophy of John Dewey and Tabletop Role-Playing Games." PhD diss., Loyola University of Chicago. https://ecommons.luc.edu/luc_diss/4025.

Hallwylska museet. 2014. "Lajvare intar Hallwylska museet." Last modified on September 25, 2023. https://hallwylskamuseet.se/press/lajvare-intar-hallwylska-museet/.

Halvorsen, Morten. 1997. "Jeg var en førstegangslaiber på Kybergenesis!" *Imagonem,* (15) June. https://www.scribd.com/document/52400602/Imagonem-15-web.

Harding, Tobias. 2012. "Ideellt Arbete i Kultursektorn En Förstudie För Myndigheten För Kulturanalys." *Förstudie. Myndigheten för Kulturanalys*, January 1. https://liu.diva-portal.org/smash/record.jsf?pid=diva2%3A563304&dswid=6293

Hartz-Karp, Janette, Patrick Anderson, John Gastil, and Andrea Felicetti. 2010. "The Australian Citizens' Parliament: Forging Shared Identity Through Public Deliberation." *Journal of Public Affairs* 10: 353–371.

Harviainen, J. Tuomas. 2007. "Live-Action, Role-Playing Environments as Information Systems: An Introduction." *Information Research* 12 (4): 12–4

Harviainen, J. Tuomas. 2016. "Political Larps, or Larps about Politics?" In *Larp Politics: Systems, Theory, and Gender in Action*, edited by Kaisa Kangas, Mika Loponen, and Jukka Särkijärvi. Ropecon ry. https://nordiclarp.org/w/images/6/6a/2016_Larp_Politics.pdf.

Harviainen, J. Tuomas, Rafael Bienia, Simon Brind, Michael Hitchens, Yaraslau I. Kot, Esther MacCallum-Stewart, David W. Simkins, Jaakko Stenros, and Ian Sturrock. 2018. "Live-Action Role-Playing Games." In *Role-Playing Game Studies: Transmedia Foundations*, edited by José Zagal and Sebastian Deterding. Routledge.

Hassel, Jostein. 1997. "Kybergenesis. En reise in i de mørke irrganger av menneskets sinn". *Imagonem* (15) June. https://www.scribd.com/document/52400602/Imagonem-15-web.

Helin, Elsa. 2016. "My Sister, Malala." In *#Feminism: A Nano-Game Anthology*, edited by Misha Bushyager, Lizzie Stark, and Anna Westerling. Pelgrane Press, Ltd.

Holkar, Mo. 2016. "Larp and Prejudice: Expressing, Erasing, Exploring, and the Fun Tax." In *Larp Realia: Analysis, Design, and Discussions of Nordic Larp*, edited by Jukka Särkijärvi, Mika Loponen, and Kaisa Kangas. Ropecon ry.

Hollander, Aaron T. 2021. "Blessed Are the Legend-Makers: Experimentation as Edification in Dungeons & Dragons." *Political Theology* 22 (4): 316–331. https://doi.org/10.1080/1462317X.2021.1890933.

Hopeametsä, Heidi. 2008. "24 Hours in a Bomb Shelter." In *Playground Worlds*, edited by Markus Montola and Jaakko Stenros. Ropecon.

Hugaas, Kjell Hedgard. 2019. "Investigating Types of Bleed in Larp: Emotional, Procedural, and Memetic." *Nordiclarp.org*, January 25. https://nordiclarp.org/2019/01/25/investigating-types-of-bleed-in-larp-emotional-procedural-and-memetic/.

Hugaas, Kjell Hedgard. 2024. "Bleed and Identity: A Conceptual Model of Bleed and How Bleed-Out from Role-Playing Games Can Affect a Player's Sense of Self." *International Journal of Role-Playing* 15: 9–35. https://doi.org/10.33063/ijrp.vi15.323.

Huizinga, Johan. 1955. *Homo ludens: A Study of Play Element in Culture*. Beacon Press.

ISAGA Conference. 2024. "Welcome to the International Simulation and Gaming Association's (ISAGA) Conference 2024!"https://isaga2024.com/.

Iuama, Tadeu Rodrigues. 2022. "Anthropophagic Reflexes in Brazilian Larp Scenes – Tadeu Rodrigues Iuama." Transformative Play Initiative. *YouTube*, December 3. https://www.youtube.com/watch?v=7xF_cdFk8dk.

Järvelä, Simo. 2012. "The Golden Rule of Larp." In *States of Play: Nordic Larp around the World*, edited by Juhana Pettersson. Pohjoismaisen roolipelaamisen seura. nordiclarp.org/w/images/a/a0/2012-States.of.play.pdf.

Jennstål, Julia, and Per-Ola Öberg. 2019. "The Ethics of Deliberative Activism: In Search of Reasonableness and Dialogic Responsiveness in Provocative Art Exhibitions." *Policy Studies* 40 (6): 648–661. https://doi.org/10.1080/01442872.2019.1599840.

Jennstål, Julia, Katrin Uba, and PerOla Öberg. 2021. "Deliberative Civic Culture: Assessing the Prevalence of Deliberative Conversational Norms." *Political Studies* 69 (2): 366–389.

Johansson, Karin, Raquel Robinson, Jon Back, Sarah Lynne Bowman, James Fey, Elena Márquez Segura, Annika Waern, and Katherine Isbister. 2024. "Why Larp? A Synthesis Article on Live Action Roleplay in Relation to HCI Research and Practice." *ACM Transactions in Computer-Human Interactions* 31 (5): 64:1–64:35. https://doi.org/10.1145/3689045.

Jonnmyren, Olof, and Hans Lindberg. 1997. "Manlig Monopolisering i Uppluckring – Röster Om Könsroller Och Manligt Monopoli Levande Rollspel." *Fëa Livia* (16).

Josefsson, Erika. 2019. "Kulturministern: Alla borde prova på politik." *Göteborgs-Posten*, February 4. https://www.gp.se/kulturministern-alla-borde-prova-pa-politik.165c8e1d-8481-4e2c-b5f5-55703a19e9e6.

Kaljonen, J. P., and Johanna Raekallio. 2012. "Dublin2: the EU's Asylum Policy in Miniature." In *States of Play: Nordic Larp around the World*, edited by Juhana Pettersson. Pohjoismaisen roolipelaamisen seura. nordiclarp.org/w/images/a/a0/2012-States.of.play.pdf.

Kangas, Kaisa. 2015. "Processing Political Larps – Framing Larp Experiences with Strong Agendas." In *The Knudepunkt 2015 Companion Book*, edited by Charles Bo Nielsen and Claus Raasted. Rollespilsakademiet.

Kangas, Kaisa. 2017. "Playing the Stories of Others." In *Once Upon a Nordic Larp… Twenty Years of Playing Stories*, edited by Martine Svanevik, Linn Carin Andreassen, Simon Brind, Elin Nilsen, and Grethe Sofie Bulterud Strand. Knutepunkt.

Kangas, Kaisa, Mika Loponen, and Jukka Särkijärvi, eds. 2016. *Larp Politics: Systems, Theory, and Gender in Action*. Ropecon ry. https://nordiclarp.org/w/images/6/6a/2016_Larp_Politics.pdf

Kapitany, Rohan, Tomas Hampejs, and Thalia R. Goldstein. 2022. "Pretensive Shared Reality: From Childhood Pretense to Adult Imaginative Play." *Frontiers in Psychology* 13 (28 February 2022): 774085. https://doi.org/10.3389/fpsyg.2022.774085.

Kemper, Jonaya. 2017. "The Battle of Primrose Park: Playing for Emancipatory Bleed in Fortune & Felicity." *Nordiclarp.org*, June 21. https://nordiclarp.org/2017/06/21/the-battle-of-primrose-park-playing-for-emancipatory-bleed-in-fortune-felicity/.

Kemper, Jonaya. 2018. "More Than a Seat at the Feasting Table." In *Shuffling the Deck: The Knutpunkt 2018 Color Printed Companion*, edited by Annika Waern and Johannes Axner. ETC Press.

Kemper, Jonaya. 2020. "Wyrding the Self." In *What Do We Do When We Play?* edited by Eleanor Saitta, Johanna Koljonen, and Jukka Särkijärvi. Solmukohta.

Kemper, Jonaya, Mo Holkar, Yeonsoo Julian Kim, Aina Skjønsfjell Lakou, Kat Jones, and Ross Cheung. 2018. "Larpers of Color Panel – Unlocking the Spectrum | Knutpunkt 2018." *Nordic Larp. YouTube*, March 20. https://www.youtube.com/watch?v=3RXOAPhiOGc.

Kemper, Jonaya, Eleanor Saitta, and Johanna Koljonen. 2020. "Steering for Survival." In *What Do We Do When We Play?*, edited by Eleanor Saitta, Jukka Särkijärvi, and Johanna Koljonen. Solmukohta.

Kessock, Shoshana. 2014. "Cultural Appropriation and Larp." In *The Cutting Edge of Nordic Larp*, edited by Jon Back. Knutpunkt.

Klabbers, Jan H. G. 1999. "Three Easy Pieces: A Taxonomy on Gaming." In *The International Simulation & Gaming Research Yearbook Volume 7: Simulations and Games for Strategy and Policy Planning*, edited by Danny Saunders and Jackie Severn. Kogan Page.

Klanac, Emelie, and Sally Ståh. 2016. "The Circle of Life." *Stockholm Scenario Festival*. https://scenariofestival.se/archive/scenarios-2016/the-circle-of-life/.

Klenell, Johannes. 2019. "Johannes Klenell: Vi har en ny kulturminister – och hon är skogsalv." *Arbetaren*, January 21. https://arbetet.se/2019/01/21/vi-har-en-ny-kulturminister-och-hon-ar-skogsalv/.

Knobloch, Katherine R., and John Gastil. 2015. "Civic (Re) Socialisation: The Educative Effects of Deliberative Participation." *Politics* 35 (2): 183–200.

Koljonen, Johanna. 2007. "Eye-Witness to the Illusion: An Essay on the Impossibility of 360° Role-Playing." In *Lifelike*, edited by Jesper Donnis, Morten Gade, and Line Thorup. Projektgruppen KP07.

Koljonen, Johanna. 2008. "The Dragon Was the Least of It: Dragonbane and LARP as Ephemera and Ruin." In *Playground Worlds: Creating and Evaluating Experiences of Role-Playing Games*, edited by Markus Montola and Jaakko Stenros. Ropecon ry.

Koljonen, Johanna. 2011. "On Games: Painting Life with Rules – Johanna Koljonen." *Nordic Larp Talks. YouTube*, March 11. https://www.youtube.com/watch?v=UOVf06NCBGQ.

Koljonen, Johanna. 2019. "An Introduction to Bespoke Design." In *Larp Design: Creating Role-Play Experiences*, edited by Johanna Koljonen, Jaakko Stenros, Anne Serup Grove, Aina D. Skønsfjell, and Elin Nilsen. Landsforeningen Bifrost.

Koljonen, Johanna. 2020. "Larp Safety Design Fundamentals." *JARPS: Japanese Journal of Analog Role-Playing Game Studies* 1: *Emotional and Psychological Safety in TRPGs and Larp* (September 21): 3e–19e. https://doi.org/10.14989/jarps_1_03e.

Koljonen, Johanna, Jaakko Stenros, Anne Serup Grove, Aina D. Skjønsfjell, and Elin Nilsen, eds. 2019. *Larp Design: Creating Role-Play Experiences*. Landsforeningen Bifrost.

Korhonen, Maija. 2015. *Ulkoavaruuden muukalaiset ja enemmistön tyrannia.* Otavan opisto. https://roolipelikirjasto.fi/book/16.

Kranzberg, Melvin. 1986. "Technology and History: 'Kranzberg's Laws.'" *Technology and Culture* 27 (3): 544–560. https://doi.org/10.2307/3105385.

Kulturföreningen Fogelstad. 2024. "Kvinnliga Medborgarskolan." https://fogelstad.org/kvinnliga-medborgarskolan/.

Lajvbyrån. 2025. "Välkommen till Lajvbyrån." https://lajvbyran.se/.

Lajvhistoria. n.d. "Lajvhistoria: Ockulta Medborgarbyrån (2016)." Lajvhistoria. se. Accessed January 15, 2025. https://lajvhistoria.se/lajv/Ockulta_Medborgarbyran.466.

LajvVerkstaden. 2025a. "Franska Revolutionen." Accessed January 15, 2025. https://lajvverkstaden.se/produkt/franska-revolutionen/.

LajvVerkstaden. 2025b. "Lajv som Kultur." https://lajvverkstaden.se/.

Lampo, Marjukka. 2015. "Ecological Approach to the Performance of Larping." *International Journal of Role-Playing* 5: 35–46.

Laycock, Joseph P. 2015. *Dangerous Games: What the Moral Panic over Role-Playing Games Says about Play, Religion, and Imagined Worlds.* University of California Press.

Lehto, Tanja. 2016. "Where Can Political Larp Go?" In *Larp Politics: Systems, Theory, and Gender in Action*, edited by Kaisa Kangas, Mika Loponen, and Jukka Särkijärvi. Ropecon ry.

Leonard, Diana J., Jovo Janjetovic, and Maximilian Usman. 2021. "Playing to Experience Marginalization: Benefits and Drawbacks of "Dark Tourism" in Larp." *International Journal of Role-Playing* (11): 25–47. https://doi.org/10.33063/ijrp.vi11.282.

Levin, Hilda. 2023. "Bridging Historical and Present-Day Queer Community through Embodied Role-playing." *International Journal of Role-Playing* 14: 82–90.

Levine, Peter. 2018. "Deliberation or Simulated Deliberation?" *Democracy and Education* 26 (1). https://democracyeducationjournal.org/home/vol26/iss1/7.

Lo, Jane C. 2015. "Learning to Participate through Role-Play: Understanding Political Simulations in the High School Government Course." PhD diss., University of Washington. https://hdl.handle.net/1773/33766.

Losilla, Sergio. 2024. "Rules, Trust, and Care: the Nordic Larper's Risk Management Toolkit." In *Liminal Encounters: Evolving Discourse in Nordic and Nordic Inspired Larp*, edited by Kaisa Kangas, Jonne Arjoranta, and Ruska Kevätkoski. Ropecon ry.

Masek, Leland, and Jaakko Stenros. 2021. "The Meaning of Playfulness: A Review of the Contemporary Definitions of the Concept across Disciplines." *Eludamos* 12 (1): 13–37.

McCallum-Stewart, Esther. 2016 "Role-Play." In *Debugging Game History: A Critical Lexicon*, edited by Henry Lowood and Raiford Guins. The MIT Press.

McDiarmid, Rob. 2015. "Writing Game Economies for Larp." In *The Wyrd Companion Book 2015*, edited by Sarah Lynne Bowman. Wyrd Con.

Montola, Markus. 2010. "The Positive Negative Experience in Extreme Role-playing." In *Proceedings of DiGRA Nordic 2010: Experiencing Games: Games, Play, and Players.* Stockholm, Sweden, August 16, 2010. https://dl.digra.org/index.php/dl/article/view/500.

Montola, Markus, Jaakko Stenros, and Annika Waern. 2009. *Pervasive Games: Theory and Design.* Morgan Kaufmann.

Moreno, Jonathan D. 2014. *Impromptu Man: J.L. Moreno and the Origins of Psychodrama, Encounter Culture, and the Social Network.* Bellevue Literary Press.

Müller, Maya. 2011. "From Subculture to Mainstream." In *Think Larp: Academic Writings from KP2011,* edited by Thomas Duus Henriksen, Christian Bierlich, Kasper Friis Hansen, and Valdemar Kølle. Rollespilsakademiet.

Munthe-Kaas, Peter. 2010. "System Danmarc. Political Action Larp". In *Nordic Larp,* edited by Jaakko Stenros and Markus Montola. Fëa Livia.

Nakamura, Lisa. 1995. "Race in/for Cyberspace: Identity Tourism and Racial Passing on the Internet." *Works and Days* 13 (1–2): 181–193.

National Museum of American Diplomacy. n.d. "Diplomacy Simulations." Accessed January 15, 2025. https://diplomacy.state.gov/education/diplomacy-simulations/.

Nelson, Jonas. 1996a. "Jonas Nelson Svarar." *StrapatS* (40) November. https://alexandria.dk/sv/magazines?issue=743

Nelson, Jonas. 1996b. "Örnstedt, Sjöstedt, Hellqvist och Jag." *StrapatS* (35) May. https://alexandria.dk/sv/magazines?issue=749

Nelson, Jonas. 1997. "Vilka är Egentligen de Övergivna. Sverox (1) October.

Nobel Prize Museum. 2017. *Rollspel i genetik & etik.* Nobelmuseet. https://www.nobelprize.org/uploads/sites/2/2025/05/nobelmuseum-skolmaterial-rollspel-genetik-lararhandledning.pdf.

NRK. 1997. *Dagsrevyen.* March 25, 1997. https://tv.nrk.no/serie/dagsrevyen/sesong/199703/episode/FAKN20008497#t=1316s.

Örnstedt, Didi and Björn Sjöstedt. 1997. *De övergivnas armé.* Norstedts.

Østerskov Efterskole. n.d. "Et år på Østerskov." Accessed January 16, 2025. https://osterskov.dk/.

Pesce, Nicole Lyn. 2022. "Dungeons & Dragons is on a Roll: D&D Direct Went Viral, and Hasbro Bought D&D Beyond for Almost $150M." *MarketWatch,* April 21. https://www.marketwatch.com/story/dungeons-dragons-is-on-such-a-roll-hasbro-bought-d-d-beyond-for-almost-150-million-in-cash-11649877741.

Peterson, Jon. 2012. *Playing at the World. A History of Simulating Wars, People and Fantastic Adventures from Chess to Role-Playing Games.* Unreason Press.

Peterson, Jon. 2022. *The Elusive Shift. How Role-Playing Games Forged Their Identity.* The MIT Press.

Pettersson, Juhana, ed. 2014. *Life under Occupation: A Documentation Book for the Larp Halat Hisar.* Pohjoismaisen roolipelaamisen seura.

Pettersson, Juhana. 2021a. "Baltic Warriors: Helsinki." In *Engines of Desire: Essays on Larp as the Art of Experience,* edited by Juhana Pettersson. Pohjoismaisen roolipelaamisen seura.

Pettersson, Juhana. 2021b. "Saving the Baltic Sea with Larp." In *Engines of Desire: Essays on Larp as the Art of Experience,* edited by Juhana Pettersson. Pohjoismaisen roolipelaamisen seura.

Piven, Frances Fox, and Richard A. Cloward. 2005. "Rule Making, Rule Breaking, and Power." In *The Handbook of Political Sociology: States, Civil Societies, and Globalization*, edited by Thomas Janoski, Robert R. Alford, Alexander M. Hicks, and Mildred A. Schwartz. Cambridge University Press.

Plan International and FN förbundet. n.d. "Klimatrollspel." https://plansverige. org/app/uploads/2017/07/klimatrollspel.pdf.

Pohjola, Mike. 2004. "Autonomous Identities: Immersion as a Tool for Exploring, Empowering, and Emancipating Identities." In *Beyond Role and Play*, edited by Markus Montola and Jaakko Stenros. Ropecon ry.

Pohjola, Mike. 2016. "Monsters as Metaphors." *Nordic Larp Talks. YouTube*, September 18. https://www.youtube.com/watch?v=QNblu2Ij3fE.

Pöllänen, Sonja, and Jonne Arjoranta. 2021. "'Whose Were Those Feelings?' Affect and Likenessing in Halat Hisar Live Action Role-Playing Game." *International Journal of Cultural Studies* 24 (6): 899–916.

Pothong, Kruakae, Larissa Pschetz, Ruth Catlow, and Sarah Meiklejohn. 2021. "Problematising Transparency Through LARP And Deliberation." In *Proceedings of the 2021 ACM Designing Interactive Systems Conference*, 1682–1694. https://doi.org/10.1145/3461778.3462120.

Rantanen, Teemu. 2016. "Larp as a Form of Political Action – Some Insights from Theories of Political Science." In *Larp Politics: Systems, Theory, and Gender in Action*, edited by Kaisa Kangas, Mika Loponen, and Jukka Särkijärvi. Ropecon ry.

Rislund, Staffan. 1997. "Tillbaka till Forntiden?" *Fëa Livia* (16).

Roberts, Catherine and Philip R. Stone. 2014. "Dark Tourism and Dark Heritage: Emergent Themes, Issues and Consequences." In *Displaced Heritage: Responses to Disaster, Trauma, and Loss*, edited by Ian Convery, Gerard Corsane, and Peter Davis. Boydell & Brewer.

Rombot, Olifia, Titin Sunaryati, and Dewi Ariani. 2018. "Increasing Democratic Attitude of Students through Role Play Method in Civics Learning." In *Proceedings of the 6th International Conference on Information and Education Technology*, 97–101. https://doi.org/10.1145/3178158.3178174.

Rumore, Danya, Todd Schenk, and Lawrence Susskind. 2016. "Role-Play Simulations for Climate Change Adaptation Education and Engagement." *Nature Climate Change* 6 (8): 745–750. https://doi.org/10.1038/nclimate3084.

Saitta, Eleanor, Marie Holm-Andersen, and Jon Back, eds. 2014. *The Foundation Stone of Nordic Larp*. Knutpunkt. https://nordiclarp.org/w/ images/8/80/2014_The_Foundation_Stone_of_Nordic_Larp.pdf

Sanders, Lynn. 1997. "Against Deliberation." *Political Theory* 25 (3): 347–376. https://doi.org/10.1177/0090591797025003002.

Schirch, Lisa. 2005. *The Little Book of Strategic Peacebuilding: A Vision and Framework for Peace With Justice.v* Good Books.

Seter, Magnus. 2024. *Outside the Box. How Sweden Conquered the World of Role-Playing Games*. Fandrake.

Sharing Sweden. 2025. "Welcome to Electionville – The Democracy Game." https://sharingsweden.se/toolkits/electionville.

Standberg, Margarethe. 2011. 'Bred markering' *Blikk*. November 30. https://www. blikk.no/bred-markering/178636

Stenros, Jaakko. 2014. "What Does 'Nordic Larp' Mean?" In *The Cutting Edge of Nordic Larp*, edited by Jon Back. Knutpunkt.

Stenros, Jaakko. 2017. "The Game Definition Game: A Review." *Games and Culture* 12 (6) 499-520.

Stenros, Jaakko, and Markus Montola, eds. 2010a. *Nordic Larp*. Fëa Livia.

Stenros, Jaakko, and Markus Montola. 2010b. "The Paradox of Nordic Larp Culture." In *Nordic Larp*, edited by Jaakko Stenros and Markus Montola. Fëa Livia.

Stenros, Jaakko, and Markus Montola. 2011 "The Making of Nordic Larp: Documenting a Tradition of Ephemeral Co-Creative Play." In *Proceedings of Think Design Play, DiGRA 2011 Conference*. DiGRA Digital Library.

Stenros, Jaakko, and Markus Montola, eds. 2017. *College of Wizardry: The Magic of Participation in Harry Potter Larps*. Pohjoismaisen roolipelaamisen seura.

Stenros, Jaakko, Martin Eckhoff Andresen, and Martin Nielsen. 2016. "The Mixing Desk of Larp: History and Current State of a Design Theory." *Analog Game Studies* 3 (6).

Stevens, Rachel. 2015. "Role-Play and Student Engagement: Reflections from the Classroom." *Teaching in Higher Education* 20 (5): 481–492. https://doi.org/10.1080/13562517.2015.1020778.

Strand, Annica, Frida Gamero, and Sofia Stenler. 2015. "Last Will – Make Us Your Slaves, but Feed Us." *Nordiclarp.org*, February 2. https://nordiclarp.org/2015/02/27/last-will-make-us-your-slaves-but-feed-us/.

Suffragette! An International Larp about the Fight for the Vote in 1912. n.d. "Home." Accessed January 15, 2025. https://suffragettelarp.wordpress.com/.

Sutton-Smith, Brian. 1997. *The Ambiguity of Play*. Harvard University Press.

Svenska institutet. 2025. "Electionville firar två år!" https://si.se/electionville-firar-tva-ar/.

Sveriges Radio, 2012. 'P1 uppmärksammar 30 år av aids i Sverige' Press release dated March 30. https://mb.cision.com/Main/123/9241872/181.pdf

The New York Times. 1947. "Model U.N. Sessions Held at Swarthmore." *The New York Times*, April 6, 54.

Toft, Ida, and Sabine Harrer. 2020. "Design Bleed: A Standpoint Methodology for Game Design." In *Proceedings of DiGRA 2020 Conference: Play Everywhere*. https://dl.digra.org/index.php/dl/article/view/1278.

Torner, Evan. 2013. "Transparency and Safety in Role-Playing Games." In *The Wyrd Con Companion Book 2013*, edited by Sarah Lynne Bowman and Aaron Vanek. Wyrd Con.

Torner, Evan. 2019. "Designing a Character Description." In *Larp Design: Creating Role-Play Experiences*, edited by Johanna Koljonen, Jaakko Stenros, Anne Serup Grove, Aina Skjønsfjell, and Elin Nilsen. Landsforeningen Bifrost.

Torner, Evan. 2024. "RPG Theorizing by Designers and Players." In *The Routledge Handbook of Role-playing Game Studies*, edited by José P. Zagal and Sebastian Deterding. Routledge.

Townser, Henry Piers, and J Li. 2019. "Describing What Actually Happens in a Larp." In *Larp Design: Creating Role-Play Experiences*, edited by Johanna Koljonen, Jaakko Stenros, Anne Serup Grove, Aina Skjønsfjell, and Elin Nilsen. Landsforeningen Bifrost.

Trammell, Aaron. 2023. *The Privilege of Play. A History of Hobby Games, Race, and Geek Culture*. New York University Press.

Turkington, Moyra. 2016. "Rehearsing Difference." In *Larp Politics: Systems, Theory, and Gender in Action*, edited by Kaisa Kangas, Mika Loponen, and Jukka Särkijärvi. Ropecon.

UNA-UK. 2023. "Model UN Portal." Accessed January 16, 2025. https://una.org.uk/get-involved/learn-and-teach/model-un-portal.

United Nations. n.d. "Model United Nations." United Nations. Accessed January 15, 2025. https://www.un.org/en/mun.

Vår skyldighet: Ett lajv om fredsmötet i Varberg 1915. n.d. "Hem." Accessed 22 November 2024. https://varskyldighet.wordpress.com/.

Waern, Annika, Markus Montola, and Jaakko Stenros. 2009. "The Three-Sixty Illusion: Designing for Immersion in Pervasive Games." *Proceedings of CHI 2009*, Boston, USA.

Wei, Eva, and Rosalind Göthberg. 2015. "Beyond the Barricades." *Stockholm Scenario Festival*. https://scenariofestival.se/archive/scenarios-2015/beyond-the-barricades/.

Weidenfeld, Matthew C., and Kenneth E. Fernandez. 2017. "Does Reacting to the Past Increase Student Engagement? An Empirical Evaluation of the Use of Historical Simulations in Teaching Political Theory." *Journal of Political Science Education* 13 (1): 46–61. https://doi.org/10.1080/15512169.2016.1175948.

Westborg, Josefin. 2023. "The Educational Role-Playing Game Design Matrix: Mapping Design Components onto Types of Education." *International Journal of Role-Playing* 13: 18–30.

Westborg, Josefin, and Sarah Lynne Bowman. In press. "GM Screen: The Didactic Potential of RPGs." German: "Das didaktische Potential von Rollenspielen." In *#eduRPG. Rollenspiel als Methode der Bildung*, edited by Frank J. Robertz and Kathrin Fischer. SystemMatters Publ. Academia.edu. https://www.academia.edu/109659917/GM_Screen_The_Didactic_Potential_of_RPGs.

Whittington, Richard. 2006. "Completing the Practice Turn in Strategy Research." *Organization Studies* 27 (5): 613–634. https://doi.org/10.1177/0170840606064101.

Wisemee. n.d. "The History of the First MUN." https://www.wisemee.com/history-of-the-first-mun/.

Worl, Jessica. 2022. "The Political Classroom in Practice: Roleplaying Deliberations in a Political Ecology Course." *Deliberative Citizenship Initiative*, July 14. https://deliberativecitizenship.org/blogposts/the-political-classroom-in-practice-roleplaying-deliberations-in-a-political-ecology-course/.

Wright, Jennifer Cole, Daniel E. Weissglass, and Vanessa Casey. 2020. "Imaginative Role-Playing as a Medium for Moral Development: Dungeons & Dragons Provides Moral Training." *Journal of Humanistic Psychology* 60 (1): 99–129. https://doi.org/10.1177/0022167816686263.

Young, Iris Marion. 2022. *Inclusion and Democracy*. Oxford University Press.

Zagal, José P., and Sebastian Deterding. 2024. "Definitions of 'Role-Playing Games.'" In *The Routledge Handbook of Role-Playing Game Studies*, edited by José P. Zagal and Sebastian Deterding. Routledge.

CHAPTER 11

Mapping the Design Terrain between Live Action Role-Playing Games and Deliberative Events for Democratic Skill Development

Sarah Lynne Bowman, PerOla Öberg,
Karin Johansson and Annika Waern

INTRODUCTION

Societies across the world are facing a crisis in democracy (Arato and Cohen 2022). The filtering out of alternative viewpoints by selective social media algorithms, breakdowns in civil discourse in online spaces, and rapid spread of misinformation have led to extreme polarization and a mistrust of the democratic process. Such polarization amplifies perceived differences between people (McCoy, Rahman, and Somer 2018; McCoy and Somer 2021), which has led to a troubling rise in violent militantism in many countries. These outcomes undermine the process of democracy,

DOI: 10.1201/9781003641353-15

which we define as equal participation in enlightening collective will-formation informing decision-making based on equal participation among those concerned (Warren 2017). The major challenge, given such an understanding of democracy, is the lack of functioning communication among society members who have different perceptions of reality and perceive themselves as having different interests. Thus, society members find it difficult, if not impossible, to discuss and evaluate policy options in order to find solutions to political problems that could be at least provisionally accepted by many in their community.

The growing literature on the practices surrounding various deliberative events is one area of research that takes up this challenge: society members with conflicting preferences meet to discuss sensitive policy issues in town meetings, mini-publics, deliberative polls, or similar events. These events are almost exclusively rooted in deliberative democracy, a normative theory that holds that society members should engage in "mutual communication that involves weighing and reflecting on preferences, values, and interests regarding matters of common concern" (Bächtiger et al. 2018, 2). A large body of literature evaluating deliberative events has shown that, under the right conditions, people are willing to deliberate, which can reduce affective and issue polarization and help participants form consistent values and reflected preferences (Dryzek et al. 2019). At the same time, when and under what conditions this is the case is still being explored, as deliberation can take many forms depending on the context and the participants involved. Advocates for deliberative democracy also acknowledge that much remains to be done in refining the findings of the field (Dryzek et al. 2019, 1146).

In this paper, we explore the possibilities for the development of knowledge about deliberative skills and how they can be advanced by exploring possible cross-fertilization between two areas of research that have not yet met to the extent we think is desirable, namely research on deliberative events and live action role-playing (larp).

Unlike most deliberative events, larp is considered fictional and is played while taking the perspective of a fictional person who may have political beliefs different from one's own. larps are physically enacted "co-creative experiences in which participants immerse into fictional characters and realities for a bounded period of time and improvise through spontaneous, emergent playfulness" (Bowman 2022a). While pretend play and storytelling are essential aspects of human culture, larp emerged from specific subcultural lineages that have led to unique design theories and practices (Johansson et al. in press), which distinguish them from e.g., designs based on democratic theory such as deliberative democracy (Rantanen 2016). Still, larps are often also political. In the avant-garde experimental movement Nordic larp and adjacent communities, such events are often organized as a tool to raise awareness about political issues (see e.g., Kangas, Loponen, and Särkijärvi 2016), whether current or historical, or simulate a political situation, real or imaginary. Such larps are considered *political larps* (Johansson et al. in press).

The purpose of this study is to identify areas in which practices in deliberative events and larps overlap as spaces for practicing skills relevant to democracy, as well as areas in which they differ, investigating how the two fields might enhance one another. Our goal is to map the design terrain between both in an effort to compare, contrast, and possibly combine insights. Tension points are also of interest, e.g., how larps often emphasize emotional escalation and intensified conflicts, whereas deliberation often focuses on de-escalation, although both aim to avoid psychological overwhelm that might cause participants to become unable to continue engaging or for the activity to break down (see e.g., Brown 2014).

This work is motivated by recent research on larps and deliberative events demonstrating their potential for cultivating prosocial skills and raising awareness on political issues, as explored later in this paper. While collaborative embodied storytelling and deliberative discussion are human activities that transcend culture, the communities surrounding larp and deliberative events have developed theory, practice, and empirical research that suggest a potentially fruitful overlap and design space between them. Additionally, while we are ultimately interested in investigating whether the design of deliberative larps might lead to behavioral change and active participation in political activities in daily life (Waern and Munthe-Kaas 2013), such questions are beyond the scope of the current study and reserved for later experimental work.[1]

The paper is organized as follows. First, we provide brief descriptions of deliberative events and larps, as well as introductions to relevant theories, to help readers understand these research fields. In this section, we demonstrate that these are two distinct and largely unrelated fields. Next, we compare and contrast the key findings on democratic skill development identified by each field of research. We find that the two fields have provided overlapping lessons on building deliberative skills from different perspectives and with diverse motivations. This motivates us to establish potential learning objectives and desired outcomes of *deliberative larps*, then discuss design considerations when combining the two. In the same section, we discuss the challenges that these considerations may pose. Finally, based on this discussion, we conclude with suggestions for establishing a new research agenda.

DELIBERATIVE EVENTS AND LARP

Deliberative Events: Normative Roots, Theory, and Live Events

Deliberative events are rooted in a normative democratic theory emphasizing that a healthy democracy needs spaces conducive to society members' reflective political expressions, as opposed to unreflective and impulsive ones (Fishkin 2018). Alarmingly, current democracy has been diagnosed to suffer from a deficiency of such spaces, producing an unhealthy climate where reflective opinions are either nonexistent or rare, while biased political thinking (e.g., Taber and Lodge 2006), in combination with an inability or unwillingness to listen to opinions of others, characterizes public opinion formation and democratic life. At the same time, a growing line of deliberative research experimenting with innovations beyond classic democratic institutions has demonstrated that society members *can* make reflective political judgments and engage in an exchange of reason-giving if conditions are right (Dryzek et al. 2019).

Deliberative theory is based on the constructivist premise that interests and preferences regarding political issues are not "objective" or predetermined, but rather formed through social interaction. Therefore, merely aggregating people's interests in voting procedures will not necessarily produce decisions that everyone can accept as being in their best interests (Habermas 1994). A democratically legitimate procedure must also ensure reasoned and equal deliberation aimed at mutual understanding and, if possible, consensus (Habermas 1998). The core idea is that, when citizens disagree morally, they should reason together to reach mutually acceptable decisions (Gutmann and Thompson 1996, 1). This emphasis on communicative action as opposed to strategic action (Habermas 1984) has been described as "talk-centric" compared to the "vote-centric" aggregative model (Chambers 2003).

In his "two-track model," Jürgen Habermas argued that deliberation should precede formal decision-making and occur primarily through informal, diffuse collective communication in the public sphere (Habermas 1994). Although the core idea is simple, the meaning and implications are complex (Gutmann and Thompson 1996, 1). The challenge lies in making this work in contexts of difference and disagreement (Chambers 2003). In other words, it is about dealing with the fact that moral conflict in politics is unavoidable and determining how to address it (Gutmann and Thompson 1996).

Deliberative theory has been the subject of extensive debate (Mutz 2008). One of the most prominent and constructive critics has been Iris Marion Young. She has argued that overly demanding deliberative practices can exclude marginalized voices in particular and reinforce or create new unequal power relations (Young 2002). Her critique has significantly impacted how deliberative theory has evolved over the years. For example, its original emphasis on "rational" reason-giving has evolved to accept many kinds of communication, so long as they still feature a claim and justification in communication/dialogue with an audience. This means that storytelling, emotional expression, self-interests, and certain forms of rhetoric are accepted as normatively legitimate in deliberation. Furthermore, the previous aim for consensus has shifted to the notion that there is "no deliberation without contestations"; in other words, if everyone agrees, deliberation is not occurring. Similarly, the aim to produce consensus has shifted to developing a better understanding of one's own and others' values, or perhaps a meta-consensus, i.e., a common understanding of the problem and what arguments that are relevant, which can clarify and strengthen contesting values (Niemeyer and Dryzek 2007; Niemeyer et al. 2024). This development has given rise to a new type of criticism, which claims that the concept of deliberation has become so diluted that it is no longer useful (Scudder and White 2023). While we acknowledge the broader contemporary understanding of deliberative theory, we maintain that "not all talk is deliberation" (Chambers 2012, 58). Additionally, we acknowledge that deliberation cannot solve all conflicts (cf. Mouffe 1999) and that other forms of political participation, such as protesting, also fulfill important democratic functions under certain conditions (Young 2001; Scudder and White 2023). However, these are not in focus here.

Thus, the emphasis in deliberation is on providing spaces for people to refine their thinking, listen to the perspectives of others, and be prepared to change their opinions if other arguments are persuasive. Importantly, not all human behavior related to political participation can be understood as reason-giving communicated to a relevant audience. Thus, deliberation is a specific practice and skill set that differs from other forms of engagement, e.g., forms of activism that assert one position as superior to others. The democratic deliberation is argued by John Dryzek (2012) to be *authentic* (no coercion or manipulation in reason-giving), *inclusive* (usually including "those affected"), and *consequential* (it should make a difference for collective decision-making). Not all deliberation is democratic, e.g., if it excludes people who are affected (Chambers 2012; Öberg 2022). Furthermore, deliberation is not the same thing as debate (Beauvais 2020), as it intends to foster greater understanding rather than winning an argument. Thus, deliberation is not a debate or negotiation that one should try winning, but an exchange of reasons and considerations, with options weighed against each other, aiming to find common ground, if not always consensus.

The main components of democratic deliberation, which are equal and non-hierarchical, are thus:

1. **Opinion stating, justifying, and explaining claims:** A claim refers to one's position on the issue, i.e., what they want to happen or believe to be true based on their own experience and gathered evidence. Such explanations should be honest and authentic rather than strategic, manipulative, or coercive.

2. **Listening, trying to understand,** not intentionally misinterpreting.

3. **Openness to change or adjusting one's claim,** but only if convinced by others' considerations.

Deliberative events, for example Citizen Assemblies and *mini-publics*, are mainly organized as traditional political conversations between participants over a specific political theme advertised in the invitation. They range from around 50 to 500 invited people aiming to roughly mirror the community, hence aiming to be a "mini-public." These events take place face to face and/or online. Their lengths vary from half a day, a weekend, or several weekends during a year. While some events have limited sessions, permanent assemblies do exist, with rotating participation. These events feature fact briefings that form the basis of the discussion and about which all participants should agree to accept, e.g., balanced booklets that feature multiple perspectives on an issue and introductory issue videos. They may also have politicians, experts and/or advocacy group presentations that all participants attend (Fishkin et al. 2021; Curato et al. 2021; Grönlund and Setälä 2024).

While discussions sometimes happen in the larger group plenum, the deliberations are often facilitated in smaller subgroups (10–15). Deliberation can be over one issue, e.g., a road construction, or several, e.g., the most contested topics in the current presidential election. These topics may be connected to democratic institutions, e.g., when reflecting on citizen's initiatives or preparing for a referendum, or unconnected, e.g., "Who should pay for climate change?" or "What are our responsibilities for future generations?" Ideally, deliberation is consequential, in that the outcome of the event has an impact on the larger political world. Therefore, sometimes these events aim to make a common statement or policy proposal to be published or sent to parliaments for consideration.

larp: Transformative and Political

Live action role-playing can be studied from many different aspects. Since this paper focuses on their potential to contribute to deliberative skill development, we will focus on larp's ability to provide players with a *transformational container* (Baird and Bowman 2022), in which cognitive, affective, and behavioral skills can be trained through play (Bowman 2014). *Bleed* theory is helpful in understanding the psychological mechanisms underpinning such change. For example, in *procedural bleed*, certain actions spillover from the character's behavior to the player's and vice versa (Hugaas 2019, 2024), e.g., the embodied practice of reason-giving and listening.

Alternatively, *memetic bleed* (Hugaas 2019, 2024), formative concepts and ideologies spillover to a player's everyday consciousness from the larp experience and vice versa, e.g., the political perspective of one's character influencing the player's beliefs. Unlike the popular notion on social media (Milner 2016), memes here refer to entire systems of thought that influence our ideological standpoints, e.g., the foundational ideologies of different political affiliations. Political standpoints can affect design (Toft and Harrer 2020) in terms of the topics chosen for the larp and the intentionality behind them, as well as play, in terms of how players engage with the larp before, during, and after play. Such effects extend beyond larp communities; researchers have observed the *role-play effect* since the 1960s, in which people portraying characters with different views while discussing political issues leads to greater attitude change than exposure to similar information without the role-taking (Elms 1967), e.g., memetic *bleed-out* (Hugaas 2019).

Designers of political larps often leverage this potential, whether consciously or intuitively, to increase the impactfulness of the experience. The process of role-playing inherently involves perspective taking, in which the player compartmentalizes their own identity to greater or lesser degrees when adopting the viewpoint of another person. Sometimes, these characters have entirely different backgrounds, social contexts, and belief systems from the player's, e.g., having a marginalized background the player does not share (Leonard, Janjetovic, and Usman 2021). While a person can never fully understand another's perspective, thinking, feeling, and reacting as the character can increase a player's empathy for individuals from similar circumstances after the larp.

A meaningful player experience does not require one's character to succeed in their goals (i.e., "win"), especially if the larp explores the human condition or societal power structures. The player may "win" a deep insight or satisfyingly tragic narrative even when their character loses everything. Embodying a character who fails or suffers can become a *positive negative* experience for the participant (Hopeametsä 2008; Montola 2010) in which they experience *positive discomfort* leading to insights after the larp. Such impacts are sometimes enhanced when paired with debriefing and other forms of post-game processing (Bjørkelo and Jørgensen 2018).

Larps are not always intended or perceived by participants to be political. Still, they are often designed from certain perspectives, and may in fact raise awareness on political themes among participants and/or the media and the general public (see e.g., examples in Kangas, Loponen, and Särkijärvi 2016). Larps can cover a subject linked to political issues, current or historical, or simulate a political situation, real or imaginary (Rantanen 2016). This subject matter makes it possible to include, encourage, and demonstrate the use of skills necessary in politics in most types of larps, including writing and giving speeches, organizing a protest, practicing negotiation, debating, and engaging in common decision-making (e.g., Lehto 2016). A notable example involving a form of deliberation is *Parliament of Shadows*, which was played in the European Parliament together with public officials with an emphasis on political play as close as possible to real life – including the use of real life topics of discussion – but with a supernatural twist (Pettersson 2018).

J. T. Harviainen (2016) offers a typology of political larps, based on organization theory (Whittington 2006):

1. **Practices: Politics at Play.** Larps that include dynamics of politicking, such as intrigue or negotiation, but with no explicit political or activistic intentions (common in fantasy or vampire larps);

2. **Praxis: Illustrating Oppressive Structures.** Larps with some critical or political dimensions, that e.g., illustrate oppressive structures, but that are not explicitly designed to have a political impact beyond the event itself; and

3. **Practitioners: Influencing Players.** Larps that aim to influence players beyond the larp, e.g., changing participant behavior.

While many political larps falls under the first category of Practices and are not designed for political impacts, we should not assume that the lasting effects are not occurring in an incidental fashion; indeed, many of the relevant studies on the impacts of role-playing games (RPGs) focus on more traditional titles played in leisure environments, e.g., *Dungeons & Dragons* (1974). Since the 1990s, popular larps based on the *Vampire: the Masquerade* franchise have emphasized Machiavellian politicking in a "World of Darkness" much like our own (see e.g., *Mind's Eye Theatre*, By Night Studios 2014). Within the fiction of these games, most characters exist within hierarchies headed by a Prince who often has the ultimate fiat, although the Domain usually has a Primogen Council, which may deliberate on current issues depending on the session. Other *Vampire* games explore alternative political structures, such as fiercely individualistic or communally oriented factions opposing the strictures of traditional vampire society.

Similarly, fantasy larps often feature kingdoms with hierarchies and political positions. Interestingly, in some cases, high-ranking political positions confer in-game status, but also some degree of off-game community management responsibility (see e.g., Budai and Hammock 2014). In such situations, political representation happens both inside and outside the fiction; thus, some degree of transfer may be happening, e.g., social responsibility or leadership skills.

Alternatively, political larps emerging from the Nordic larp (Stenros and Montola 2010) and adjacent communities often fall under the second Praxis or third Practitioners categories. The Nordic larp movement has been particularly impactful since 1997 when the annual Nordic larp Knutepunkt/Solmukohta conference series began, which rotates between Norway, Sweden, Denmark, and Finland, and hundreds of associated zines, books, magazines, and videos have been published over the years. Educational larp (edu-larp) is also burgeoning in the Nordics, with the Edu-larp Conference hosted every year since 2014 before Knutepunkt/Solmukohta. Thousands of Swedish schoolchildren have experienced curriculum-specific edu-larp from organizations such as LajvVerkstaden (2025b) and Lajbyrån (2025), and Denmark has two boarding schools taught in part or in whole through larp pedagogy: Østerskov Efterskole (n.d.) and Efterskolen Epos (n.d.).

Practitioners within these communities often organize larps with explicitly political themes without easy answers or win conditions, e.g., explicit activistic and political purposes (Kangas, Loponen, and Särkijärvi 2016). Some examples include larps about immigration (*Europa* 2001; see Fatland 2016), environmental issues (*Baltic Warriors* 2015; see Arjoranta 2015; Pettersson 2015); occupation (*Halat Hisar* 2013, 2016; see Pettersson 2014; Pöllänen and Arjoranta 2021); and the outbreak of HIV/AIDS (*Just a Little Lovin'* 2011; Groth, Grasmo, and Edland 2021). While technically a leisure community, many members of Nordic larp have strong connections to art, academia, journalism, political groups, and other forms of influence in the world outside of the subculture. Notably, while originating in the Nordics, the term is used to refer to larps influenced by or contributing to this subcultural discourse (Stenros 2014). Furthermore, many larps occurring in the Nordics do not fall under this classification, e.g., fantasy boffer, World of Darkness, and others.

Anecdotal evidence asserts that participation in larps has increased political engagement in a few high-profile cases. When a former Sverok larper, Amanda Lind, became Swedish Minister of Culture, she presented her larp background as an asset, explaining it provided a good foundation for engaging with politics (Erlandsson 2019), and that larp had opened doors for her and contributed to her collaborative skills (Josefsson 2019). Similarly, the former Minister of International Development of Norway, Heikke Holmås, has attended several Nordic larps, explicitly stating that larp has a great deal of political potential in helping people understand each other's perspective, and can change the world (Halvorsen 1997).

Since our recommended design work in this paper aims to increase democratic skills in participants, we consider it educational in nature, whether played in informal, non-formal, or formal contexts (Baird 2022; Westborg 2023), thus falling under the third Practitioners category.

Deliberative Play

Some efforts have been made to incorporate play into deliberation (Craig 2023). Some researchers argue that elements of game design, *gamification*, are helpful in deliberative events. In the broadest sense, to gamify something means the application of techniques, tools, and lessons from games. The result is not necessarily a full-fledged game but something that resembles or evokes games in certain respects.

According to Gastil and Broghammer (2021), past research has found that game mechanics can motivate lay society members to participate, deliberate, and engage constructively with public institutions while simultaneously motivating agencies and policymakers to be more responsive to public input (Gordon et al. 2017; Hassan and Hamari 2019; Lerner 2014; Mayer 2009; Thiel 2016; Tolmie et al. 2014). However, Gastil and Broghammer (2021) argue that the literature remains under-theorized (Hassan 2017; Morschheuser et al. 2017). Specific game elements are not clearly connected to desired outcomes, and studies have not clarified the mediating mechanisms through which these game elements operate (Boyle et al. 2016; Giessen 2015; Thiel 2016). Addressing that deficiency, Gastil and Broghammer (2021, 12) specify several ways that game design can change public behaviors or attitudes.

A dichotomy exists between games and play (Caillois 1961). Gamification has strengths as a design approach, but can be problematic in terms of pro-social skill development, as it often focuses on shallow, extrinsically motivated, and competitive behaviors (Mekler et al. 2017; Andrade et al. 2016). Larps can be designed to instead build more on a playful approach, i.e., *playification*, with focus on collaborative playful exploration, interactive storytelling, and co-creation (Johansson et al. 2024, this volume). Larp elements could very well be a way to employ playification to deliberative events and some initial experimentation along these lines has already been explored, which will be discussed in the design section.

As the above illustrates, research on deliberative events and larp are two distinct fields, with only a few examples of overlaps. Deliberative events are rooted in a normative theory of democracy, explicitly aiming to develop deliberative skills and be part of democratic systems. Larp is essentially a social activity and a hobby for many people. It is more akin to an art form, such as improvisational theater. A specific larp may be built around a real or imagined political problem, requiring participants to engage in political behavior. However, unlike deliberative events, this political issue is rarely the main reason for conducting or participating in a larp. Despite this diversity, several theoretical and empirical similarities between the fields exist that are not sufficiently explored in research or practice. In the following sections, we will elaborate on these points and discuss the way forward, including what is possible and what obstacles need to be addressed.

DELIBERATIVE SKILLS DEVELOPMENT IN DELIBERATIVE EVENTS AND IN LARPS

Empirical research on deliberative events is extensive, and the literature on RPGs is expanding. This section does not aim to cover or review all findings in both fields. Instead, the goal is to map some of the most important skill formations and to illustrate key overlapping findings.

Skills Development in Deliberative Events

Evidence-based research on deliberative democracy has focused on several aspects drawn from normative deliberative theory. Studies on deliberative processes have primarily focused on various deliberative events, for example mini-publics (Curato et al. 2021), which involve society members in political decision-making processes by providing them with unbiased and diverse viewpoints, expert information, and a safer space to deliberate and reason together (Goodin and Dryzek 2006).

Studies have focused on how deliberation in mini-publics affects individuals' values and attitudes by boosting the coherence of their policy attitudes, democratic legitimacy beliefs, political efficacy, complexity of thinking, and the quality of their political knowledge and judgments (Fishkin 2018; Grönlund, Setälä, and Herne 2010; Himmelroos and Christensen 2014; Jennstål 2019; Lindell et al. 2017; Luskin et al. 2002; Muradova 2020; Suiter et al. 2016). Findings suggest that deliberation in mini-publics often leads to higher-quality political attitudes, increased political efficacy and political knowledge, and higher civic engagement among participating society members (Farrar et al. 2009; Grönlund, Setälä, and Herne 2010; Knobloch and Gastil 2015; Luskin et al. 2002).

Some mini-publics are intentionally designed to study how certain design components impact deliberation and the development of deliberative skills. In addition, various forms of controlled experiments are increasingly used in order to identify causality, i.e., how certain institutional designs impact behavior (Grönlund and Herne 2022; Werner and Muradova 2022). These experiments study the consequences of taking part in deliberative discourse, how opinions change during deliberation, often with a focus also on civic virtues central to deliberative democracy, e.g., social and political trust, political efficacy, political knowledge, and readiness to participate in politics. For summaries, see for example Suiter et al. (2020).

Skills Development in larps

While the field of RPG studies is still quite young (see e.g., Zagal and Deterding 2024), evidence-based research on their benefits has increased in recent years, including the potential of larp as a vehicle for transformation in leisure, educational, and therapeutic contexts. Such evidence is often qualitative in nature, drawn from autoethnographies, participant-observation ethnographies, and/or participant interviews, with few large-scale quantitative studies available to date. The results of these studies confirm the theorized potential of RPGs to serve as vehicles for practicing democratic skills (see e.g., Garcia 2016; Haarman 2022, 2023) and cultivating moral development (see e.g., Hollander 2021). For overviews, see for example see Bowman et al. (2024).

While many of these studies focus on tabletop RPGs rather than the more embodied larp, the process of role-playing itself is the important factor. However, greater embodiment may enhance these impacts in some cases due to its somatic nature, e.g., transfer of skills occurring (Westborg and Bowman in press) after an experience of procedural bleed (Hugaas 2019, 2024), as may thorough debriefing emphasizing the desired impact (Crookall 2014).

Notably, while much of the empirical research focuses on personal change, often from a therapeutic perspective, larps can lead to social transformation in interesting ways, e.g., group development; social cohesion; forming affinity groups (Eklund 2015) and social identities; feeling more connected to other players; or engaging in play, design, and/or social activities together after the larp. While the leisure practice itself may have the inherent potential for such bonding, interestingly, affinity groups have also been observed to form in mandatory RPGs within primary and secondary formal education (Cullinan 2024). Such experiences can have lasting positive effects on the social group beyond the activity. Thus, the next section will emphasize both personal and social development.

CONNECTIONS BETWEEN SKILL DEVELOPMENT IN DELIBERATION AND LARP

Connections between some of the findings on deliberative skills in research on deliberation and analog RPGs – including tabletop RPGs and larp – are summed up in Table 11.1. Importantly, many of these impacts overlap and could fit into multiple categories. While this list is not comprehensive of all empirical research, we highlight similarities found in key examples from the respective literatures in these ostensibly different fields. This examination of the relevant literature gives rise to several intriguing observations. In particular, we can see that researchers have observed the central outcomes of deliberative research in role-play research despite the fact that the research has not been driven by normative or positive deliberative theory. Nor have the results been interpreted from a perspective based on deliberative theory, and often not even related to any explicit understanding of alternative models of democracy at all. The clear overlap between the skill-building that occurs in RPGs and deliberation raises hopes that combining design practices from both could strengthen participants' capacities and their ability to connect, discuss, and collaborate with others around political activities. In the long run, this overlap could help us better understand how to improve communication between opposing groups of society members.

One important concept present in both fields is self-efficacy, which refers to an individual's confidence in their own abilities within a specific context (Bandura 2002). Political scientists have refined this concept to include *internal efficacy,* meaning an individual's perception of competence regarding their ability to understand and effectively participate in political activities (Bowler and Donovan 2002; Morrell 2005); and *external efficacy,* meaning an individual "perceptions of the responsiveness of the political system to their demands" (Morelle 2005). Both topics relate to feelings of empowerment and agency, which are key affordances larp often offers to participants, i.e., the perception of one's competence and ability to meaningfully and effectively enact change within a game environment. Such experiences can often transfer to feelings of empowerment to a player's daily identity (see e.g., Bowman 2010) or a greater sense of overall perceived competence when engaging with a specific subject matter or

TABLE 11.1 Connections between deliberative skills developed in deliberative events and analog role-playing games

Deliberative skills	Deliberative events	Role-playing games
Improved factual/political knowledge of an issue or political system, e.g., systems thinking	**Knowledge of the issue at hand** (Burkhalter, Gastil, and Kelshaw 2002; Luskin, Fishkin, and Jowell 2002; Grönlund and Setälä 2024, 299)	**Subject matter revision** (Mochocki 2014) **Working with subject matter in game** (Cook, Morgan, and Gremo 2016)
Improved deliberative skills (arguing and listening; problem solving)	**Analytical capacities**, including information processing skills; reflective and logical thinking; and increased cognitive complexity of political reasoning (Jennstål 2019) **Communication skills**, including the capacity to articulate one's views, construct persuasive arguments, and engage in a discussion with others (Burkhalter, Gastil, and Kelshaw 2002; Suiter et al 2016)	**Decision making skills** (Daniau 2016; Varrette et al. 2023) **Complex problem solving** (Kallam 1984; Zayas and Lewis 1986; Bowman 2010; Dyson et al. 2015; Daniau 2016; Atanasio 2020; Varrette et al. 2023) **Improved communication skills** (Enfield 2007; Daniau 2016; Katō 2019) **Debate/persuasion** (Daniau 2016) **Practicing democratic skills** (Adams 2013) **Practicing prosocial behaviors/social skills/Social Emotional Learning (SEL)** (Meriläinen 2012; Rosselet and Stauffer 2013; Sargent 2014; Helbig 2019; Katō 2019; Atanasio 2020; Davis and Johns 2020; Ruff 2021; Varrette et al. 2023; Bartenstein 2022a, 2022b, 2024; Atherton et al. 2024); especially **without serious repercussions for mistakes** (Pitt et al. 2023)
Improved understanding and consistency of participants' own considerations (moral reflection)	**Better alignment between one's own values, beliefs and preferences** (Niemeyer and Dryzek 2007; Niemeyer et al. 2024; Veri and Niemeyer 2025)	**Critical thinking** (Daniau 2016) **Balancing self-interests with community responsibility** (Wright, Weissglass, and Casey 2020)

(Continued)

Improved intrinsic motivation/ self-determination, empowerment, and/or agency of the participant (internal and external efficacy)	**Self-confidence,** including increased participant self-confidence with respect to what they can achieve in politics (Suiter et al. 2020), building readiness to participate in politics (Grönlund et al. 2010; Grönlund and Herne 2022), including building capacity for traditionally marginalized groups (Curato et al. 2017, 31)	**Increased motivation/self-determination** (Bowman and Standiford 2015; Algayres 2018; Walsh and Linehan 2024) **Self-confidence** (Abbott, Stauss, and Burnett 2021; Varrette et al. 2023; Walsh and Linehan 2024) including **confidence/coping when making mistakes** (Abbott, Stauss, and Burnett 2021) **Perceived competence/self-efficacy/seeing oneself as successful/ capable/having agency** (Bowman and Standiford 2015; Davis and Johns 2020; Atanasio 2020; Daniau 2016; Abbott, Stauss, and Burnett 2021; Varrette et al. 2023; Causo and Quinlan 2021; Hixson, West, and Eike 2024) **Increased engagement** (Bowman and Standiford 2015; Varrette et al. 2023; Cullinan 2024) **Agency/empowerment** (Daniau 2016; Wright, Weissglass, and Casey 2020; Abbott, Stauss, and Burnett 2021; Varrette et al. 2023)
Understanding the considerations of others: perspective-taking and empathy	**Emotional capacity and empathy,** including Other-regarding empathic feelings toward the other side of a public policy debate, including perspective taking (Muradova 2021) and regarding future generations (Kulha et al. 2021)	**Perspective taking** (Cook, Gremo, Morgan 2016) **Empathy** (Daniau 2016; Rivers et al. 2016; Bagés, Hoareau, and Guerrien 2021)
Understanding how to reconcile the values and interests of others	**Forging mutual respect and understanding** across polarized and divided enclaves (Grönlund, Herne, and Setälä 2015; Fishkin et al. 2021)	**Connecting despite differences** (Katō 2019)

TABLE 11.1 (Continued)

Deliberative skills	Deliberative events	Role-playing games
Development of group identity and community building	**Developing positive feelings** between members of in-groups and out-groups (Luskin et al. 2012) **Developing shared collective identity** (Felicetti et al. 2012; Hartz-Karp et al. 2010, including **across cultural and geographical divides** (Knobloch and Gastil 2015)	**Camaraderie/group cohesion/connectedness** (Zayas and Lewis 1986; Katō 2019; Abbott, Stauss, and Burnett 2021; Causo and Quinlan 2021) **Feelings of belonging** (Sargent 2014) **Development of affinity groups** (Cullinan 2024)
Development of norm formation of the group	**Generating generalizable moral principles** for group deliberation (Grönlund et al. 2015). **Forming meta-consensus**, i.e. common recognition of relevant considerations (Niemeyer and Dryzek 2007).	**Group development** (Daniau 2016) **Group consensus building** (Wright, Weissglass, and Casey 2020)
Impacting participants' political beliefs or worldview after the event	(Some) **long-time positive effects** on participants' involvement, opinion change (Van der Does and Jacquet 2023) and **mutual understanding** (Andersen and Hansen 2007)	**Moral development** (Wright, Weissglass, and Casey 2020)
Impacting participants' motivation to engage and/or actual political behavior in the outside world after the event	Deliberating society members can and do **influence public policy** (Curato et al. 2017, 29)	**Engaging in political organizing** after the event (Levin 2023) **Making active changes afterward** (Lehto 2024)

activity, as well as their *intrinsic motivation* to do so (Ryan 1982) (see e.g., in edu-larp, Bowman and Standiford 2015). Similarly, positive experiences within deliberative events can sometimes motivate participants to engage in collective political action after the event.

Potential Learning Objectives and Desired Outcomes for Deliberative Larp Design

Based on the overlapping objectives of lap and deliberative events, the following learning objectives and outcomes can be seen as desirable in deliberative larp design. The skills can be associated to psychological domains, with the understanding that in practice, these domains overlap: *cognitive*, i.e., primarily intellectual; *affective*, i.e., primarily emotional; or *behav ioral*, i.e., primarily impacting behavior and/or interaction with others (see e.g., Bowman 2014; Bowman et al. 2024).

As demonstrated above, research on deliberative events and larp is very extensive. Therefore, this section does not aim to cover or review all findings in both fields. Instead, the goal is to map some of the most important skill formations related to these two fields and to illustrate key overlapping findings. In the context of deliberative theory, we organize the various skills into five main categories: (1) basic knowledge for relevant considerations; (2) forming, understanding, and communicating one's own values and preferences; and (3) acknowledging the values and preferences of others; (4) developing group cohesion; and (5) integration of transformative impacts. Each of these can be further divided into subcategories, which gives us a total of six aspects: (A) factual and (B) behavioral knowledge; (C) the participant's own preferences and (D) willingness to engage; and (E) understanding others' considerations and (F) reconciling different preferences; (G) group identity and community building, and (H) norm formation of the group; and finally, (H) impacts on participants' political beliefs or worldview; and (I) impacts on participants' motivation to engage and/or actual political behavior.

The final category deals specifically with longer-term transformation, often as a result of participating in the previous activities, which can have a significant impact on participants outside of the event or game. For example, citizens can become more active as a result of participating in deliberative events. Players who have played a certain role in a larp can also be affected as individuals and feel more confident engaging in real political contexts. The recommended learning objectives and desired outcomes are.

Applying Basic Knowledge and Skills

A. Improved factual/political knowledge of an issue or a political system (systems thinking).
   Primary domain: *cognitive.*

B. Improved deliberative skills (arguing and listening; problem solving).
   Primary domains: cognitive, behavioral.

Forming and Communicating Opinions

C. Improved understanding and consistency of participants' own considerations (moral reflection).
   Primary domain: *cognitive.*

D. Improved intrinsic motivation/self-determination, empowerment, and/or agency of the participant (internal and external efficacy).
   Primary domains: cognitive, affective, behavioral.

Listening to and Understanding Others

E. Understanding the considerations of others: perspective-taking and empathy.
   Primary domains: cognitive, affective.

F. Understanding how to reconcile the values and interests of others.
   Primary domains: cognitive, affective.

Developing Group Cohesion

G. Development of group identity and community building.
   Primary domains: cognitive, affective, behavioral.

H. Development of norm formation of the group.
   Primary domains: cognitive, behavioral.

Integration of Transformative Impacts

I. Impacting participants' political beliefs or worldview after the event.
   Primary domain: cognitive, affective.

J. Impacting participants' motivation to engage and/or actual political behavior in the outside world after the event.
   Primary domains: cognitive, affective, behavioral.

Notably, the cognitive domain is likely utilized in each of the outcomes, whereas behavioral and affective may or may not be present. This suggests that deliberative behavior should always feature a cognitive dimension, even if views are presented in an emotional way or interpersonal behaviors are also emphasized.

Note that these impacts vary in terms of their sphere of influence. Mo Turkington (2016) suggests that political larps could have an impact in three areas of life: the *personal*, the *communal*, and/or the *public sphere*. Such a classification is similar to spheres of impact mentioned in John Paul Lederach's (2014) formulation of conflict transformation, which envisions conflict as an opportunity to envision positive futures. For Lederach, conflict is a dynamic system within which we can enact short- and long-term change processes that occur at the *personal, relational, structural,* and/or *cultural* levels, sometimes simultaneously.

Conflict is inherent to all human interaction and political discussions are inherently rife with conflict due to contrasting worldviews on often high-stakes topics that affect the discussion participants. In skill development for political discussions, we can choose approaches grounded in *conflict management* (de-escalating/making less visible); *resolution* (trying to solve); or *transformation* (collaborating on win-win solutions). Deliberation would fall into conflict transformation because it is time consuming and works to get everyone on board with the process to envision long-term change processes, even if consensus is not possible. From this perspective, deliberating on important topics connected to Lederach's four spheres can be an important tool in social transformation.

Thus, we have arranged these learning objectives as a range in terms of scope, i.e., their relative sphere of influence, and their temporality, i.e., whether the impact is observable during the event or after. Our list begins with temporary impacts observable during the event, moving from the *personal*, e.g., application of knowledge; to the *interpersonal*, e.g., communicating one's views and listening to others' perspectives; and the *social*, e.g., group development and cohesion during the event. Finally, we transition to *longer-term impacts* integrated into players' daily life, indicative of changes in beliefs, social responsibility, and/or political engagement.

Notably, while often a larp only impacts one individual's worldview and thus minimally affects the world at large, participants can also choose to enact change individually or in groups as a result of takeaways from the event. Such actions can ultimately have impacts at the structural and cultural levels (Lederach 2014), e.g., the individual making change within a governmental system, the individual leading an organizing effort for political purposes, or members of the group engaging in collective political action. While we do have preliminary examples from both fields, such larger-scale effects are more difficult to track and more data collection is needed especially on the long-term impacts of larp.

The next step is to explore the design possibilities and challenges of combining deliberative events and larps for this purpose.

COMBINING ROLE-PLAYING AND DELIBERATION: DESIGN CONSIDERATIONS

How Can Larp Enhance Deliberation?

We posit that larps can be used to create a safer environment where diverse opinions may be more freely expressed and explored. Larps may also provide conducive spaces for different kinds of reason-giving, for example encouraging storytelling and narratives. In addition, RPGs create opportunities for enhanced perspective-taking, which is inherent in the design and development of roles and can help foster greater empathy (Leonard, Janjetovic, and Usman 2021) and metareflection (Levin 2020).

Larps often focus on cultural and artistic engagement, which may include various forms of creation: imaginative scenarios, storytelling, emergent improvisational play, alternative identities, artistic scenography, costumes, props, and other forms of expression. These elements encourage spontaneous role-play while interacting with changing developments in collaboration with co-players, who often improvise in unpredictable ways. In line with current deliberative theory, such creative and artistic spaces foster not only fact-based argumentation but also alternative and less formal modes of communication such as storytelling, narratives, testimony, and humor. Such modes are important since an acceptance of only neutral language of rational reason-giving might disadvantage already marginalized groups (e.g., Sanders 1997; Young 2001).

Researchers have found that legitimate reasoning in deliberation can be articulated through storytelling, bodily expressions, and artistic aspects (Jennstål and Öberg 2019), all of which are present in larp as a medium. Storytelling combines intellectual aspects with empathic and embodied approaches (Turkington 2016), and has the potential to help especially marginalized groups feel more comfortable engaging in deliberation, as personal experience and counternarratives can be foregrounded as valid forms of reasoning. Furthermore, empathy, active listening, perspective-taking, and taking initiative are examples of central skills for both democratic deliberation (Bächtiger et al. 2018, Bächtiger and Parkinson 2019) and larp, which suggests a fruitful nexus point for design.

Pothong et al. (2021) conclude that larp provides a deliberative playground for exploring different possible consequences and choices. Furthermore, they state that the co-creational, open-ended, and emotional dimensions of larp could complement and enhance deliberation. However, designing larps training democratic skills requires a nuanced design for reflexive player agency and conscious usage of deliberative democracy theories (Pothong et al. 2021). In another case study, RPGs, as a method in civic planning processes, encouraged dialogues to foster empathy, nurture consequence awareness, and cultivate civic creativity among participants (Gordon, Haas, and Michelson 2017).

Deliberation scholar Peter Levine (2018a, 2018b) claims that fostering deliberative discussion in a meaningful way in educational situations can be difficult for various reasons. He cites case studies by Crocco et al. (2018) in which they describe difficulties such as the facilitators having unrealistic expectations about the level of deliberation possible; existing classroom dynamics and contexts; students having fixed attitudes and lacking developed deliberative skills; majority positions within the group dominating less common ones, leading to an unbalanced power dynamic; and performative rather than authentic behavior. Challenges such as these make it important to design experiences that feel consequential and relatable to student's lives rather than overly charged with existing political rhetoric (Levine 2018a).

Levine identifies two types of classroom deliberation: (1) real decisions and (2) simulated or hypothetical decisions. In either case, students can either act as themselves or role-play fictional or historical characters. He suggests that role-play can be an effective way to create engagement and enhance the quality of the deliberative discussions, particularly if "students role-play powerful decision-makers, rather than playing themselves in a discussion that has no political impact" (Levine 2018a, p. 1).

A key element of larp and all role-play is that players act not as themselves but adopt characters. Playing fictional characters means participants do not need to represent their own views, but rather imagine the perspective of another person, which decreases the social consequences and may lead to greater engagement. In other words, role-playing confers *alibi* e.g., "it wasn't me expressing those views, but my character" (Deterding 2018). Furthermore, students can be tasked with playing characters that adopt the *mantle of the expert* (Heathcote and Bolton 1995), see e.g., in secondary school (Hyltoft 2010) and higher education (Cox and Lewis 2023; Hixon, West, and Eike 2024), i.e., individuals with greater expertise than they do. Such enactments can help players feel more confident expressing viewpoints, as they are able to borrow the authority of the character during the scenario.

How Can Deliberation Enhance Larp?

Techniques in deliberative events can be borrowed in service of more sustained positive impacts on democratic attitudes and behaviors in larp. Teemu Rantanen (2016) proposes developing larps designed for deliberation in which multiple views are shared. Systematic study would require consciously designed larps in which the organizers cannot only focus on their own political message, but might, for example, give their players agency to freely shape the framing of their characters and the game in general (Rantanen 2016). He proposes that inspiration for such larps can be drawn from deliberative democracy scholars, with the examples of Thompson (2008), Grönlund, Herne, and Setälä (2015), Carpini, Cook, and Jacobs (2004), and Mercier and Landemore (2012). While few have answered Rantanen's call thus far, this theoretical grounding is a promising line of inquiry.

Current political larp design is often driven by debate and designed to enhance polarization between characters. These strategies do not cohere well with democratic deliberation, which focuses more on reason-giving and listening, and strives toward depolarization. So while the two can be combined, special design considerations need to be explored and developed, e.g., emphasizing the deliberative skill development of the player over divergent character goals and dramatic story arcs.

Similarly, as larps featuring long meetings or discussions can sometimes become less engaging for larpers due to lack of simultaneous interaction, design innovations from larp on this topic are worth investigating (see e.g., Axner and Vejdemo 2016). Can larp techniques add interest to deliberative processes? Examples might include pausing to hear the inner thoughts of quiet characters (*monologuing*), engaging in flashback scenes, or physically acting out a point being made rather than only describing it. How might such additions affect the outcomes of deliberation? Furthermore, in terms of tone, including humor in deliberative larp could provide interesting results; while humor can be beneficial for discussions (Basu 1999), it might lead to less respectful deliberative communication.

Ultimately, we believe that overall practices, design methods, and theories related to larp can innovate democratic deliberation, as they have done e.g., in health care simulation (Standiford 2014). Examples include innovating character creation structures, safety structures, meta-techniques (Stark 2014; Koljonen et al. 2019), and transformative RPG design principles (Bowman, Diakolambrianou, and Brind 2024). Other fruitful lines of inquiry include investigating literature on other forms of role-playing not associated with larp subcultures, such as in simulation, e.g., studies on facilitation (Leigh 2024; Kriz 2010; de Wijse-van Heeswijk and Kriz 2023; de Wijse-van Heeswijk 2021); debriefing (Crookall 2010, 2014, 2023; Roungas et al. 2018; de Wijse-van Heeswijk et al. 2025); and deliberative simulations (Levine 2018a, 2019b). Also of interest are role-playing scenarios developed by the Reacting to the Past Consortium, e.g., role-playing scripts on the development of early American democracy (Weidenfeld and Fernandez 2017). Thus, while the intersection of larp and deliberation is of particular interest to us, a thorough map of the wider design terrain would also prove fruitful.

Conditions for Deliberation and Implications for Design Factors
Both fields of research have widely accepted the idea that design matters. Changing the rules of a game, adding new characters, or altering the setting will likely change the behavior of the participants in a larp. Similarly, the design of deliberative events determines how they are conducted. Since political behavior and the practice of deliberative skills are at the core of deliberative research, these events are often organized as experiments in which groups deliberate under different design conditions (Grönlund and Herne 2022). Below, we will focus on some of the most important design factors for deliberative events that may also be important to consider in relation to role-playing: (1) the format (length and venue); (2) recruiting participants (diversity and representativeness); (3) information provided, including issue complexity; (4) implementing deliberative norms (including facilitation); and (5) decision rules and integration into decision-making. In relation to each design aspect, we discuss to what extent they are also important in game design, and what challenges they present.

Format: Venue and Length

Most mini-publics have used single venues, with all participants meeting in the same building. Depending on the number of participants, the entire group often meets in a large hall for the plenary session, while most of the actual deliberation takes place in smaller subgroups. While this approach usually works well, it is not without problems. First, these events are expensive. Second, some practical obstacles, such as the conditions during the COVID-19 pandemic, can make in-person deliberation impossible.

Online events, however, have opened up opportunities to organize deliberations that include people living far apart in different regions of the world. Consequently, online deliberations, as well as combination events, have become increasingly common. At the same time, it is clear that designing an online or in-person deliberative event impacts how the deliberation and facilitation work. In-person meetings can foster deeper connections and a sense of common purpose. While possible online, these outcomes are more difficult and require more advanced facilitation (Willis et al. 2023). Online engagement also brings up concerns about inclusion, as access to technology and a suitable place to participate can differ significantly, which can affect participation and behavior (Curato et al. 2021, 25; Grönlund and Setälä 2024, 301). On the other hand, physical presence can prove exclusionary for some in terms of accessibility.

The length of events is strongly connected to venue options. Most events so far have lasted more than one day but less than four days. Approximately one-quarter of all mini-publics in Europe have met for four to ten days or more (Curato et al. 2021, 26). Although organizing longer events is costly and difficult, effective deliberation requires time. Important reflections among participants with long-term effects cannot be expected to occur if the event lasts only a few hours (Dryzek et al. 2019). Consequently, many well-known examples of successful deliberation involved meetings that spanned several days over a period of time – sometimes up to a year (Farrell and Suiter 2021).

Similar issues are connected to larps. Short larps are likely less impactful than longer ones simply due to length of time spent playing with others, although high-intensity short larps can be impactful. Participation in person can be difficult, especially due to economic (Ford 2020) or accessibility factors (Kessock 2017). Online larp can be accessible, but some players find it less immersive or connective. Such larps are usually shorter, as screen time can be exhausting for participants.

Thus, in both deliberation and larp, the length of time commitment and physical location can have strong design implications.

Recruitment of Participants

Most deliberative events aim to bring together a group of society members that is somewhat representative of a particular community. However, achieving representativeness can be problematic when an event can only gather a limited number of participants. Consequently, it is common to combine random sampling with quotas for specific groups (Curato et al. 2021, 22). Nevertheless, it is difficult to avoid the overrepresentation of individuals or personality traits that make one more inclined to engage in deliberation (Jacquet 2017). For example, certain groups, such as young people or immigrants, are harder to recruit for deliberative events. This naturally impacts how deliberation works and its outcomes (Grönlund and Setälä 2024; Jennstål 2018). Nevertheless, organizers often strive to include all types of voices, even those typically considered extreme or uncomfortable (Grönlund and Setälä 2024). While diversity of viewpoints can lead to increased empathy and counteract polarization, it can also lead to difficult-to-handle contestation and confrontation (Grönlund, Herne, and Setälä 2015).

Additional challenges arise with regard to recruiting players for deliberative larps. The term "larp" in itself can be a hindrance, as among some members of the public, as it often connotes fantasy escapism in a negative way and is used derogatorily when discussing adult pretend play (Klenell 2019). Furthermore, as political larps are opt-in, they also have selection bias issues; Nordic larpers in particular tend toward progressive politics. Certain event settings, such as larp festivals, make it impossible (or at least complicated) to make use of random selection and control groups. Depending on the design, it might be difficult to project how the actual game will play out, producing unexpected outcomes, as we have seen also in some mini-publics (Niemeyer 2011, 126).

While acknowledging these and other challenges, hosting larps as deliberative experiments also comes with some advantages. It is of course impossible to avoid selection bias among participants, but the fact that the bias is not necessarily connected to willingness to participate in deliberation can be used as an opportunity to complement deliberative experiments. Importantly, we may learn how otherwise apolitical society members, or at least unlikely to participate in mini-publics, react to various designs, e.g., what kind of designs have empowering and mobilizing effects (or not).

This consideration leads to questions about the target audience and goals of organizing larps based on these themes. Who would benefit most from learning these skills? Can larp as an activity attract these populations effectively? Do we aim for participants with a wide range of political views, or mainly focus on alternative views in the character design? One strategy for wider reach is to design a scenario for a general adult population, then try it out in multiple contexts, e.g., for larpers in informal learning environments such as festivals; for non-larpers in non-formal settings, e.g., museums, community centers, government offices; and for students in formal ones, e.g., classrooms.

Creating an environment that feels inclusive for marginalized participants is another challenge. While role-playing can lead to empathy for others, players should not assume they understand another's perspective fully. Furthermore, when playing characters with backgrounds different from one's own, issues can arise if the character has a marginalized identity that the participant does not share. For example, people with a limited understanding of a perspective may lean on stereotypes (Leonard, Janjetivic, and Usman 2021) or appropriate someone else's culture in an offensive way (Kessock 2014; Eddy 2020). Therefore, complex power dynamics accompany all kinds of role-taking involving tragedies, minority identities, or oppressed groups.

A related concern is how leisure larping is a fairly homogeneous hobby. For example, after analyzing the international Larp Census (2015), which mostly featured Western countries, Christopher Amherst (2016) drew the conclusion that "the 'default' is a white male, between the ages of 20 and 34, who participates as cast/crew in live combat fantasy campaigns." While gender parity is more common in Nordic larp, the long-standing stereotype that RPGs are a primarily cis White-male middle-class activity might dissuade people with more marginalized identities from attending.

Larp can sometimes be experienced as empowering, especially for participants from marginalized backgrounds. Jonaya Kemper (2017, 2020) discusses the empowering experience of *emancipatory bleed*, e.g., playing a character who is able to challenge oppressive structures through play in ways that feel unavailable in daily life. However, the same author has also described the difficulties people of color often experience in feeling included in the larp community (Kemper 2018).

How can deliberative larp be designed in a way that signals inclusivity? Who writes these games, informed by what research, and in collaboration with which groups? Just as deliberation should include those affected, so too should the design of scenarios based on relevant political positions to the degree possible, e.g., hiring cultural consultants, sensitivity readers, and/or include designers from represented backgrounds (Kemper 2018).

In some cases, unequal power dynamics may make democratic deliberation impossible, such as in wars when at least one actor does not accept even the existence of another actor. We also acknowledge that peaceful deliberative processes are not always possible in areas of escalated conflict and political crisis, although notably, deliberation has been important in certain peace negotiations (see e.g., Jennstål 2012). In a less extreme example, if a facilitator holds a power position over members of the group, e.g., a teacher in a classroom, participants may feel reticent to deliberate. Thus, power dynamics will be important to consider during both the design and facilitation phases.

The Issue: Complexity and Provided Information
Deliberative events are organized around policy problems, which can range from practical, local issues to more abstract, principled ones (Curato et al. 2021). Regardless of the issue, it must be significant enough to generate interest and engagement. However, the complexity of the issue can prevent participants from engaging in meaningful discussions, thereby reducing the quality of deliberation (Niemeyer et al. 2024). To help participants, basic, unbiased information on the issue at hand is provided. The type of information provided, as well as how and by whom it is provided, can affect the conditions for deliberation (Barabas2004). For instance, under certain circumstances, experts may silence participants (Bogler, 2012), though more interactive expert hearing formats do not seem to cause this issue (Leino et al. 2022).

Similarly, excessive information or complexity of tasks may cause cognitive overload for players preparing for and playing larps. For example, edu-larp designer Michał Mochocki (2013a, 2013b) recommends far shorter character sheets than usual in larp in order to focus on learning goals and avoid inhibiting the players. He also suggests using larp primarily as subject matter revision rather than the players' first or primary interaction with the material (Mochocki 2013a). Because larp has additional cognitive demands due to the role-taking and fiction, the amount of information provided before a deliberative larp and the length of time required to learn it must be carefully considered.

Establishing and Implementing Norms for Interaction
Designing facilitation is often key to implementing deliberative norms and is considered indispensable to deliberative practice (Moore 2012). While

free discussions without rules can lead to increased polarization, facilitation can prevent this from happening (Strandberg et al. 2019). However, facilitation can also backfire (Escobar 2019). Excessive facilitation can distort the deliberation process and negatively impact substantive argumentation (Moore 2012; Escobar 2019). Alternatively, self-moderation, in which participants establish and enforce norms themselves, has proven highly effective. However, without such enforcement, issues can arise.

While important for civil discourse, the concept of depolarization can have negative connotations, especially for people concerned with human rights. Extreme polarization and radicalization tend to focus upon limiting the rights of some people in favor of others, in some cases, also the right for them to exist at all, i.e., anti-democratic beliefs. For many people, these two poles are not equivalent and should not be compared. One position fundamentally aims to exclude, while the other aims to include. Therefore, designing a deliberative larp would likely need to exclude extreme positions focusing on restricting human rights, as well as players who hold such positions, lest the activity fall apart or become hostile. Lessons from successful deliberative events managing to hold space for such polarities could be informative here.

This tension is one worth exploring, especially when considering issues with participation bias. Are "all opinions/reasons equivalent" when some are clearly intended for exclusion and oppression? Can deliberation be considered inclusive under such conditions? How might such events backfire, such as making marginalized participants feel less heard or feel less empowered to make consequential decisions due to power dynamics? Can conditions of authenticity be said to be present if one party in the discourse feels belittled or harmed by another, even within the conditions of "polite" discourse, e.g., power moves/inequitable power dynamics, micro-aggressions, etc.?

The type of interaction that the norms of various deliberative spaces imply is also important. Design factors that encourage an interplay of fact-based argumentation and storytelling can lead to more reflective political judgments (Black 2008). Events that encourage participants to imagine the world from opposing viewpoints can positively impact cognitive complexity (Muradova and Arceneaux 2022, 279). However, democratic deliberation itself is a normative ideal and therefore limited. Democracy as a preferable way to govern communities historically may have developed based on limited sources and certain ways of thinking. Our notions of democracy may be shaped by beliefs developed by the ancient Greeks and Enlightenment philosophers, but do not reflect, e.g., indigenous ways of collective will-formation that are also democratic in nature (Graeber and Wengrow 2021; Mendonça and Asenbaum 2025).

As different methods can reflect the same values; institutions are context-dependent. As Mark Warren argues (2017), democracy should be understood as certain functions, but that these functions may work distinctly in different contexts (and hence need to be adjusted to context). While "an exchange of reasons" or "explanation and justification of initial preferences" are at the core of deliberation, various methods exist to formulate, express, and communicate reasons, which might very well be context-dependent. On the other hand, it is a pivotal democratic idea that we should constantly disagree over normative values and how they are accomplished, so such questioning the foundation of democracy is actually part of the democratic process. Thus, like game design, we should consider democratic deliberation iterative rather than fixed, in spite of its roots, and therefore be open to deliberative larp evolving in form.

Collective Decision-Making, Collaboration, and Escalation/De-Escalation
A primary design consideration for deliberative events is the purpose of the deliberations. When deliberations involve public statements or decisions rather than secret ballots or individual statements, participants develop greater knowledge of the issue and understanding of compromise in politics, as well as an increased appreciation for democratic institutions (Grönlund, Setälä, and Herne 2010). Simultaneously, informing participants that they will make a final decision, for example, by voting, might induce strategic behavior, directing them toward fixed positions and predetermined votes. Similarly, introducing a vote during the process might disrupt dialogic exchange and undermine the quality of the deliberative process, especially in short deliberative events (Felicetti et al. 2016; Veri and Niemeyer 2025). However, there are also indications that group building can mitigate these effects (Veri and Niemeyer 2025). Similarly, in larps that feature competition, a collaborative group-building approach off-game could make such conflicts less contentious.

A larger issue related to deliberative larp design is the emphasis on de-escalation of contentious intensity inherent to successful deliberation. Larps tend to lean toward heightened drama, conflicts, and disagreements, i.e., escalation. Rantanen (2016) describes how this conflict-based larp design could potentially clash with trying to create a positive deliberative climate. Deliberation builds on values such as mutual respect, good faith, and should not be propagandistic. Active listening and considering the viewpoints of others tend to de-escalate rather than escalate, e.g., resulting in depolarization.

Thus, democratic deliberation stands in contrast to other forms of political exchange, such as debate. Within larp, debating, characters with strong, hard-to-change opinions and propagandistic elements are common. Those features can provide interesting game situations, but might not be beneficial for democratic deliberation purposes. Furthermore, playing a scenario in which characters respectfully listen to one another's views might not appeal to some larpers, especially if they enjoy larps with escalated conflicts. Alternatively, if another player escalates emergently through play, it may be difficult for players to avoid matching that intensity; to use an extreme and unrealistic example that nonetheless could happen in emergent play, if one of the characters is holding a grenade, the situation is likely to escalate unless the player makes the out-of-character decision to *steer* toward de-escalation (Montola, Stenros, and Saitta 2015).

These competing norms in the two communities could potentially become a challenge in combining larp and deliberation, and thus require design consideration. How can we maintain interest and a certain degree of emotional engagement without the deliberative activity falling apart?

Ultimately, while necessarily imperfect, we believe that the potential offered by deliberative larp is valuable nonetheless and may indirectly contribute to strengthening civil society and the resilience of our democracies.

While these initial considerations provide certain challenges in design deliberative larps, we believe the potential benefits motivate further research in the area.

IMPLICATIONS FOR A NEW RESEARCH AGENDA

Based on the above sections, we propose more focus on bridging democratic deliberation and larp, with some future research explorations suggested in this section.

Categorizing and Defining Aspects of Larp and Deliberation

Many different ways exist to categorize different larps and larp-like methods. There is a need for defining, categorizing, and clarifying what is meant with deliberation, larps, and the combination of the two. Such definitions should also distinguish larp from other forms of educational role-play and simulation featuring deliberative elements, while also acknowledging similarities in practice.

Analyzing larps in Relation to Deliberation

A rich plethora of political larps exist, including ones that directly engage with deliberation, as well as some evidence of role-playing used to train deliberative skills. However, more research is needed on what makes them both effective together. We propose considering what design aspects each contains that can enhance the other, such as genres, facilitation, safety mechanisms, debriefing strategies, moderation level, participant agency, and more.

For example, while players in larps may have a comparatively wider range of actions to take within the game, participants in deliberative events are often expected to produce policy recommendations at the end of the event. Such a constraint may limit play, but have more lasting impacts on the political process, i.e., be more consequential than events transpiring in a fictional larp (see e.g., Knobloch and Gastil 2015). On the other hand, trying to insert such consequentiality without the collective intentionality of the group, or in a way that is not well-aligned with the rest of the fiction, can actually detract from the experience. While such consequentiality outside of the larp will be difficult to replicate in a fictional scenario, one middle ground would be to research larps with deliberative elements in which the discussion has a strong impact on the game world, e.g., collectively deliberating on which system of governance to adopt.

Furthermore, while acknowledging that measuring the effects of larps is a difficult task, we propose that more qualitative and quantitative scientific research on different approaches to designing larp and deliberative events is needed.

Analyzing Larp Like-Deliberation Activities and Deliberation Events

Studying deliberation itself can inform larp design, whether attending events themselves or intensively interviewing organizers to uncover more implicit design practices not present in the literature. Of special interest would be events or skill-training methods that already include role-play elements.

Combining Knowledge on Larp Design and Deliberation Events

The Nordic larp and adjacent communities are skilled at sharing design ideas, learning from each other, and from previous larp designs, e.g., when designing political larps. Research on deliberation and deliberative events also holds important insights. Many useful concepts from political studies, such as framing and coercion, can be generative in relation to designing political larps (Harviainen 2016). We argue that combining the two areas can enhance both deliberation events and political larp design, especially when designing based on theory backed by empirical studies.

Establishing Design Implications and Tools for Deliberation larps

Such knowledge can establish methods for designing deliberative larps with the potential for strong impacts. For example, we could expand the Mixing Desks of larp (Stenros, Andresen, and Nielsen 2016) and edu-larp (Bowman 2022b): larp design tools that categorize design strategies based on different factors. These mixing desks could be expanded to include political and deliberative aspects in larps.

Expanding Strategies for Inclusion

While larp communities are relatively tolerant compared with other subgroups, fostering inclusion requires stepping beyond tolerance, consistently learning about the needs of others, and adapting. Deliberation has similar challenges, in that people from privileged backgrounds likely feel more comfortable sharing their opinions in groups. An important design space to explore is what practices both larp and deliberation have developed in terms of fostering inclusion and whether participants from marginalized backgrounds have found these practices effective or welcoming, e.g., strategies for facilitation, moderation, and psychological safety. Perhaps this area is another in which larp and deliberation can learn from one another.

CONCLUSION

Our study is based on the premise that the current democratic crisis is largely due to a lack of effective communication among society members with different perceptions of reality. Therefore, improving our understanding of the conditions necessary for effectively communicating values and preferences is crucial for grasping and addressing the crisis. To this end, we examined ways to enhance our understanding of such communication by merging research on deliberation and larps. Ultimately, we hope this chapter serves as an initial guide for determining when and how to use larps in research to help participants develop deliberation and democratic engagement skills.

It should be noted that embracing a deliberative normative theory is not a prerequisite for this endeavor. We can investigate empirical questions, such as "Under what circumstances or with what design factors can the skills highlighted in deliberative theory be developed through role-playing?" without making normative statements. Additionally, investigating such empirical questions does not imply that other types of political participation are ignored. For instance, protests play an important role in democratic systems and can even fulfill deliberative functions.

Furthermore, we acknowledge that human interaction, especially in politics, is often marked by contradictions and conflict. These divisions are often rooted in perceived political identities, where society members may view others with the same identity as friends and those with different identities as enemies (Mouffe 1999). However, we do not believe that political identities, along with the values and preferences associated with them, are unchangeable or objective. They are shaped and changed by particular circumstances, which can be influenced by design factors.

Political theorists Scudder and White (2023, 103) formulate this view as follows: "Thus, a world of friend and enemy is not presumed from the start: rather, it takes shape through a mutually reenforcing blend of technology and the social-psychological dynamics of resentment, self-righteousness, and a sense of being persistently threatened." In other words, even if we assume that conflict is the hallmark and fundamental driver of politics, focusing on communication between groups in society becomes essential to understanding our world. Without some kind of considerations being formulated and exchanged, it becomes difficult to identify different political identities and interests. In other words, it becomes impossible to distinguish friends from enemies (Erman 2009).

In this chapter, we demonstrated that political larp and deliberative events are spaces where relevant democratic skills can be practiced. These findings should inform our future design strategies and can be of service to other researchers exploring the fruitful terrain between the two practices in service of democratic education. Researchers can, for example, employ a research-through-design approach (Zimmerman, Forlizzi, and Evenson 2007) to design, run, and iterate upon larp experiments based on deliberative theory. Such explorative design processes including studies of designed prototypes informed by current deliberative theory and empirical findings, can serve as a meeting point between larp and deliberation.

ACKNOWLEDGEMENTS

This research is co-funded by the European Union's Horizon Europe project Larpocracy: Developing Spaces for Deliberation and Democratic Skills through Role-playing. Larpocracy integrates perspectives from researchers on game studies, larp design, transformative play, political science, and human-computer interaction. The project aims to explore larp in relation to democratic processes, including deliberative events, and how the combination can promote civic outcomes related to democratic participation.

AUTHOR DISCLOSURE

Sarah Lynne Bowman has contributed extensive composition and citations in several drafts.

PerOla Öberg has contributed extensive composition and citations in several drafts.

Karin Johansson has contributed composition in early drafts, revisions in later drafts, and citations.

Annika Waern has contributed brainstorming and comments in several drafts.

NOTE

1 Neither larp nor deliberation design is politically neutral; some norms do exist and underlie the event. We acknowledge that deliberation is normative, that is, it asserts a norm that favors democratic engagement that emphasizes the communication of relevant considerations, personal testimony, and active listening. Our investment here is not to prove that deliberation always works or solves all democratic problems. We seek to explore how political participation is conditioned by context, and how we might design contexts with conditions that allow participants to, for example, better express themselves and understand others' perspectives. Our interest is in creating spaces in which democratic engagement can occur that reduce polarization and increase mutual understanding. We recognize that other forms of democratic engagement are important (Scudder and White 2023), and welcome research and applications of larp design that promote other activities that support the enhancement of democratic values and processes.

REFERENCES

Abbott, Matthew S., Kimberly A. Stauss, and Allen F. Burnett. 2021. "Table-Top Role-Playing Games as a Therapeutic Intervention with Adults to Increase Social Connectedness." *Social Work with Groups* 45 (1): 16–21.

Adams, Aubrie S. 2013. "Needs Met through Role-Playing Games: A Fantasy Theme Analysis of Dungeons & Dragons." *Kaleidoscope: A Graduate Journal of Qualitative Communication Research* 12 (6): 69–86.

Algayres, Muriel Gaelle. 2018. "A Study of Active Learning in Educational Roleplaying Games and Students' Motivation." In *Proceedings from Teaching for Active Learning: TAL2018*, edited by Christopher Kjær, Donna Hurford, and Lotte Dyhrberg O'Neill. Syddansk University.

Amherst, Christopher. 2016. "Representation and Social Capital: What the Larp Census reveals about Community." In *Larp Realia: Analysis, Design, and Discussions of Nordic Larp*, edited by Jukka Särkijärvi, Mika Loponen, and Kaisa Kangas. Ropecon ry.

Andersen, Vibeke Normann, and Kasper M. Hansen. 2007. "How Deliberation Makes Better Citizens: The Danish Deliberative Poll on the Euro." *European Journal of Political Research* 46 (4): 531–556.

Andrade, Fernando R.H., Riichiro Mizoguchi, and Seiji Isotani. 2016. "The Bright and Dark Sides of Gamification." In *Intelligent Tutoring Systems: Lecture Notes in Computer Science*, Springer International Publishing.

Arato, Andrew, and Jean L. Cohen. 2022. *Populism and Civil Society: The Challenge to Constitutional Democracy.* Oxford University Press.

Arjoranta, Jonne. 2015. "Larp as Playful Resistance." Paper presented at Adult Play, University of Tampere, Finland, May 10–12, 2015.

Atanasio, Joseph F. 2020. "Why Older Adventurers Can Beat a Lich: How Dungeons & Dragons Empowers Older Adults." In *Integrating Geek Culture into Therapeutic Practice: The Clinician's Guide to Geek Therapy*, edited by Anthony M. Bean, Emory S. Daniel Jr., and Sarah A. Hays. Fort Worth, TX: Leyline Publishing.

Atherton, Gray, Rhys Hathaway, Ingela Visuri, and Liam Cross. 2024. "A Critical Hit: Dungeons and Dragons as a Buff for Autistic People." *Autism*, August 21.

Axner, Theo, and Susanne Vejdemo. 2016. "Design Strategies for Discussion-Heavy Larps." In *Larp Realia: Analysis, Design, and Discussions of Nordic Larp*, edited by Jukka Särkijärvi, Mika Loponen, and Kaisa Kangas. Helsinki: Ropecon ry.

Bächtiger, André, John S. Dryzek, Jane Mansbridge, and Mark Warren, eds. 2018. *The Oxford Handbook of Deliberative Democracy.* Oxford Handbooks. Oxford University Press.

Bächtiger, André, and John Parkinson. 2019. *Mapping and Measuring Deliberation: Towards a New Deliberative Quality.* Oxford Academic Press.

Bagès, Céline, Natacha Hoareau, and Alain Guerrien. 2021. "Play to Reduce Bullying! Role-Playing Games Are a Useful Tool for Therapists and Teachers." *Journal of Research in Childhood Education* 35 (4): 631–641.

Baird, Josephine. 2021. "Role-playing the Self: Trans Self-Expression, Exploration, and Embodiment in (Live Action) Role-Playing Games." *International Journal of Role-Playing* 11: 94–113.

Baird, Josephine. 2022. "Learning About Ourselves: Communicating, Connecting and Contemplating Trans Experience through Play." *Gamevironments* 17: 355-402.

Baird, Josephine, and Sarah Lynne Bowman. 2022. "The Transformative Potential of Immersive Experiences within Role-Playing Communities." *Revista de Estudos Universitário* 48: 1–48.

Bandura, Albert. 2002. "Social Foundations of Thought and Action." In *The Health Psychology Reader*, edited by David F. Marks. Sage.

Barabas, Jason. 2004. "How Deliberation Affects Policy Opinions." *American Political Science Review* 98 (4): 687–701.

Bartenstein, Lennart. 2022a. "Larp in Cognitive Behavioral Psychotherapy (CBT)." *Video Poster Presented at the Transformative Play Initiative Seminar 2022: Role-Playing, Culture, and Heritage*, October 20–21, 2022. Online.

Bartenstein, Lennart. 2022b. "Larp in Cognitive Behavioral Therapy: Making Larp a Standard Method." *Nordiclarp.org*, April 22.

Bartenstein, Lennart. 2024. "Live Action Role Playing (Larp) in Cognitive Behavioral Psychotherapy: A Case Study." *International Journal of Role-Playing* 15 (June): 92–126.

Basu, Sammy. 1999. "Dialogic Ethics and the Virtue of Humor." *Journal of Political Philosophy* 7 (4): 378-403.

Beauvais, Edana. 2020. "Deliberation and Non-Deliberative Communication." *Journal of Deliberative Democracy* 16 (1): 4–13.

Bjørkelo, Kristian A., and Kristine Jørgensen. 2018. "The Asylum Seekers Larp: The Positive Discomfort of Transgressive Realism." In *Proceedings of Nordic DiGRA 2018*.

Black, Laura W. 2008. "Deliberation, Storytelling, and Dialogic Moments." *Communication Theory* 18 (1): 93–116.

Bogler, Alexander. 2012. "The Paradox of Participation Experiments." *Science, Technology & Human Values* 3 (5): 506–527.

Bowman, Sarah Lynne. 2010. *The Functions of Role-playing Games: How Participants Create Community, Solve Problems, and Explore Identity*. McFarland & Company, Inc.

Bowman, Sarah Lynne. 2014. "Educational Live Action Role-Playing Games: A Secondary Literature Review." In *Wyrd Con Companion Book 2014*, edited by Sarah Lynne Bowman. Wyrd Con.

Bowman, Sarah Lynne. 2022a. "Introduction to Transformative Game Design." Transformative Play Initiative. *YouTube*, January 5.

Bowman, Sarah Lynne. 2022b. "The Mixing Desk of Edu-Larp." Transformative Play Initiative. *YouTube*, July 21.

Bowman, Sarah Lynne, and Andhe Standiford. 2015. "Educational Larp in the Middle School Classroom: A Mixed Method Case Study." *International Journal of Role-Playing* 5: 4–25.

Bowman, Sarah Lynne, Elektra Diakolambrianou, and Simon Brind, eds. 2024. *Transformative Role-Playing Game Design*. Acta Universitatis Upsaliensis. Transformative Play Research 1. Uppsala University Publications.

Bowman, Sarah Lynne, Josephine Baird, Kjell Hedgard Hugaas, Elektra Diakolambrianou, and Taisto Suominen. 2024. "Chapter 7: Research in Transformative Game Design." In *Transformative Role-playing Game Design*.

Acta Universitatis Upsaliensis, edited by Sarah Lynne Bowman, Elektra Diakolambrianou, and Simon Brind. Transformative Play Research 1. Uppsala University Publications.

Bowler, Shaun, and Todd Donovan. 2002. "Democracy, institutions and attitudes about citizen influence on government." *British Journal of Political Science* 32 (2): 371–390.

Boyle, Elizabeth A., Thomas Hainey, Thomas M. Connolly, et al. 2016. "An Update to the Systematic Literature Review of Empirical Evidence of the Impacts and Outcomes of Computer Games and Serious Games." *Computers & Education* 94: 178–192.

Brown, Maury. 2014. "Pulling the Trigger on Player Agency: How Psychological Intrusion in Larps Affect Game Play." In *The Wyrd Con Companion Book 2014*, edited by Sarah Lynne Bowman. Wyrd Con.

Budai, Sarah, and Kristin Hammock. 2014. "The State of Amtgard." In *The Wyrd Con Companion Book* 2014, edited by Sarah Lynne Bowman. Wyrd Con.

Burkhalter, Stephanie, John Gastil, and Todd Kelshaw. 2002. "A Conceptual Definition and Theoretical Model of Public Deliberation in Small Face-to-Face Groups." *Communication Theory* 12 (4): 398–422.

By Night Studios. 2014. *Mind's Eye Theatre: Vampire: The Masquerade Quick Start Guide*. By Night.

Caillois, Roger.1961. *Man, Play, and Games*. University of Illinois Press.

Carpini, Michael X. Delli, Fay Lomax Cook, and Lawrence R. Jacobs. 2004. "Public, Deliberation, Discursive Participation, and Citizen Engagement: A Review of the Empirical Literature." *Annual Review of Political Science* 7 (7): 315–344.

Causo, Francesco, and Elly Quinlan. 2021. "Defeating Dragons and Demons: Consumers' Perspectives on Mental Health Recovery in Role-playing games." *Australian Psychologist*, March 12.

Chambers, Simone. 2003. "Deliberative Democratic Theory." *Annual Review of Political Science* 6 (1): 307–326.

Chambers, Simone. 2012. "Deliberation and Mass Democracy." In *Deliberative Systems*, edited by John Parkinson and Jane Mansbridge. Cambridge University Press.

Cook, Mike P., Ryan Morgan, and Matthew Gremo. 2016. "Implementing Tabletop Gaming in the English Classroom: Promoting Literacy Through Interactive Gameplay." *Minnesota English Journal* 1–27.

Cox, Jason, and Lillian Lewis. 2023. "Whose Art Museum?: Immersive Gaming as Irruption." *The Journal of Social Theory in Art Education* 42: 52–63.

Craig, Robert T. 2023. "Introduction: Deliberative Play." *American Behavioral Scientist* 67 (8): 951–962.

Crocco, Margaret, Avner Segall, Anne-Lise Halvorsen, and Rebecca Jacobsen. 2018. "Deliberating Public Policy Issues with Adolescents: Classroom Dynamics and Sociocultural Considerations." *Democracy and Education* 26 (1): Article 3.

Crookall, David. 2010. "Serious Games, Debriefing, and Simulation/gaming as a Discipline." *Simulation & Gaming* 41: 898–920.

Crookall, David. 2014. "Engaging (in) Gameplay and (in) Debriefing." *Simulation & Gaming* 45 (4–5): 416–427.

Crookall, David. 2023. "Debriefing: A Practical Guide." In *Simulation for Participatory Education: Virtual Exchange and Worldwide Collaboration*, edited by M. Laura Angelini and Rut Muñiz. Springer International Publishing.

Cullinan, Maryanne. 2024. "Surveying the Perspectives of Middle and High School Educators Who Use Role-Playing Games as Pedagogy." *International Journal of Role-Playing* 15 (June): 127–41.

Curato, Nicole, David Farrell, Brigitte Geißel, et al. 2021. "Deliberative Mini-Publics: Core Design Features." In *Deliberative Mini-Publics: Core Design Features*, edited by Nicole Curato David Farrell, Brigitte Geißel, et al. Bristol University Press.

Curato, Nicole, John S. Dryzek, Selen A. Ercan, Carolyn M. Hendriks, and Simon Niemeyer. 2017. "Twelve Key Findings in Deliberative Democracy Research." *Daedalus* 146 (3): 28–38.

Daniau, Stéphane. 2016. "The Transformative Potential of Role-Playing Games: From Play Skills to Human Skills." *Simulation & Gaming* 47 (4): 423–444.

Davis, Adam, and Adam Johns. 2020. "Dungeons, Dragons, and Social Development." In *Integrating Geek Culture into Therapeutic Practice: The Clinician's Guide to Geek Therapy*, edited by Anthony M. Bean, Emory S. Daniel Jr., and Sarah A. Hays. Fort Worth, TX: Leyline Publishing.

Deterding, Sebastian. 2018. "Alibis for Adult Play: A Goffmanian Account of Escaping Embarrassment in Adult Play." *Games and Culture* 13 (3): 260–279.

de Wijse-van Heeswijk, Marieke. 2021. "Ethics and the Simulation Facilitator: Taking your Professional Role Seriously." *Simulation & Gaming* 52 (3): 312–332.

de Wijse-van Heeswijk, Marieke, and Willy C. Kriz. 2023. "Design Science Perspective on Formative Evaluation in Simulation Games." In *Simulation for Participatory Education: Virtual Exchange and Worldwide Collaboration*, edited by M. Laura Angelini and Rut Muñiz. Springer International Publishing.

de Wijse-van Heeswijk, Marieke, Joeri van Laere, Friedrich Trautwein, et al. 2025. "Debriefing as a Leverage Point for the Transfer of Simulation Game Learning Outcomes to Reality: Building Blocks before and during Debriefing that Enhance Learning Transfer." In *Transferring Gaming and Simulation Experience to the Real World*, edited by Toshiko Kikkawa, Willy Christian Kriz, Junkichi Sugiura, and Marieke de Wijse-Van Heeswijk. Translational Systems Sciences. Springer.

Dryzek, John S. 2012. *Foundations and Frontiers of Deliberative Governance.* Oxford University Press.

Dryzek, John S., André Bächtiger, Simone Chambers, et al. 2019. "The Crisis of Democracy and the Science of Deliberation." *Science* 363 (6432): 1144–1146.

Dyson, Scott Benjamin, Yu-Lin Chang, Hsueh-Chih Chen, Hsiang-Yu Hsiung, Chien-Chih Tseng, and Jen-Ho Chang. 2016. "The Effect of Tabletop Role-playing Games on the Creative Potential and Emotional Creativity of Taiwanese College Students." *Thinking Skills and Creativity* 19 (March): 88–96.

Eddy, Zoë Antoinette. 2020. "Playing at the Margins: Colonizing Fictions in New England Larp." *Humanities* 9 (4): 143.

Efterskolen Epos. N.d. "Start." https://efterskolen-epos.dk/.

Eklund, Lina. 2015. "Bridging the Online/Offline Divide: The Example of Digital Gaming." *Computers in Human Behavior* 53: 527–535.

Elms, Alan C. 1967. "Role Playing, Incentive, and Dissonance." *Psychological Bulletin* 68: 132–148.

Enfield, George. 2007. "Becoming the Hero: The Use of Role-Playing Games in Psychotherapy." In *Using Superheroes in Counseling and Play Therapy*, edited by L. C. Rubin. Springer Publishing Company.

Erlandsson, Anna. 2019. "Debattinlägg: 'Bara bra med en spelnörd som kultur-minister!'" *SVT Nyheter*, 22 January 22.

Erman, Eva. 2009. "What Is Wrong with Agonistic Pluralism? Reflections on Conflict in Democratic Theory." *Philosophy & Social Criticism* 35 (9): 1039–1062.

Escobar, Oliver. 2019. "Facilitators: The Micropolitics of Public Participation and Deliberation." In *Handbook of Democratic Innovation and Governance*, edited by Stephen Elstub and Oliver Escobar. Edward Elgar Publishing.

Farrar, Cynthia, Donald P. Green, Jennifer E. Green, David W. Nickerson, and Steven Shewfelt. 2009. "Does Discussion Group Composition Affect Policy Preferences? Results from Three Randomized Experiments." *Political Psychology* 30 (4): 615–647.

Farrell, David M., and Jane Suiter. 2021. *Reimagining Democracy: Lessons in Deliberative Democracy From the Irish Front Line*. Cornell University Press.

Fatland, Eirik. 2016. "Europa – Larp Presentation by Eirik Fatland." Larpwriter Summer School. *YouTube*.

Felicetti, Andrea, John Gastil, Janette Hartz-Karp, and Lyn Carson. 2012. "Collective Identity and Voice at the Australian Citizens' Parliament." *Journal of Public Deliberation* 8 (1): Article 5: 1–27.

Felicetti, Andrea, Simon Niemeyer, and Nicole Curato. 2016. "Improving Deliberative Participation: Connecting Mini-Publics to Deliberative Systems." *European Political Science Review* 8 (3): 427–448.

Fishkin, James S. 2018. *Democracy When the People Are Thinking: Revitalizing Our Politics Through Public Deliberation*. Oxford University Press.

Fishkin, James, Alice Siu, Larry Diamond, and Norman Bradburn. 2021. "Is Deliberation an Antidote to Extreme Partisan Polarization? Reflections on 'America in One Room.'" *American Political Science Review* 115 (4): 1464–1481.

Ford, Kol. 2020. "Mind the Gap: Barriers to Larping for People from Backgrounds of Structural Poverty." Presentation at Solmukohta 2020. Nordic Larp. YouTube, April 10.

Garcia, Antero. 2016. "Teacher as Dungeon Master: Connected Learning, Democratic Classrooms, and Rolling for Initiative." In *The Role-Playing Society: Essays on the Cultural Influence of RPGs*, edited by Andrew Byers and Francesco Crocco. McFarland.

Gastil, John, and Michael Broghammer. 2021. "Linking Theories of Motivation, Game Mechanics, and Public Deliberation to Design an Online System for Participatory Budgeting." *Political Studies* 69 (1): 7–25.

Giessen, Hans W. 2015. *Serious Games Effects: An Overview. Procedia-Social and Behavioral Sciences* 174: 2240–2244.

Goodin, Robert E., and John S. Dryzek. 2006. Deliberative Impacts: The Macro-Political Uptake of Mini-Publics. *Politics & Society* 34 (2): 219–244.

Gordon, Eric, Jason Haas, and Becky Michelson. 2017. "Civic Creativity: Role-Playing Games in Deliberative Process." *International Journal of Communication* 11: 3789–807.

Graeber, David, and David Wengrow. 2021. *The Dawn of Everything: A New History of Humanity*. Penguin UK.

Grönlund, Kimmo, and Kaisa Herne. 2022. "Experimental Methods." In *Research Methods in Deliberative Democracy*, edited by Selen A. Ercan, Hans Asenbaum, Nicole Curato, and Ricardo F. Mendonça. Oxford University Press.

Grönlund, Kimmo, Kaisa Herne, and Maija Setälä. 2015. "Does Enclave Deliberation Polarize Opinions?" *Political Behavior* 37 (4): 995–1020.

Grönlund, Kimmo, and Maija Setälä. 2024. "Chapter 19: Deliberative Mini-publics." In *Handbook of Comparative Political Institutions*, edited by Vatter, Adrian and Rahel Freiburghaus. Edward Elgar Publishing.

Grönlund, Kimmo, Maija Setälä, and Kaisa Herne. 2010. "Deliberation and Civic Virtue – Lessons from a Citizen Deliberation Experiment." *European Political Science Review* 2 (1): 95–117.

Groth, Anna Emilie, Hanne "Hank" Grasmo, and Tor Kjetil Edland. 2021. *Just a Little Lovin': The Larp Script*. Drøbak.

Gutmann, Amy, and Dennis Thompson. 1996. *Democracy and Disagreement*. Harvard University Press.

Gygax, Gary, and Dave Arneson. 1974. *Dungeons & Dragons*. TSR, Inc.

Haarman, Susan. 2022. "Dungeons & Dragons & Dewey: The Potential for Dramatic Rehearsal and Civic Outcomes in Tabletop Role-Playing Games." *Philosophical Studies in Education* 53: 56–70.

Haarman, Susan. 2023. *Dungeons & Dragons & Dewey: Toward a Ludic Pedagogy of Democratic Civic Life Through the Philosophy of John Dewey and Tabletop Role-Playing Games*. PhD. diss., Loyola University Chicago.

Habermas, Jurgen. 1984. *The Theory of Communicative Action: Vol. 1, Reason and the Rationalization of Society*. Beacon Press.

Habermas, Jurgen. 1994. "Three Models of Democracy." *Constellations* 1 (1): 1-10.

Habermas, Jurgen. 1998. *Between Facts and Norms: Contributions to a Discourse Theory of Law and Democracy*. MIT Press.

Halvorsen, Morten. 1997. "Jeg var en førstegangslaiber på Kybergenesis!" *Imagonem* (15): 50–55.

Hartz-Karp, Janette, Patrick Anderson, John Gasti, and Andrea Felicetti. 2010. "The Australian Citizens' Parliament: Forging Shared Identity through Public Deliberation." *Journal of Public Affairs* 10 (4): 353–371.

Harviainen, J. Tuomas. 2016. "Political Larps, or Larps about Politics?" In *Larp Politics: Systems, Theory, and Gender in Action*, edited by Kaisa Kangas, Mika Loponen, and Jukka Särkijärvi. Solmukohta 2016, Ropecon ry.

Hassan, Lobna. 2017. "Governments Should Play Games: Towards a Framework for the Gamification of Civic Engagement Platforms." *Simulation & Gaming* 48 (2): 249–267.

Hassan, Lobna, and Juho Hamari. 2019. "Gamification of E-participation: A Literature Review." In *Proceedings of the 52nd Hawaii International Conference on System Science*. AIS eLibrary. 3077–3086.

Heathcote, Dorothy, and Gavin M. Bolton. 1995. *Drama for Learning: Dorothy Heathcote's Mantle of the Expert Approach to Education*. Heinemann.

Helbig, Kate. A. 2019. "Evaluation of a Role-Playing Game to Improve Social Skills for Individuals with ASD." Ph.D. Diss., University of Southern Mississippi, USA.

Himmelroos, Staffan, and Henrik Serup Christensen. 2014. "Deliberation and Opinion Change: Evidence from a Deliberative Mini-public in Finland." *Scandinavian Political Studies* 37 (1): 41–60.

Hixson, Sarah West, and Rachel J. Eike. 2024. "Mixed-Methods Assessment of an Apparel Edu-Larp Rooted in Self-Determination Theory." *International Journal of Fashion Design, Technology and Education* 18 (1): 1–13.

Hollander, Aaron T. 2021. "Blessed Are the Legend-Makers: Experimentation as Edification in Dungeons & Dragons." *Political Theology* 22 (4) (Feb 26): 1–16.

Hopeametsä, Heidi. 2008. "24 Hours in a Bomb Shelter." In *Playground Worlds*, edited by Markus Montola and Jaakko Stenros. Ropecon.

Hugaas, Kjell Hedgard. 2019. "Investigating Types of Bleed in Larp: Emotional, Procedural, and Memetic." *Nordiclarp.org*, January 25.

Hugaas, Kjell Hedgard. 2024. "Bleed and Identity: A Conceptual Model of Bleed and How Bleed-Out from Role-Playing Games Can Affect a Player's Sense of Self." *International Journal of Role-playing* 15: 9-35.

Hyltoft, Malik. 2010. "Four Reasons Why Edu-Larp Works." In *LARP: Einblicke*, edited by Karsten Dombrowski, 43–57. Zauberfeder Ltd.

Jacquet, Vincent. 2017. "Explaining Non-participation in Deliberative Mini-Publics." *European Journal of Political Research* 56 (3): 640–659.

Jennstål, Julia. 2012. "Traits & Talks: Lessons about Personality and Deliberation from the Negotiations between Nelson Mandela and FW de Klerk." Ph.D. diss., Acta Universitatis Upsaliensis.

Jennstål, Julia. 2018. "Deliberative Participation and Personality: The Effect of Traits, Situations, and Motivation." *European Political Science Review* 10 (3): 417–440.

Jennstål, Julia. 2019. "Deliberation and Complexity of Thinking: Using the Integrative Complexity Scale to Assess the Deliberative Quality of Minipublics." *Swiss Political Science Review* 25 (1): 64–83.

Jennstål, Julia, and Per-Ola Öberg. 2019. "The Ethics of Deliberative Activism: In Search of Reasonableness and Dialogic Responsiveness in Provocative Art Exhibitions." *Policy Studies* 40 (6): 648–661.

Johansson, Karin, Johanna Koljonen, Jaakko Stenros, PerOla Öberg, and Sarah L. Bowman. In Press. "Playing a Role in Democracy: Political Live Action Role-Playing Games, Activism, and Deliberation." In *Education and Role-Playing Games: Theory and Pedagogy*, edited by Susan Haarman. CRC Press.

Josefsson, Erika. 2019. "Kulturministern: Alla borde prova på politik." *Göteborgs-Posten*, February 4.

Kangas, Kaisa, Mika Loponen, and Jukka Särkijärvi, eds. 2016. *Larp Politics: Systems, Theory, and Gender in Action*. Solmukohta 2016, Ropecon ry.

Kallam, Michael L. 1984. "The Effects of Simulation Game Play upon Oral Language Development and Internalisation of Locus of Control among Mildly Handicapped Adolescents." PhD diss., Oklahoma State University. ProQuest Dissertations and Theses Global.

Katō, Kōhei. 2019. "Employing Tabletop Role-Playing Games (TRPGs) in Social Communication Support Measures for Children and Youth with Autism Spectrum Disorder (ASD) in Japan: A Hands-On Report on the Use of Leisure Activities." *Japanese Journal of Analog Role-Playing Game Studies* (0): 23–28.

Kemper, Jonaya. 2017. "The Battle of Primrose Park: Playing for Emancipatory Bleed in Fortune & Felicity." *Nordiclarp.org*, June 21.

Kemper, Jonaya. 2018. "More Than a Seat at the Feasting Table." In *Shuffling the Deck: The Knutpunkt 2018 Color Printed Companion*, edited by Annika Waern and Johannes Axner. ETC Press.

Kemper, Jonaya. 2020. "Wyrding the Self." In *What Do We Do When We Play?*, edited by Eleanor Saitta, Johanna Koljonen, Jukka Särkijärvi, Anne Serup Grove, Pauliina Männistö, and Mia Makkonen. Solmukohta.

Kessock, Shoshana. 2014. "Cultural Appropriation and Larp." In *The Cutting Edge of Nordic Larp*, edited by Jon Back. Knutpunkt.

Kessock, Shoshana. 2017. "The Absence of Disabled Bodies in Larp." In *Once Upon a Nordic Larp... Twenty Years of Playing Stories*, edited by Martine Svanevik, Linn Carin Andreassen, Simon Brind, Elin Nilsen, and Grethe Sofie Bulterud Strand. Oslo, Norway: Knutepunkt 2017.

Klenell, Johannes. 2019. "Johannes Klenell: Vi har en ny kulturminister – och hon är skogsalv." *Arbetaren*, January 21.

Knobloch, Katherine R., and John Gastil. 2015. "Civic (Re) Socialisation: The Educative Effects of Deliberative Participation." *Politics* 35 (2): 183–200.

Koljonen, Johanna, Jaakko Stenros, Anne Serup Grove, Aina D. Skjønsfjell, and Elin Nilsen, eds. 2019. *Larp Design: Creating Role-Play Experiences*. Landsforeningen Bifrost.

Kriz, Willy Christian. 2010. "A Systemic-Constructivist Approach to the Facilitation and Debriefing of Simulations and Games." *Simulation & Gaming* 41 (5): 663–680.

Kulha, Katariina, Mikko Leino, Maija Setälä, Maija Jäske, and Staffan Himmelroos. 2021. "For the Sake of the Future: Can Democratic Deliberation Help Thinking and Caring about Future Generations?" *Sustainability* 13 (10): 5487.

Lajvbyrån. 2025. "Välkommen till Lajvbyrån." *Lajvbyrån.se*. https://lajvbyran.se/.

LajvVerkstaden. 2025b. "Lajv som Kultur." *LajvVerkstaden.se*. https://lajvverkstaden.se/.

Larp Census. 2015. "Larp Census." *Larpcensus.org*. https://www.larpcensus.org.

Lederach, John Paul. 2014. *Little Book of Conflict Transformation: Clear Articulation of the Guiding Principles by a Pioneer in the Field*. Good Books.

Lehto, Tanja. 2016. "Where Can Political Larp Go?" In *Larp Politics: Systems, Theory, and Gender in Action*, edited by Kaisa Kangas, Mika Loponen, and Jukka Särkijärvi. Solmukohta 2016, Ropecon ry.

Leigh, Elyssebeth E., and Laurie L. Levesque. 2024. *Facilitating Simulations: Teaching Methods in Business Studies*. Edward Elgar Publishing.

Leino, Mikko, Katariina Kulha, Maija Setälä, and Juha Ylisalo. 2022. "Expert Hearings in Mini-Publics: How Does the Field of Expertise Influence Deliberation and Its Outcomes?" *Policy Sciences* 55 (3): 429–450.

Leonard, Diana J., Jovo Janjetovic, and Maximilian Usman. 2021. "Playing to Experience Marginalization: Benefits and Drawbacks of 'Dark Tourism' in Larp." *International Journal of Role-Playing* 11: 25–47.

Lerner, Josh A. 2014. *Making Democracy Fun: How Game Design Can Empower Citizens and Transform Politics.* MIT Press.

Levin, Hilda. 2020. "Metareflection." In *What Do We Do When We Play?*, edited by Eleanor Saitta, Johanna Koljonen, Jukka Särkijärvi, Anne Serup Grove, Pauliina Männistö, and Mia Makkonen. Solmukohta.

Levin, Hilda. 2023. "Bridging Historical and Present-Day Queer Community through Embodied Role-Playing." *International Journal of Role-Playing* 14: 82–90.

Levine, Peter. 2018a. "Deliberation or Simulated Deliberation?" *Democracy and Education* 26 (1): 1-4.

Levine, Peter. 2018b. "Deliberation or Simulated Deliberation? Choices for the Classroom « Peter Levine." Peter Levine: *A Blog for Civic Renewal* (April 30).

Lindell, Marina, André Bächtiger, Kimmo Grönlund, Kaisa Herne, Maija Setälä, and Dominik Wyss. 2017. "What Drives the Polarisation and Moderation of Opinions? Evidence from a Finnish Citizen Deliberation Experiment on Immigration." *European Journal of Political Research* 56 (1): 23–45.

Luskin, Robert C., James S. Fishkin, and Roger Jowell. 2002. "Considered Opinions: Deliberative Polling in Britain." *British Journal of Political Science* 32 (3): 455–487.

Luskin, Robert C., Ian O'Flynn, James S. Fishkin, and David Russell. 2012. "Deliberating Across Deep Divides." *Political Studies* 62 (1): 116–135.

Mayer, Igor S. 2009. "The Gaming of Policy and the Politics of Gaming: A Review." *Simulation & Gaming* 40 (6): 825–862.

McCoy, Jennifer, Tahmina Rahman, and Murat Somer. 2018. "Polarization and the Global Crisis of Democracy: Common Patterns, Dynamics, and Pernicious Consequences for Democratic Polities." *American Behavioral Scientist* 62 (1): 16–42.

McCoy, Jennifer, and Murat Somer. 2021. "Overcoming Polarization." *Journal of Democracy* 32 (1): 6–21.

Mekler, Elisa D., Florian Brühlmann, Alexandre N. Tuch, and Klaus Opwis. 2017. "Towards Understanding the Effects of Individual Gamification Elements on Intrinsic Motivation and Performance." *Computers in Human Behavior* 71: 525–534.

Mendonça, Ricardo Fabrino, and Hans Asenbaum. 2025. "Decolonizing Deliberative Democracy." *European Journal of Social Theory*: 0 (0): 1–22.

Mercier, Hugo, and Hélène Landemore. 2012. "Reasoning is for Arguing: Understanding the Successes and Failures of Deliberation." *Political Psychology* 33 (2): 243–258.

Meriläinen, Mikko. 2012. "The Self-perceived Effects of the Role-Playing Hobby on Personal Development – A Survey Report." *International Journal of Role-Playing* 3: 49–68.

Milner, Ryan. M. 2016. *The World Made Meme: Public Conversations and Participatory Media*. MIT Press.

Mochocki, Michał. 2013a. "Edu-Larp as Revision of Subject-Matter Knowledge." *The International Journal of Role-Playing* 4: 55–75.

Mochocki, Michał. 2013b. "Less Larp in Edu-Larp Design." In *Crossing Habitual Borders: The Official Book for Knutepunkt 2013*, edited by Katrine Øverlie Svela and Karete Jacobsen Meland. : Fantasiforbundet.

Mochocki, Michał. 2014. "Larping the Past: Research Report on High-School Edu-Larp." In *The Wyrd Con Companion Book 2014*, edited by Sarah Lynne Bowman. Wyrd Con.

Montola, Markus. 2010. "The Positive Negative Experience in Extreme Role-playing." In *Proceedings of DiGRA Nordic 2010: Experiencing Games: Games, Play, and Players*. DiGRA Digital Library.

Montola, Markus, Jaakko Stenros, and Eleanor Saitta. 2015. "The Art of Steering: Bringing the Player and the Character Back Together." *Nordiclarp.org*, March 29.

Moore, Alfred. 2012. "Following from the Front: Theorizing Deliberative Facilitation." *Critical Policy Studies* 6 (2): 146–162.

Morrell, Michael E. 2005. "Deliberation, Democratic Decision-Making and Internal Political Efficacy." *Political Behavior* 27: 49–69.

Morschheuser, Benedikt, Juho Hamari, Jonna Koivisto, and Alexander Maedche. 2017. "Gamified Crowdsourcing: Conceptualization, Literature Review, and Future Agenda." *International Journal of Human-computer Studies* 106: 26–43.

Mouffe, Chantal. 1999. "Deliberative Democracy or Agonistic Pluralism?" *Social Research* 66 (3): 745–758.

Muradova, Lala. 2021. "Seeing the Other Side? Perspective-Taking and Reflective Political Judgements in Interpersonal Deliberation." *Political Studies* 69 (3): 644–664.

Muradova, Lala, and Kevin Arceneaux. 2022. "Chapter 13 – Political Belief Formation: Individual Differences and Situational Factors." In *The Cognitive Science of Belief: A Multidisciplinary Approach*, edited by Julien Musolino, Joseph Sommer and Pernille Hemmer. Cambridge University Press.

Mutz, Diana C. 2008. "Is Deliberative Democracy a Falsifiable Theory?" *Annual Review of Political Science* 11 (1): 521–538.

Niemeyer, Simon. 2011. The Emancipatory Effect of Deliberation: Empirical Lessons from Mini-Publics. *Politics & Society* 39 (1): 103–140.

Niemeyer, Simon, and John S. Dryzek. 2007. "The Ends of Deliberation: Meta-Consensus and Inter-Subjective Rationality as Ideal Outcomes." *Swiss Political Science Review* 13 (4): 497–526.

Niemeyer, Simon, Francesco Veri, John S. Dryzek, and André Bächtiger. 2024. "How Deliberation Happens: Enabling Deliberative Reason." *American Political Science Review* 118 (1): 345–362.

Öberg, PerOla. 2022. "Chapter 16: Deliberation." In *Handbook on Theories of Governance*, edited by Christopher Ansell and Jacob Torfing. Edward Elgar.

Østerskov Efterskole. n.d. "Et år på Østerskov." *Osterskov.dk*. Accessed January 16, 2025. https://osterskov.dk/.

Pettersson, Juhana, ed. 2014. *Life under Occupation: A Documentation Book for the Larp Halat Hisar.* Pohjoismaisen roolipelaamisen seura.

Pettersson, Juhana. 2015. "Baltic Warriors: Helsinki." *Nordiclarp.org*, January 16.

Pettersson, Juhana. 2018. "Lobbying for the Dead – Vampire Larp at the European Parliament." *Nordiclarp.org*, January 23.

Pitt, Caroline, Katharine Chen, Jennifer Rubin, Dominic Gibson, and Sam Bindman. 2023. "How Youth Can Build Social and Emotional Skills with Tabletop Role-Playing Games: Research Findings and Actionable Insights." White paper, Foundry10.

Pöllänen, Sonja, and Jonne Arjoranta. 2021. "'Whose Were Those Feelings?' Affect and Likenessing in Halat Hisar Live Action Role-playing Game." *International Journal of Cultural Studies* 24 (6): 899–916.

Pothong, Kruakae, Larissa Pschetz, Ruth Catlow, and Sarah Meiklejohn. 2021. "Problematising Transparency through LARP And Deliberation." In *Proceedings of the 2021 ACM Designing Interactive Systems Conference*, edited by Wendy Ju et al., 1682–1694. Association for Computing Machinery.

Rantanen, Teemu. 2016. "Larp as a Form of Political Action: Some Insights from the Theories of Political Science." In *Larp Politics: Systems, Theory, and Gender in Action*, edited by Kaisa Kangas, Mika Loponen, and Jukka Särkijärvi, 111–118. Solmukohta 2016, Ropecon ry.

Rivers, Anissa, Ian E. Wickramasekera II, Ronald J. Pekala, and Jennifer A. Rivers. 2016. "Empathic Features and Absorption in Fantasy Role-Playing." *American Journal of Clinical Hypnosis* 58: 286–294.

Rosselet, Julian. G., and Sarah. D. Stauffer. 2013. "Using Group Role-Playing Games with Gifted Children and Adolescents: A Psychosocial Intervention Model." *International Journal of Play Therapy* 4 (22): 173–192.

Roungas, Bill, Marieke de Wijse-van Heeswijk, Sebastiaan Meijer, and Alexander Verbraeck. 2018. "Pitfalls for Debriefing Games and Simulations: Theory and Practice." In Proceedings of *Intersections in Simulation and Gaming – 21st Annual Simulation Technology and Training Conference*, edited by Anjum Naweed et al. Springer.

Ruff, Tia. 2021. "Increasing Social and Emotional Learning Competencies through Use of Tabletop Role-Playing Games." PhD diss., George Fox University.

Ryan, Richard M., 1982. "Control and Information in the Intrapersonal Sphere: An Extension of Cognitive Evaluation Theory." *Journal of Personality and Social Psychology* 43: 450–461.

Sanders, Lynn. 1997. "Against Deliberation." *Political Theory* 25 (3): 347–376.

Sargent, Michael S. 2014. "Exploring Mental Dungeons and Slaying Psychic Dragons: An Exploratory Study." Master's thesis, Smith College.

Scudder, Mary F., and Stephen K. White. 2023. *The Two Faces of Democracy: Decentering Agonism and Deliberation*. Oxford University Press.

Standiford, Andhe. 2014. "Lessons Learned from Larp: Promoting High-Quality Role-Play and Immersion in Nursing Simulation." In *The Wyrd Con Companion Book 2014*, edited by Sarah Lynne Bowman. Wyrd Con.

Stark, Lizzie. 2014. "Defining Meta-Techniques." *Leaving Mundania*, August 28.

Stenros, Jaakko. 2014. "What Does 'Nordic Larp' Mean?" In *The Cutting Edge of Nordic Larp*, edited by Jon Back. Knutpunkt.

Stenros, Jaakko, Martin Eckhoff Andresen, and Martin Nielsen. 2016. "The Mixing Desk of Larp: History and Current State of a Design Theory." *Analog Game Studies*, November 13.

Stenros, Jaakko, and Markus Montola, eds. 2010. *Nordic Larp*. Fëa Livia.

Strandberg, Kim, Staffan Himmelroos, and Kimmo Grönlund. 2019. "Do Discussions in Like-Minded Groups Necessarily Lead to More Extreme Opinions? Deliberative Democracy and Group Polarization." *International Political Science Review* 40 (1): 41–57.

Suiter, Jane, David M. Farrell, and Eoin O'Malley. 2016. "When Do Deliberative Citizens Change Their Opinions? Evidence from the Irish Citizens' Assembly." *International Political Science Review* 37 (2): 198–212.

Suiter, Jane, Lala Muradova, John Gastil, and David M. Farrell. 2020. "Scaling Up Deliberation: Testing the Potential of Mini-Publics to Enhance the Deliberative Capacity of Citizens." *Swiss Political Science Review* 26 (3): 253–272.

Taber, Charles S., and Milton Lodge. 2006. "Motivated Skepticism in the Evaluation of Political Beliefs." *American Journal of Political Science* 50 (3): 755–769.

Thiel, Sarah-Kristen. 2016, May. "A Review of Introducing Game Elements to e-Participation." In *2016 Conference for E-Democracy and Open Government (CeDEM)*, May 18–20, 2016. IEEE. 3–9.

Thompson, Dennis F. 2008. "Deliberative Democratic Theory and Empirical Political Science." *Annual Review of Political Science* 11: 497–520.

Toft, Ida, and Sabine Harrer. 2020. "Design Bleed: A Standpoint Methodology for Game Design." In *Proceedings from DiGRA '20 – Proceedings of the 2020 DiGRA International Conference: Play Everywhere*. DiGRA Digital Library. 1–18.

Tolmie, Peter, Alan Chamberlain, and Steve Benford. 2014. "Designing for Reportability: Sustainable Gamification, Public Engagement, and Promoting Environmental Debate." *Personal and Ubiquitous Computing* 18: 1763–1774.

Turkington, Moyra. 2016. "Rehearsing Difference." In *Larp Politics: Systems, Theory, and Gender in Action*, edited by Kaisa Kangas, Mika Loponen, and Jukka Särkijärvi.: Solmukohta 2016, Ropecon ry.

van der Does, Ramon, and Vincent Jacquet. 2023. "Small-Scale Deliberation and Mass Democracy: A Systematic Review of the Spillover Effects of Deliberative Minipublics." *Political Studies* 71 (1): 218–237.

Varrette, Matthew, Jack Berkenstock, Adams Greenwood-Ericksen, et al. 2023. "Exploring the Efficacy of Cognitive Behavioral Therapy and Role-Playing Games as an Intervention for Adults with Social Anxiety." *Social Work with Groups* 46 (2): 140–165.

Veri, Francesco, and Simon Niemeyer. 2025. "Deliberative Reason and the Effect of Minipublic Configurations." *European Political Science Review*: 17 (3): 530-540.

Waern, Annika, and Peter Munthe-Kaas. 2013. "Can Larp Change the World? 2027 – A Larp That Tried." In *Crossing Habitual Borders*, edited by Karete Jacobsen Meland and Katrine Øverlie Svela. : Fantasiforbundet.

Walsh, Orla, and Conor Linehan. 2024. "Roll for Insight: Understanding How the Experience of Playing Dungeons & Dragons Impacts the Mental Health of an Average Player." *International Journal of Role-Playing* 15 (June): 36–60.

Warren, Mark E. 2017. "A Problem-Based Approach to Democratic Theory." *American Political Science Review* 111 (1): 39–53.

Weidenfeld, Matthew C., and Kenneth E. Fernandez. 2017. "Does Reacting to the Past Increase Student Engagement? An Empirical Evaluation of the Use of Historical Simulations in Teaching Political Theory." *Journal of Political Science Education* 13 (1): 46–61.

Werner, Hannah, and Lala Muradova. 2022. "13 Scenario Experiments." In *Research Methods in Deliberative Democracy,* edited by Selen A. Ercan, Hans Asenbaum, Nicole Curato, and Ricardo F. Mendonça. Oxford University Press.

Westborg, Josefin. 2023. "The Educational Role-Playing Game Design Matrix: Mapping Design Components onto Types of Education." *International Journal of Role-Playing* 13: 18–30.

Westborg, Josefin, and Sarah Lynne Bowman. In press for 2025 publication. "GM Screen: The Didactic Potential of RPGs." German: "Das didaktische Potential von Rollenspielen." In *#eduRPG. Rollenspiel als Methode der Bildung,* edited by Frank J. Robertz and Kathrin Fischer. SystemMatters Publ.

Whittington, Richard. 2006. "Completing the Practice Turn in Strategy Research." *Organization Studies* 27 (5): 613–634.

Willis, Rebecca, Andy Yuille, Peter Bryant, Duncan McLaren, and Nils Markusson. 2023. "Taking Deliberative Research Online: Lessons from Four Case Studies." *Qualitative Research* 23 (4): 921–939.

Wright, Jennifer Cole, Daniel E. Weissglass, and Vanessa Casey. 2020. "Imaginative Role-Playing as a Medium for Moral Development: Dungeons & Dragons Provides Moral Training." *Journal of Humanistic Psychology* 60 (1): 99–129.

Young, Iris Marion. 2001. "Activist Challenges to Deliberative Democracy." *Political Theory* 29 (5): 670–690.

Young, Iris Marion. 2002. *Inclusion and Democracy.* Oxford University Press.

Zagal, José P., and Sebastian Deterding, eds. 2024. *The Routledge Handbook of Role-playing Game Studies.* Routledge.

Zayas, Luis H., and Bradford H. Lewis. 1986. "Fantasy Role-Playing for Mutual Aid in Children's Groups: A Case Illustration." *Social Work with Groups* 9 (1): 53–66.

Zimmerman, John, Jodi Forlizzi, and Shelley Evenson. 2007. "Research through Design as a Method for Interaction Design Research in HCI." In *Proceedings of the SIGCHI Conference on Human Factors in Computing Systems, CHI '07,* 493–502. Association for Computing Machinery.

Index

For Product Safety Concerns and Information please contact our EU
representative GPSR@taylorandfrancis.com
Taylor & Francis Verlag GmbH, Kaufingerstraße 24, 80331 München, Germany